ABOUT THE AUTHOR

Eric Holt-Giménez, Ph.D., is the executive director of Food First/Institute for Food and Development Policy. Previously, Eric served as the Latin America Program Manager for the Bank Information Center in Washington, D.C. He earned a Ph.D. in Environmental Studies from the University of California–Santa Cruz. He has taught Development Studies at the University of California in Berkeley and Santa Cruz, and for the Boston University Global Ecology Program and graduate courses in food justice, food sovereignty, and agroecology at Marylhurst University, Antioquia University in Colombia, the International University of Gastronomy in Italy, and the University of the Pacific in San Francisco, California. Prior to his work in the United States, he worked as an agroecologist with farmers' movements in Central America and Mexico for over 20 years. At Food First, Eric's research and writing has concentrated on the global food crisis, the U.S. Farm Bill, the expansion of agrofuels, land issues, racism in the food system, community food security, and social movements for food justice and food sovereignty. Eric is author and editor of the Food First books, *Land Justice: Reimagining Land, Food and the Commons in the United States* (2017), *Food Movements Unite! Strategies to Transform Our Food Systems* (2011), *Food Rebellions: Crisis and the Hunger for Justice* (2009), and *Campesino: Voices from Latin America's Farmer-to-Farmer Movement for Sustainable Agriculture* (2006), as well as many academic and magazine articles and blogs.

A FOODIE'S GUIDE TO CAPITALISM

Understanding the Political Economy of What We Eat

ERIC HOLT-GIMÉNEZ

Dev Publishers & Distributors
New Delhi

Published by
Dev Publishers & Distributors
Second Floor, Prakashdeep,
22, Delhi Medical Association Road,
Darya Ganj, New Delhi – 110 002

www.devbooks.co.in

ISBN 978-93-81406-80-9

Dev Publishers & Distributors, 2018

Printed in India.

Contents

For Manolo: friend, farmer, comrade, who taught me that hope is not negotiable.

Acknowledgments

THE IDEA FOR THIS BOOK BEGAN with a comradely email conversation with Fred Magdoff, who was interested in producing a book about food and agriculture and asked me for suggestions on a title. Feeling overwhelmed by the plethora of books on food, I replied a little flippantly, "How about, 'The *Last* Book about Food'?" Luckily, Fred brushed off my remark. Some time later, over a hearty Vermont breakfast, we went on to outline what eventually became *A Foodie's Guide to Capitalism*. The book, and my own understanding of food and capitalism, benefited greatly from Fred's insights, suggestions, and patience during a frustratingly protracted writing process as work, life, and the U.S. elections led to a stream of missed deadlines.

The silver lining in these delays was that I was able to share drafts of the manuscript with a wide range of readers. Once a week for nearly two months, Ilja Van Lammeren, Tasnim Eboute, Francesco Guerreri, McKenna Jaquemet, Ayana Crawford, and Lauren Tate Baeza met with me to review the draft chapters. Their thirst for understanding the capitalist roots of the stunning contradictions in today's food systems was invaluable for developing a text for both seasoned political economists and passionate food activists. Eva Perroni prepared the material for many of the informative boxes. Grace Treffinger and

Erik Hazard worked on the glossary. Ahna Kruzic, Alyshia Silva, and Marilyn Borchardt also contributed with suggestions and help with the text, title, and cover. Marion Nestle gave the manuscript a full read, provided many useful comments, and kindly agreed to write the Foreword. Special thanks are in order for the comrades at Monthly Review Press—Michael Yates, Martin Paddio, and Susie Day; and to Erin Clermont, whose patient editing and helpful suggestions brought this book to its published form. I especially want to thank my *compañera en la lucha y la vida*, Leonor Hurtado, whose love, support, creativity, and encouragement were the main ingredients in writing this book. Finally, thanks to everyone who, when hearing about the book project, said, "That's just what we need!"

—ERIC HOLT-GIMÉNEZ
GRATON, CALIFORNIA, APRIL 2017

Foreword

by Marion Nestle

WHEN ERIC HOLT-GIMÉNEZ ASKED ME to introduce his *Foodie's Guide to Capitalism*, I said yes right away. I love the title, I think the food movement needs this book, and I am tired of having to treat capitalism as the "C word," never to be mentioned in polite company. Those of us "foodies" who love to eat and want our food system to produce tastier, healthier, and more sustainable diets—and to provide a decent living to everyone involved in this work—need to bring capitalism out of the closet, understand the problems it causes, and deal with them front and center. Eric (if I may) has done us an enormous favor by producing this book at this time.

We are endlessly told that the American food system gives us an abundant and varied food supply that is the envy of the world. Perhaps, but these purported benefits come at a high cost: food insecurity for 45 million Americans (half of them children), obesity in nearly two-thirds of adults, incalculable damage to the quality of our soil, air, and water, and foods excessively high in calories, sugars, and salt. Capitalism may not be the only explanation for these problems, but it is a great place to begin to understand why they exist.

We need food to live. But the purpose of food companies is not to promote our life, health, or happiness; it is to make money for executives and shareholders. The United Nations may declare that humans have a right to food, "realized when every man, woman and child, alone or in community with others, has the physical and economic access at all times to adequate food or means for its procurement," but that is not how unfettered capitalism works. Capitalism turns food—a life essential—into a commodity to be sold like any other commodity. As Eric puts it:

> It doesn't matter if the food is fresh organic arugula or a Big Mac, teff from the highlands of Ethiopia, or Cheez-Whiz from Walmart. It doesn't matter whether you need it or not, whether it is good or bad for you, whether it is locally produced or traveled from afar or whether it was corralled, caged, free range, or led a happy life—if enough people *want* it (and have the money to buy it), someone will turn it into a commodity and sell it.

How did something as basic to our existence as food get transformed into an instrument for profit? This book recounts that history and explains its consequences. It addresses questions we should all be asking: Why are so many Americans too poor to buy food? Why do so many gain weight and become obese? Why has the price of fresh fruits and vegetables risen faster than that of soft drinks? Why can't beginning farmers afford to buy land? Why does the USDA consider fruits and vegetables to be "specialty crops"? Why does the vast majority of our agricultural land grow feed for animals and fuel for cars rather than food for people? Following the money is not a bad way to get to the answers to these questions.

In addressing them, Eric wants us to see the bigger picture and ask who "decides how wealth will be extracted and who will it belong to? Is it the consumer? No. Is it the worker? No. It is the capitalist. That's why the system is called capitalism and not 'laborism' or 'workerism.'"

My own work deals with the influence of the food industry on nutrition and health, the influence of capitalism, in other words, though I rarely use the term. In my experience, the C word makes students and audiences uncomfortable. They don't like having to think about politics or the power relationships that govern how food is produced, sold, and consumed. But food *is* political, and deeply so. Recognizing the uncomfortable politics behind our food system is essential if we are really going to produce food that is more sustainable, less wasteful, and healthier for body and soul—and in ways that fairly compensate everyone involved.

Let me give one example of how understanding capitalism helps in my own area, nutrition. I am especially interested in the sharp rise in obesity in the United States that began around 1980. The immediate cause was that people began eating more food, and therefore more calories. But why? Genetics did not change. What did change was the environment of food choice. A look at the bigger picture takes us back to a shift in agricultural policies to encourage farmers to grow as much food as possible. Farmers responded and increased the availability of calories in the food supply to nearly twice the average need. The "shareholder value" movement of the early 1980s caused Wall Street to value companies on the basis of higher and more immediate returns on investment. Food companies now not only had to compete to sell products in an overproduced food economy, but also had to report *growth* in profits to Wall Street every quarter.

Overproduction makes food cheap. Cheap food encourages proliferation of fast-food restaurants, consumption of more food outside the home, and creation of larger—and more caloric—food portion sizes. In this fiercely competitive food environment, companies looked for new ways to sell food. They put food everywhere: drugstores, clothing stores, bookstores, and libraries. They increased marketing to children, low-income groups, and populations in developing countries. They did everything possible to encourage overeating. Hence: obesity.

As this book makes clear, such consequences are not accidents of history. They are predictable outcomes of an economic system in which profits take precedence over any other human value. A capitalist food system keeps labor and all other costs to a minimum and provides an enormous overabundance of cheap food, consequences be damned.

A Foodie's Guide to Capitalism takes you through the capitalist food system step by step. Eric's analysis of this system may be disturbing, but stay with it. If we want to create a food movement with real power, we need to know what we are up against.

Writing in the *New York Times* late in 2016, the journalist Michael Pollan argued that "the food movement still barely exists as a political force. It doesn't yet have the organization or the troops to light up a White House or congressional switchboard when one of its issues is at stake." We need both. Most of us troops are too immersed in trying to fix the food problems that most concern us—whether they be schools, farmers' markets, SNAP (food stamps), labels, fair trade, wages, or even the farm bill—to pay attention to the bigger organizational picture.

If we want to improve our food system, we need to know what has to change and how to make that change happen. Eric urges all of us to join together with everyone else working on food issues as well as with groups working on related social causes. Let's form a united movement with real power.

Read this book. Consider its arguments. May they inspire you to join the food movement and help make it succeed.

—NEW YORK, JUNE 2017

INTRODUCTION

Do Foodies Need to Understand Capitalism?

The answer of course is yes. Everyone trying to change the food system—people fighting to end hunger, food insecurity, and diet-related diseases, as well as those working for equitable and sustainable agriculture and people who simply want access to good, healthy food—needs to know about capitalism. Why? Because we have a capitalist food system. And yet relatively few people recognize this.

This seems odd, particularly for those who identify with the food movement. After all, one wouldn't start farming without some notion of growing plants, or build a website without knowledge of web software, or roof a house without understanding construction. Yet many, if not most, food activists trying to change the food system have scant knowledge of its capitalist foundations.

In part this is because most people in the food movement are too busy trying to deal with the immediate problems of the food system. Understandably, they concentrate their efforts on one or two issues rather than the system as a whole, such as healthy food access, urban agriculture, organic farming, community-supported agriculture, local food, farmworkers' rights, animal welfare, pesticide contamination, seed sovereignty, GMO labeling . . . the list is long. These projects are often funded by philanthropic foundations favoring projects that address urgent problems and organizations that can demonstrate tangible, quantifiable results. Given the severity of the problems in our food system, this is understandable, but this focus often eclipses work to build longer-term political movements that could address the root causes of those problems. What's more, organizations often find themselves in competition for funding, making it difficult to forge diverse, cross-issue alliances dedicated to systemic change. Intrepid individuals and food entrepreneurs working on their own in specialized market niches are even less likely to address systemic issues.

But there are also larger political and ideological reasons why the food movement does not know much about capitalism. For the most part, capitalism is simply not discussed in capitalist countries—not even in university economics courses—where political-economic structures are assumed to be immutable and are rarely questioned. Until the global financial crash in 2008, it was socially awkward to mention the term *capitalism* in the United States. This is because even a perfunctory examination of capitalism immediately uncovers profound economic and political disparities, thus contradicting the commonly held notion that we live in a classless, democratic society. Those privileged enough to go to college usually need to wait until graduate school before delving into the foundational works of Ricardo, Smith, Mill, Marx, Polanyi, Keynes, and other notable scholars of our economic system. Even then, capitalism is often treated as an intellectual artifact to be studied in academic isolation rather than the dynamic social and economic system of wealth and power that constantly influences, shapes, and reshapes life around the globe.

Directed primarily (though not exclusively) to a U.S. audience, this book takes another approach. It applies a food system framework to explain some of the basic workings of capitalism, and uses a basic understanding of capitalism to understand why the food system works as it does. In the course of this analysis, social movements are discussed, showing the ways in which class interests, social perceptions, and political organization can affect outcomes in a capitalist food regime. If you are unfamiliar with this approach to understanding the world, don't be surprised. You're not alone.

In the late 1970s the United States and Great Britain introduced policies to lower taxes on corporations and the wealthy, privatize public goods, remove environmental and labor regulations, and liberalize trade. These policies encouraged the rule of what mainstream economists like to call the "free market," that is, the freedom for huge corporations to produce what and where they want, import from where they want, and stash profits where they want, all the while evading tax obligations and transferring huge environmental and health costs to society. This suite of economic policies became known as "neoliberalism" because they revived nineteenth century ideas of free markets in a twentieth century context—to the benefit of the very wealthy. Neoliberalism did more than create a new plutocracy of billionaires and the highest levels of wealth and income disparity in history. In the face of privatization and capital's growing monopoly power, the *public sphere*—that part of society where decisions are made by citizens engaged in political discussion and civic activity (rather than the market) and where public goods are shared—disintegrated. Unions were crippled, and the political influence of progressive organizations crumbled, frequently under the direct attack of well-funded reactionary forces. Although these developments are often presented as part of the "natural" evolution of the global economy, they were all based on decisions made by powerful wealthy classes to advance their own interests. Neoliberalism on a global scale became known as globalization, a class project advanced by the powerful owners of international capital we now call the 1%. Neoliberalism reinforces the notion that we are, each of us, completely responsible for whatever life outcomes we have experienced. It aims to make us as vulnerable as possible, and hence more easily exploited.

At the same time, new social movements based on gender, race, ethnicity, and environment have been growing since the 1960s. Highly fragmented, these movements tended to turn away from older forms of political organizing like unions, vanguard political parties, and politico-military organizations, which were often viewed as undemocratic and unresponsive to the politics of identity and to environmental issues. As neoliberalism gained momentum, the established organizations of the "old left" became increasingly ineffective, while established political parties, like the Republicans and the Democrats in the United States, moved steadily to the right, embracing the new model.

The combination of globalization, the demise of the old left, and the spread of new social movements broke down a lot of encrusted political orthodoxy, opening the left to issues of gender, environment, ethnicity, and race. But in affluent countries, this also produced a generation of somewhat class-blind activists with little interest in how the economic system actually works, and little understanding of the role of capitalism in the social oppressions they were fighting. Critical knowledge of capitalism—vital to the struggles of social movements through the nineteenth and twentieth centuries—largely disappeared from the lexicon of social change, precisely at a time when neoliberal capitalism was destroying the working class and relentlessly penetrating every aspect of nature and society on the planet. Many social progressives became unwitting accomplices to the rise of economic neoliberalism, giving rise to what Nancy Fraser calls "progressive neoliberalism":

> Throughout the years when manufacturing cratered, the country buzzed with talk of "diversity," "empowerment," and "non-discrimination." Identifying "progress" with meritocracy instead of equality, these terms equated "emancipation" with the rise of a small elite of "talented" women, minorities, and gays in the winner-takes-all corporate hierarchy instead of with the latter's abolition. These liberal-individualist understandings of "progress" gradually replaced the more expansive, anti-hierarchical, egalitarian, class-sensitive, anti-capitalist understandings of emancipation that had flourished in the 1960s and 1970s.[1]

The fragmentation, depolitization, and neoliberal co-optation of the food movement, however, is rapidly changing with the crumbling of progressive neoliberalism. The rise of racial intolerance, xenophobia, and organized violence from the far-right has raised concerns of neofascism, worldwide, and prompted all progressive social movements to dig deeper to fully understand the problems they confront.

Many people in the Global South, especially poor food producers, can't afford *not* to understand the economic forces destroying their livelihoods. The rise of today's international food sovereignty movement, which has also taken root among farmers, farmworkers, and foodworkers in the United States, is part of a long history of resistance to violent, capitalist dispossession and exploitation of land, water, markets, labor, and seeds. In the Global North, underserved communities of color—historically subjected to waves of colonization, dispossession, exploitation, and discrimination—form the backbone of a food justice movement calling for fair and equitable access to good, healthy food. Understanding *why* people of color are twice as likely to suffer from food insecurity and diet-related disease, even though they live in affluent Northern democracies, requires an understanding of the intersection of capitalism and racism. So does understanding why farmers go broke overproducing food in a world where one in seven people are going hungry.

As the middle class in the developed world shrinks, much of the millennial generation, underemployed and saddled with debt, will live shorter lives than their parents, due in large part to the epidemic of diet-related diseases endemic to modern capitalism. The widespread "back to the land" trend is not simply a lifestyle choice; it also responds to shrinking livelihood opportunities. And as young farmers struggle to access ever more expensive farmland, the public runs up against corporate intransigence to everything from oil pipelines and GMO labeling to foodborne illnesses and unhealthy school food. Environmentalists wage endless battles against industrial agriculture's water depletion, pollution, and inhumane treatment of animals, biodiversity loss, and carbon emissions. There is a growing desire to understand the root causes of these related and seemingly intractable problems.

Activists across the food movement are beginning to realize that the food system cannot be changed in isolation from the larger economic system. Sure, we can tinker around the edges of the issue and do useful work in the process. However, to fully appreciate the magnitude of the challenges we face in transforming our food system and what will be needed to bring about a new one in harmony with people's needs and the environment, we need to explore the economic and political context of our food system—that is, capitalist society.

This book is intended as a political-economic tool kit for the food movement—from foodies, farmers, farm justice activists, and concerned consumers to climate justice and environmental activists. It is a basic introduction to the economic system of capitalism as seen through the lens of the food system, though it's not meant to be an exhaustive treatment of either. By understanding some of the rudiments of how capitalism operates, we can better grasp why our food system is the way it is, and how we can change it. Conversely, understanding how capitalism shapes the food system can help us understand the role food plays in the structure and function of capitalism itself. These kinds of insights can help us put our different forms of activism into political perspective and recognize opportunities for building alternatives, forging alliances, taking action, and comprehending the difference between superficial and truly transformative reforms.

What is behind regional free trade agreements, carbon markets, GMOs, "sustainable intensification," and the public-private partnerships to "feed the world"? Will more organic farms and gardens, community-supported agriculture, and "voting with our forks" transform the food system? Will more certified fair trade and microfinance rebuild rural economies in the Global South? Can we fight rising land values and corporate land grabs with land trusts and voluntary responsible agricultural investment principles, or should we demand massive agrarian reform? This book will help you address these questions.

While activist jargon and the arcane language of political economy is kept to a minimum here, we will introduce essential concepts of political economy, and the terminology may seem arcane. A detailed glossary of these terms is included for convenient reference. For those who want to dig deeper into issues of capitalism, food systems, and food movements, there is plenty of reference material.

Who owns what? Who does what? Who gets what? What do they do with it?[2] These are the basic questions posed in the study of capitalism. To understanding how a capitalist food system works, we'll answer these questions by introducing selected concepts from the study of political economy, a social science that predates economics by over one hundred years.

Our study begins with a broad, historical review in chapter 1, "How Our Capitalist Food System Came to Be," which focuses on the role of agriculture in capitalist development and the role of capital in the development of agriculture over the last two centuries. The early commodification of key crops like potatoes, rice, and corn were instrumental in European colonialism, U.S. expansionism, and the rise of industrialization. Their cultivation and commodification were made possible through processes and events such as the imposition of enclosures, genocide, slavery, and indentured servitude. These were facilitated by the introduction of such revolutionary technologies as the fence (used for the enclosures), seabird droppings (to restore soil fertility), and New World crops like corn and potatoes (used to feed the growing ranks of the poor). Our study will discuss the agrarian question, the New Deal, and the Green Revolution, and will show how they all shaped the emergence of three historically linked global food regimes.

Chapter 2 starts of by addressing food as a special commodity. We'll look at its *use value* and *exchange value*. Labor, the often forgotten ingredient in our food, is fundamental to food's *surplus value*, the basis for the formation of the "capital" in capitalism. Ever wonder why organic carrots are so expensive? This chapter will help answer that question by exploring the concept of "socially necessary labor time." Why do we have Concentrated Animal Feedlot Operations (CAFOs) and genetically engineered salmon? Look to "relative surplus value" for an explanation.

The appropriation of food's value is impossible without private and corporate ownership. In our examination of "Land and Property" in chapter 3, we will look at the interrelated role that public, private, and common property have played in the construction of our food systems. Understanding "land rent" reveals how capital's cyclical crises unleash waves of land grabs and the steady financialization of farmland. Land use follows both a logic of capital and a logic of territory. We'll look at a case study in the Guatemalan highlands to see how capitalism "drills down" to access and extract resources.

Despite its capacity to generate trillions of dollars in wealth, agriculture is hard work and a risky business, made riskier with climate change. Farmers can't just pick up and move to a better location. The "disjuncture between labor time and production time" presents significant barriers to capital investment. How capitalism overcomes these barriers and avoids risks in order to profit from agriculture is nothing short of an economic marvel. Nonetheless, as the food system is steadily capitalized through a dual process called "appropriation and substitution," it falls victim to capitalism's cyclical crises. In chapter 4, "Capitalist Food and Agriculture," we'll see how governments have historically dealt with this problem, and how capital makes society pay for its devastating boom-and-bust cycles. We'll look at contract farming, CAFOs, and global warming as part and parcel of the "metabolic rift" intrinsic to capitalist agriculture. Why is capitalist agriculture considered irrational, and what would a rational agriculture look like? Agroecology, the moral economy, and the diversity of farming styles help us address this question.

How did capitalism co-evolve with inequality? In chapter 5, "Power and Privilege in the Food System: Gender, Race, and Class," we'll look at the political economic history of patriarchy, racism, and classism in the food system, analyzing the common roots of exploitation of people of color, women, and the poor. How is racial caste and whiteness itself constructed in the food system? By introducing the relationship between imperialism and the spheres of production and reproduction, we'll look at the mechanics of "superexploitation" in the production and consumption of our food. The differences of class, gender, and color in the food system also give rise to opportunities for alliances and resistance.

The list of social and environmental problems caused by capitalism—from hunger, malnutrition, global warming, and food waste—is vast. So is capitalism's list of solutions to the problems it created. In chapter 6, "Food, Capitalism, Crises, and Solutions," we'll look critically at some of the key problems and proposed capitalist solutions, applying the lessons in political economy learned in previous chapters. We also describe capitalism's new agrarian transition and compare it to the agroecological alternative.

The Conclusion to *A Foodie's Guide to Capitalism* calls for "Changing Everything" (with thanks to Naomi Klein). We revisit the nature of the capitalist food regime and look at the ways in which the fragmented food counter-movement is converging to forge a new politics of food. The contradictory role of the "nonprofit industrial complex" and the importance of building a critical transnational public sphere are discussed. Our journey through the political economy of the food system concludes with an explanation of how to distinguish between strategical and tactical alliances, and a call to change everything. I've written a personal postscript, but don't read it until you've finished the book.

For many readers, some of the concepts introduced in this book may be new and may seem counterintuitive at first, making it a challenging read. Stick with it. If we can share an analysis, we can formulate a shared strategy. If we can work strategically, we can change the world.

— 1 —

How Our Capitalist Food System Came to Be

Ill fares the land, to hastening ills a prey,
Where wealth accumulates, and men decay.

—OLIVER GOLDSMITH
THE DESERTED VILLAGE (1770)

Farming began in separate locations around the world as people domesticated plants and animals, ushering in the Neolithic Revolution some 10,000 to 12,000 years ago. Although agriculture did not completely replace hunting, gathering, or fishing, it did drive a global population explosion, creating societies that depended largely on agriculture for their survival. Centuries of co-evolution among people, plants, and animals produced a tremendous variety of cultivars, breeds, production methods, knowledge, tools, cultures, and cuisines. These also gave rise to complex systems of governance, production, and exchange. All of these produced the vast social wealth without which capitalism could never have emerged.

The continued existence of non-capitalist forms of production and social organization throughout the emergence and development of capitalism indicates that this system does not exist independently and is not the only path to human development. Nonetheless, over the course of the last three centuries it has become the world's dominant economic system and has been viewed by many as the ultimate and final stage of human economic development—even as "the end of history."[1] Agriculture continues to play a central role in capitalist production, and in capitalist development, despite the rise of manufacturing, heavy industry, information technology, and the service sector.

The Industrial Revolution and Northern Imperialism

The particular role of agriculture in capitalist development was addressed by classical political economists in seminal publications like *The Wealth of Nations*,[2] *An Essay on the Principles of Population*,[3] *The Principles of Political Economy and Taxation*,[4] and *Das Kapital*.[5] Economists like Adam Smith and David Ricardo concentrated on the nature of wealth creation, the market, and the differences of power between workers, peasants, landlords, and industrialists. Their concepts of property and commodities, the labor theory of value, land rent, and the creation of surplus value are still foundational to understanding capitalist agriculture.

Our early understandings of capitalist agriculture began in the British Isles, because in the pre-dawn of the Industrial Revolution, rural England, Wales, Scotland, and Ireland were undergoing profound transformations. Peasant communities were denied their feudal land rights by large landowners and textile manufacturers, in what came to be known as "enclosures." Karl Marx termed these the "prelude to the revolution that laid the foundation of the capitalist mode of production."[6] In order to establish pasture for commercial sheep production, enclosures destroyed common property rights, privatizing and fencing off land formerly dedicated to food cultivation, grazing, and gathering by peasant communities. The enclosures generally favored large landowners and were bitterly contested by peasants from as early as the sixteenth century, exploding in riots and rebellions in the face of the Enclosure Acts of the eighteenth and nineteenth centuries. The enclosures undermined the ability of people to feed themselves and created a destitute landless class that was obliged to work for wages. This "reserve army of labor" provided the Industrial Revolution with cheap, expendable workers.[7] But not all of the displaced peasantry went to the cities. Some became laborers or tenant farmers on the large commercial farms that characterized British "high farming," a set of intensive farming techniques introduced in the nineteenth century that relied largely on imported guano for fertilization. The larger, wealthier farms using high-farming techniques could produce more per unit of land than peasant farmers who could not afford these inputs. This tended to drive down the price of farm products, favoring larger economies of scale, and pushed more peasant farmers out of agriculture, leading to the consolidation of land ownership in larger and larger holdings.[8] (A similar process was to occur in a number of Third World countries in the 1960s and 1980s, the so-called Green Revolution, which we'll address later in this chapter.)

Once they dominated food production, large-scale farmers ensured lucrative profits by passage of the Corn Laws of 1815, which placed steep tariffs on imported grain. This kept the price of food, something most rural people had previously been able grow rather than buy, relatively high. Though this favored large landholders, the tariffs were opposed by the emerging industrialists who wanted cheap food for their workers. This was not out of altruism, but because the price of bread determined how much they would have to pay their workers. In other words, "The laborer would get wages enough to buy his crust and no more."[9]

The widespread hunger in 1845 (which preceded the Great Hunger of the Irish famine of 1846) led to the repeal of the Corn Laws, opening the British Isles to imported grain and cementing the power of the industrial sector over agriculture. The drop in grain prices did not help peasant farmers, who found it even harder to make ends meet. Agricultural land continued to concentrate in fewer and fewer hands as food production was steadily drawn into international markets. England became the world's first society in which competition, profit-maximization, and capital accumulation drove the economy.[10] This pattern was to repeat itself around the world as the demands of industry first emptied the countryside of people and wealth and then reinvested capital in the industrialization of agriculture itself.

One of the consequences of this "golden age" of British agriculture was that the British Isles ceased to be self-sufficient in food production. But then, it didn't need to be. Britain accumulated wealth by enforcing its own favorable terms of trade, subsidizing exports, keeping wages low, and prohibiting colonies from industrializing, forcing them to buy the empire's own manufactured products. Called "mercantilism" or "mercantile capitalism" these imperial trade strategies became a common characteristic of Western empires. Britain steadily conquered other territories for their raw materials and fertile lands, subjugating vast areas and people to its own mercantile project, a furthering of what Marx called "primitive accumulation"—primitive in the sense of *original.* Referred to as "accumulation by dispossession" by David Harvey, primitive accumulation continues to this day in the expropriation of land and resources, mainly in the Global South for privatization under neoliberal regimes.[11] This simultaneously created consolidated landholdings, capitalist-oriented farmers, and a class of laborers that had to sell their labor power to survive.

Although wheat was imported mainly from North America and Ukraine, as Western Europe industrialized it came to depend more and more on colonies in the Global South for food and raw materials. This had a profound impact on food systems throughout the imperial orbit, affecting landscapes, diet, and cuisine. For example, in their diet working-class Britons largely replaced beer, which supplied important calories and nutrients and could be locally sourced, with tea and sugar, which had to be imported.[12] This fit nicely into the mercantilist-industrial transition, providing a caffeine-and-sugar fix to workers—subsisting almost exclusively on bread—to dampen hunger and maintain productivity during the long hours spent working in the factories.[13] It also created a rapidly expanding market for the tea and sugar plantations steadily transforming Asia and the Americas into vast, slave-powered monocultures.

The role of food, both its production and consumption, was thus central to colonial "capital accumulation" in which wealth, technology, social organization, and political power steadily built in the centers of empire. Non-food agricultural products like cotton and tobacco also played essential roles, but it is not an exaggeration to say that seventeenth-century European capitalism would never have emerged without non-European food and beverage crops such as maize, potatoes, rice, sugar, and tea.

Take potatoes, for example. Tubers were the caloric foundation of Andean civilization. Just a few of the Andes' four thousand varieties were taken to Europe by Spanish conquistadores. Potatoes spread across Western Europe, in large part because they out-produced wheat, barley, and oats at least four times over.[14] Further, peasants could leave them in the ground, harvesting them as needed. This gave potatoes a distinct advantage over European grains that had to be harvested and stored, leaving farmers vulnerable to hungry armies and voracious tax collectors. Though potatoes did not replace grains, they are sometimes credited for saving Western Europe from periodic famines. On the other hand, the overreliance on just a few varieties—along with poverty, absentee landlord arrangements, and a market incentive to export food in times of hunger—also placed the potato at the center of Ireland's Great Famine.[15]

Maize, a staple for indigenous peoples from Mesoamerica to North America, was brought to Africa in the 1500s where it quickly spread farmer-to-farmer, revolutionizing agriculture.[16] It was less popular in Europe, however, because people thought it wasn't as nutritious as barley or wheat.[17] But slave traders stocking up in West Africa discovered that it stored better and kept more slaves alive in the horrendous Atlantic passage than did wheat, barley, or potatoes. This made the slave trade more viable, leading to the expansion of the brutal slave plantations in the Americas.[18]

The role of rice in slavery and plantation agriculture is also tragic. The first rice cultivated in North America was likely brought from Africa, not Asia. European colonists had no idea how to cultivate or process it. West Africans were experts at sophisticated forms of floodplain and tidal irrigation and adept at the difficult and arduous process of hand milling. Rice-producing slaves were initially able to exchange knowledge of rice cultivation for land. This arrangement ended when the plantation owners finally learned the technology. African rice became a staple for the enslavement of the very farmers who shared the secrets of its cultivation.[19]

Even fertilizer, one of the hallmarks of capitalist agriculture, really took off in Europe with the importation of Peruvian guano—the nutrient-rich excrement of bats and seabirds found mostly on remote islands—and the scientific endorsement by Justus von Liebig in his book *Organic Chemistry in Its Application to Agriculture and Physiology*. Not only did guano usher in British high farming, it became a highly profitable colonial business, thanks in part to the slave and convict labor used to dig it. Historian Charles Mann calls it the key ingredient of Europe's very first "Green Revolution."[20]

Slavery and Capitalism

Although slavery was commonly thought of as a pre-capitalist form of production, historians are now demonstrating that it played a pivotal role in the development of industrial capitalism in the first half of the nineteenth century.[21] Slavery made possible a cheap, plentiful supply of cotton for the burgeoning textile mills.

Prior to slavery, capitalist agriculture failed to keep up with the growing demand for cotton because capitalists couldn't force the peasantry to grow it on an industrial scale. In the southern United States, white settlers had exterminated and driven off indigenous populations to appropriate their land, a strategy that left them without a workforce. The enslavement and translocation of Africans from West Africa to North America and the Caribbean was capitalism's answer to the labor shortage.

The lucrative profits from the U.S. slave trade circulated through a thriving banking sector and were reinvested in Northern industry, which then sold industrial products from plows to clothing back to the South. Fortunes accrued and were further reinvested in genocidal

Guano Imperialism

During the mid-nineteenth century, the capitalist world economy converged around the guano trade, which brought together the United States, Britain, Peru, and China in a system of extreme ecological and human exploitation. Justus von Liebig, along with other prominent agronomists of the time, highlighted how capitalist agriculture had fundamentally altered the nutrient cycle leading to a drastic loss of soil nutrients. This nutrient deficit was experienced with particular acuity in the United States—especially among farmers in Upstate New York and in the southeastern plantation economy, who suffered from a paucity of natural fertilizers. As Britain had already established a monopoly on Peruvian guano supplies, the United States pursued, first unofficially and then as part of deliberate state policy, imperial annexation of any islands thought to contain this potent natural fertilizer, rich in nitrogen and phosphorus. In 1856 the U.S. Congress passed the Guano Islands Act, allowing U.S. capitalists to seize ninety-four islands, rocks, and keys from around the globe between 1856 and 1903, marking an important early chapter in the history of American ecological imperialism. Sixty-six of these were officially recognized by the Department of State as U.S. appurtenances (property attachments), with nine remaining as U.S. possessions today. Despite the millions of tons of guano that were excavated and exported internationally, the excrement failed to provide the United States with the quantity and quality of natural fertilizer it required. The exhaustion of agricultural soil under capitalist agriculture in the eastern United States thus became one of the key drivers for westward expansion.

projects for westward expansion. The centrality of slavery and dispossession for the emergence of modern capitalism flies in the face of many myths about our food system. As historian Sven Beckert points out,

> It was not the small farmers of the rough New England countryside who established the United States' economic position. It was the backbreaking labor of unremunerated American slaves in places like South Carolina, Mississippi, and Alabama . . . After the Civil War [and abolition], a new kind of capitalism arose, in the United States and elsewhere. Yet that new capitalism—characterized first and foremost by states with unprecedented bureaucratic, infrastructural, and military capacities, and by wage labor—had been enabled by the profits, institutions, networks, technologies, and innovations that emerged from slavery, colonialism, and land expropriation.[22]

Slavery had a tremendous influence on food systems around the world. Enslaved Africans were highly skilled farmers who not only grew rice, cotton, sugar, and tobacco, but were also expected to grow food for themselves as well as the plantation owners, for whom they also had to cook. The famed southern cooking and "soul food" of the United States is an African-American invention with deep roots in slavery.

After the hard-fought abolition of slavery, many former slaves were forced into sharecropping, through Jim Crow laws that segregated, discriminated against, incarcerated, and exploited former slaves. Sharecropping was an extractive system that recreated certain slave-like conditions among those who worked the land but did not require the landowners to pay for the reproduction of the labor force, that is, the costs of raising and maintaining the laborer before, during, and after their productive life. In spite of this, by dint of backbreaking work, frugality, and cooperation among themselves, African Americans by 1910 had acquired 15 million acres of farmland. Nevertheless, the systematic abuse of civil and human rights left African-American farmers vulnerable to the cyclical crises of capitalist agriculture, leading to the Great Migrations of 1910–1930 and 1940–1970. Millions of African Americans left the rural South for northern cities in the United States.

Agrarian Wisdom

African crops and agrarian wisdom were the basis for wealth not only in the United States but also in Brazil. Even though the introduction of rice into the Western Hemisphere is most often associated with its arrival in South Carolina shortly after the founding of that colony in 1670, rice was grown in Brazil approximately one century earlier.[23] Other crops of African origin were found in Brazil as early as 1560, including okra, pigeon peas, black-eyed peas, millet, sorghum, yams, and African oil palm. But rice had the greatest agricultural and cultural impact. French historian Jean Suret-Canale observed that the importation of crops and food-processing technology and nutritional practices from Africa to Brazil laid the cornerstone for civilization in Brazil. As one Brazilian official stated, "It is Africa that civilised Brazil."[24] Three-quarters of enslaved Africans brought to Brazil between 1548 and 1560 came from the rice-growing region of Senegambia. Rice was grown as a plantation and subsistence crop in Brazil. It was an important source of food for the maroons who escaped slavery.

The enslaved Africans' knowledge base on rice production was extensive. Enslaved African farmers in South Carolina knew much more about rice production than the plantation owners. In 1670, approximately a hundred enslaved Africans were brought by the first white settlers to reach South Carolina. Evidence exists that rice was grown there from the beginning of the colony's existence. Africans' technology and labor created a multimillion-dollar industry that eventually provided the revenue for the Industrial Revolution. African seeds and knowledge also supported the development of rice production in Louisiana. According to historian Gwendolyn Hall, two slave ships from Senegambia arrived in Louisiana in 1719 carrying several barrels of rice seed that probably came from that region.[25]

Jonathan Green conveys the ingenuity of Africans coming into South Carolina. "All the earth was moved by people only using sweetgrass baskets. They moved earth larger than the Great Wall of China . . . larger in volume than the pyramids."[26] However, once the enslavement of Africans by Europeans began, Europeans stole the credit for introducing rice and the technology for growing it. The Portuguese were said to have introduced rice from Asia into Africa. Not until the twentieth century was this misinterpretation corrected.[27] Several indigenous wild rice varieties were found throughout Africa.[28] The main improved variety of rice grown in Africa was *Oryza glaberrima*, which was of a different species than the main variety developed in Asia, *Oryza sativa*.

The Food Regime

By the end of the nineteenth century, mercantilism, colonialism, and industrialization had all combined in a new form of global capitalism that spread powerfully, if unevenly, around the earth. The empires of Europe expanded their military and economic might in Africa, Asia, and the Americas in new and violent ways. The massive increase in commodity production required the liberalization (deregulation) of markets so that goods and money could flow freely without being hindered by tariffs and trade barriers. Financial and banking systems, communications, transport, society, culture, and language were all swept into the dynamic system of capitalist relations. The flow of cheap raw materials from the colonies to the centers of imperial power transformed livelihoods, territories, and systems of governance as food, land, and labor became global commodities.

All of the institutions, treaties, and regulations shaping and governing food on a global scale made up the first colonial "food regime," a uniquely capitalist phenomenon.[29] It was the first regime to dominate the world's food systems. It followed the logic and served the interests of Northern capitalism.

To say it dominated the world's food systems does not mean that every local and regional food system was completely integrated into the colonial food regime. Most of the world's people still traded and ate their food as they had done for centuries—except when they produced global goods, or were hired (or forced) to harvest an export crop, or ate any of the international commodities circling the globe, like sugar, coffee, wheat, rice, and maize. The colonial food regime was the first *hegemonic* regime, however, in that it was ubiquitous, and had consolidated a powerful set of institutions and rules that influenced food production, processing, and distribution on a world scale.

New technology and free markets are often touted as the main factors for the development of capitalism. But when we look at the emergence of the capitalist food system, we see that *regulation* in the form of the enclosures that privatized the production and flow of goods, and the violent *dispossession* of land and resources by state-financed armies, and the *exploitation* of labor by coercive means such as poverty and slavery allowed the system to emerge. This pattern of regulation, dispossession, exploitation, technological development, and market expansion was to repeat itself many times throughout the development of capitalism. As we'll see, these patterns also characterize food regimes today.

Capitalism's Agrarian Question

Capitalism is a system in which most goods and services are produced to be bought and sold as commodities in a market. Labor is supplied by people who have no way to make a living on their own and must sell what they do have—their ability to work, that is, labor power. In capitalism, value is created by bringing labor, resources, technology, and markets together to create commodities that are sold for more than it cost to produce them. Capital, in turn, is profit in search of more profit. Value is extracted and wealth is accumulated in this process and turned again into capital. Capitalism as a system must either grow or die. Because capital is always in motion as owners compete for more profits and a greater share of the market, capitalism expands constantly. This is why land, labor, and other resources are often forcibly and violently colonized by capital through dispossession (such as the enclosures) or war. Expanding markets and access to resources are very high priorities of the system as a whole, as well as for individual business owners and managers. These priorities are then posited as social necessities and this gives rise to the view that our economic well-being is best measured by our economic growth rate, irrespective of how such growth destroys the environment, lives, or entire cultures and societies. Disasters such as hurricanes add to the gross domestic product (GDP) because of the economic activity of rebuilding. So do private prisons, the illegal drug trade, and the war on drugs. On the other hand, the work traditionally done at home by women, such as cooking and cleaning, child-rearing and care of the family—all essential to capitalism—are not part of the GDP. Neither is food grown for self-consumption, nor food that is bartered or given away.

When capitalism emerged, most people in the world were peasant farmers. The challenge for capitalism was how to use the tremendous social and environmental wealth held in rural societies to develop industry, which was much more profitable to capital than peasant farming. At first, large landholders sought to monopolize the supply of wool to meet the demands of industry. The original strategy for accomplishing this was to separate the producer (the peasant) from the means of production (the land). The forcible displacement of large sectors of the peasantry created a mass of paupers that became a potential labor force. Later, agriculture itself was industrialized, which required capital from the industrial sector, more land, cheap labor, and cheap food, all largely expropriated and extracted from the peasantry.

In his book *The Agrarian Question* (1899), the Czech-German philosopher Karl Kautsky rigorously addressed the role of agriculture in the nineteenth century development of capitalism. Kautsky believed that peasant agriculture was inferior to industrial agriculture and destined to disappear in what he called the "agrarian transition." He thought that some peasant farms could remain under capitalism because peasant families would "self-exploit" by producing food at

What Is Capital Anyway?

The notion of "capital" has generated considerable conceptual and theoretical debate. Capital can mean many things. Many people confuse capital with money. Though money can be capital, capital takes other forms as well, and is even more basic to capitalist relations of production and value-generation than is money. One way of thinking about capital is as "value in search of more value." A person or a firm has accumulated some measure of wealth—which is simply an accumulation of value—and uses this to produce or obtain more wealth. Money is usually involved—to make more money. So the accumulation of capital becomes a self-propelling process or circuit; the surplus wealth accumulated in one stage becomes the investment to produce more wealth in the next stage:

Suppose "M" represents money and "C" represents a commodity, like grain, kale, or gardening rakes. Someone takes money, buys a commodity with it, and then sells it for money, represented by the equation:

M-C-M

Actually, the point of capitalism is to sell the commodity for more money than they to produce it, so,

spent M-C-M′

Here M′ represents a sum larger than M, the increase representing the money profit. Over the whole circuit/process, capitalists appropriate this value, able to do so because they hold monopoly ownership of the means of production that everyone else depends upon.

Capital is not just profit, however. Capital can take many forms as it moves through this circuit: it can be money in the form of cash or credit, commodities in the form of raw materials, tools, and factories, as well as the labor embodied in commodities, including machinery. It also embodies the social relationships between the workers and the owners of the capital being produced! What's important to note is that these things are only considered capital when they are part of this circuit and when its various phases move seamlessly into one another. Money sitting in one's pocket or bank account or idle workers at factories are not considered capital because they aren't actively moving through this circuit.

Competition, and the drive to increase one's capital, making more money and wealth, to make more money and wealth is intrinsic to capitalism. To compete, capitalists must cut costs, by using more efficient technologies or processes, and/or paying their workers less. This will give them an advantage, until their competitors do the same. Then, the only way to out-compete their competitors is to get bigger and to access new markets. This is why capitalism is in constant expansion.

But why can't capitalist businesses just stay the same size? Why can't capitalism produce a lot of small businesses instead of consolidating into bigger and bigger operations? The simple answer is because capitalist businesses eventually saturate their markets when people can't consume products as fast as capitalists produce them. Goods and savings pile up and capital stagnates. Workers are laid off, which further reduces demand. The only solution is to find new markets, or take over someone else's market. That is the foundation of competition.

labor costs that were below the going agricultural wage and thus be able to compete with industrial agriculture, which had to pay full wages. But because peasants also needed money, they would also work for wages, providing cheap labor, thus subsidizing industrial development in the countryside and providing a market for industrial goods.[30] Contrary to the many happy narratives of modern economic progress, none of this happened seamlessly.

Russian agronomist Alexander Chayanov worked for the Ministry of Land Reform in the Soviet Union after the October Revolution and had access to vast stores of agricultural data. He claimed that the inevitable disappearance of the peasantry was a statistical illusion stemming from ignorance regarding the internal dynamics of peasant production and the ways peasant families grew, divided, and grew again across generations. He concluded that economists were wrong to treat peasant farms as if they were underdeveloped capitalist enterprises, stressing that rather than seeking profit, peasant families strove for a balance between the number of working family members and the amount of food they needed to maintain the family. They could sell some of their goods on the market, but would avoid taking market risks. He believed that under the right conditions, peasant farming could be just as productive (or more so, depending on the measure of productivity) than industrial agriculture.[31]

Debates on the "Agrarian Question" were a matter of life and death for millions of peasants throughout the twentieth century as both capitalist and socialist countries raced to industrialize. Although modern agriculture needed seasonal peasant labor (available at low cost because the peasantry still fed itself), it also had to move the vast masses of peasants out of the countryside to make way for industrial agriculture. This was accomplished by the forces of the market, politics, violence, or a combination of all three. Nonetheless, nations had tremendous difficulty accomplishing this task. People stubbornly hung on to their farms and their way of life. Despite the peasantry's reputation for being conservative, violent peasant rebellions for land and against injustice have been common throughout modern history. Major wars of liberation—most against capitalism—were fought by peasants in Mexico, China, Algeria, Vietnam, and Cuba.[32]

Of course, rural people also make up most of the military forces of governments around the world and few nations, even industrialized countries, can afford to dismiss or take them for granted. In the late 1960s at the height of the Cold War, the anti-colonial wars of liberation, and the counterinsurgency programs of the Western powers, sociologist Teodor Shanin wrote: "Day by day, the peasants make the economists sigh, the politicians sweat and the strategists swear, defeating their plans and prophecies all over the world—Moscow and Washington, Peking and Delhi, Cuba and Algeria, the Congo and Vietnam."[33]

The hotly contested Agrarian Question of the nineteenth and twentieth centuries—and the role of small-scale producers in society—have persisted until the present day. Just how, when, or whether small-scale production would or should disappear is still unresolved. This is because, despite widespread agricultural industrialization and the massive displacement of the peasantry, the world has about as many small-scale and peasant farmers today as it did over a hundred years ago. More than 70 percent of the world's food is produced by small family farms on less than 25 percent of the world's arable land.[34] Most of these farmers, primarily women, are poor and thus make up about 70 percent of the world's hungry people.

Understanding these contradictions is impossible without understanding the way capitalism interacts with our food system. The 30 percent of the world's food *not* produced by small-scale farmers is mostly produced by huge, highly capitalized, industrial agribusiness operations. These farms have tremendous economies of scale that give them an advantage in the global marketplace. They constantly upgrade their technologies and farm larger and larger areas to stay competitive in capitalist food markets. This is very good business for the multinational corporations that supply seeds, fertilizer, pesticides, irrigation, and farm equipment. It is also good business for large purchasers of agricultural products, especially the large grain traders like Cargill and Archer Daniels Midland (ADM) that earn only pennies per ton of grain traded and need to buy and sell billions of tons to make a profit.

Despite their great size, however, there is only so much technology these large farms can absorb before this input market of fertilizers, pesticides, herbicides, and machinery becomes saturated. When this happens farms either have to get even bigger (thus creating a demand for bigger farm machinery, precision agriculture services, and more labor-saving technologies) or small farms must be consolidated into large farms capable of buying the large-scale inputs. Agribusinesses are capitalist enterprises. They need to constantly grow. For this reason, behind their promises to "feed the world," agribusinesses are eager to increase their market share by expanding large-scale industrial agriculture into the 70 percent of the world's food that is still produced by small-scale and peasant farmers.

Capitalist agriculture's large-scale industrial operations have been very effective at producing cheap food. The mass production of cheap food brings down the cost of labor by making the worker's "food basket" less expensive. This stimulates industrial growth. Cheap food also means that workers can afford to buy more new products coming from industry. Of course, large farms and factories produce much more than workers eat or buy. This drives market expansion, nationally and globally, as capital seeks out more and more consumers. (Though capitalist agriculture has been adept at producing cheap food, it is not energy or water efficient, is not good at providing living wage jobs, and is rife with negative social and environmental consequences that mainstream economists call "market failures" and "externalities." More on these later.)

The agrarian transition is a continual process. It is also continually resisted by peasants, pastoralists, and small-scale producers around the world, who are forging other forms of production that challenge the capitalist food system.

The Second Global Food Regime: "Breadlines Knee-Deep in Wheat"

Throughout the nineteenth century most people in the world were still farmers who got most of their food from their own farms. There was, of course, a tremendous diversity of practices around the world—from slash-and-burn agriculture, to floating gardens and flooded rice, to farms that used animal traction and fertilized with cover crops and animal manure. There was also a diversity of work and tenure arrangements, from family farms to plantation agriculture, and multiple forms of tenant farming, sharecropping, and traditionally managed communal land.

The first food regime, rocked by international events, began to change at the dawn of the twentieth century, culminating in profound transformations by the 1950s and the dawn of a second global food regime.

The first global tremor was the First World War, fought among colonial powers. The United States, a latecomer that had largely turned its colonies and land grabs into states, did not initially join the fight. Agriculture in the United States was in its golden age. Farmers enjoyed prices that allowed them to cover their costs of production and provide a decent livelihood. This was known as "parity." In 1914—on the eve of the war—a bushel of corn bought five gallons of gasoline. No one suspected that seven years later it would take two bushels just to buy one gallon.[35]

Most Americans wanted to stay out of the war, and U.S. banks and steel companies were making windfall profits supplying capital and armaments to England and France. Farmers also saw prices and profits rise as Europeans relied more and more on food from the United States. But when German U-boats sank U.S. supply ships going to Europe, the United States entered the "War to End All Wars."

High wartime grain prices, plentiful credit, and new Ford tractors led to an agricultural boom in the United States. Land values rose dramatically. Farmers took out second, third, and fourth mortgages and bought more land to take advantage of the boom. Financing flowed and land speculation was rampant. Fortunes were made on Wall Street as well as in the North American heartland. Then the war ended.

After the Armistice of 1918, European farmers began growing food again, leading to a global oversupply and a crash in international grain and cotton prices. Capital investment abandoned agriculture, bursting the speculative land bubble. Overextended on their loans, with crop prices hopelessly below the costs of production, farmers began going broke at the height of the Roaring Twenties, when Wall Street was getting rich. Throughout the 1920s corporate profits rose by 62 percent while wages for workers rose only 9 percent. By 1929 the wealthiest 10 percent of the U.S. population controlled 34 percent of the country's wealth, as much as the bottom 42 percent.[36] (Compare these figures to today's global distribution of wealth, in which eight individuals own as much wealth as the poorest half of the world!)

The boom-bust cycle of the "Agricultural Depression" turned out to be a prelude to the 1929 stock market crash and the Great

Depression. The Great Depression only made things worse for agriculture. In recessionary times the capitalist market simply dries up because of lack of demand, leading producers to cut back production. However, for farmers, with their high fixed costs, the response to a decline in prices provokes an increase rather than a decrease in production.

Trying desperately to farm their way out of debt, farmers produced even more food, which only drove prices further downward. But no matter how much cheap food they produced, the millions of people who were out of work (up to one in four by 1932) still could not afford to buy it. Farmers dumped milk on highways, slaughtered sheep in the fields, and plowed crops into the ground, desperately trying to cut their losses and bring up prices. Long breadlines of hungry, destitute people wound through the nation's cities even as grain rotted in silos across the country. The phrase "breadlines knee-deep in wheat" epitomized the brutal market logic of overproduction within a highly productive food regime in the grip of an economic depression.[37]

President Franklin Delano Roosevelt tried to pull the United States out of the Great Depression by implementing a series of policies that became known as the New Deal. He began with the Agricultural Adjustment Act (AAA), which tried to return to "parity prices" that gave farmers the same purchasing power they had before the First World War. The Secretary of Agriculture sought to manage supply through "set-asides" that paid farmers to take land out of production, and marketing agreements that limited the amount each farmer could produce. The AAA levied taxes on processors and middlemen, who then passed costs on to industry and the public.

The problem of agriculture was not lack of production, but low prices. The problem of food access was not high prices, but unemployment. The New Deal pumped federal money into job creation programs, attempting to put money back into people's pockets to kick-start the economy. The first national food assistance programs were also initiated to deal with both overproduction and poverty. It was the dawn of the second food regime. The agricultural policies of the New Deal set the institutional and regulatory framework for the relation between food, agriculture, government, and capitalism for the next half-century. According to George Naylor, an Iowa farm leader:

> New Deal farm programs involved conservation-supply management to avoid wasteful, polluting overproduction; a price support that actually set a floor under the market prices rather than sending out government payments; grain reserves to avoid food shortages and food price spikes; and a quota system that was fair to all farmers and changed the incentives of production. "Parity" was the name associated with these programs because it meant the farmer would be treated with economic equality and prices would be adjusted for inflation to remove the destructive cost-price squeeze and the need for farmers to overproduce their way out of poverty and debt. It was understood that the farmer's individual "freedom" to do whatever he or she wished with the land would be tempered for the good of all farmers and society. A social contract was established.[38]

The Second World War eventually pulled the U.S. economy out of the Depression. The country's labor surplus disappeared overnight. Women headed for the factories. Agriculture could not meet peak seasonal labor demands. The United States needed hundreds of thousands of workers for planting, weeding, and harvest.

The nation found its ideal workforce in Mexico. Able to execute quick, precise, repetitive movements while bent over all day long under the hot sun for months at a time—despite physical pain—Mexican peasants kept the U.S. food system running. Without them, the United States could not have fought the war. Brought in under the Mexican Farm Labor Program Agreement of 1942 (later the Bracero Program), over two decades, some 4.6 million Mexican farmers transformed U.S. agriculture.[39] Mexican labor was cheap. Because of their foreign citizenship and their contract stipulations, workers were prohibited from organizing or seeking redress against the rampant labor violations that plagued U.S. agriculture. It was not the first or the last time the United States would rely on cheap immigrant labor. The

Waves of Labor

The history of early agricultural industrialization in the United States is inextricably linked to the history of immigrant labor. There have been four major waves of immigration in U.S. history, the events and policies of which have shaped—and continue to shape—the conditions of laborers in the agricultural system.

FIRST WAVE: 1600–1800

Born from the acute need for cheap labor to work and develop the land, indentured servitude operated as the primary mechanism for European immigration to the United States during the early seventeenth century. It served as a labor system for both Europe's "surplus" people—the rootless, the unemployed, the criminal—and those willing to sell their labor and freedom for a fixed term of four to seven years in exchange for free passage and board. Indentured servants were quantitatively important in the early colonies that produced staple crops for export, but as the price of indentured agricultural labor increased over time, colonial landowners turned to African slave labor as a cheaper alternative.[40] The Trans-Atlantic Slave Trade Database conservatively estimates that approximately 12.5 million slaves arrived in the United States between 1500 and the end of the Civil War in 1865, the majority of them brought to the southern colonies and states where the warm climate and long growing season made slave labor profitable. After the end of the Civil War, during the Reconstruction Era, the U.S. government passed laws to prohibit slavery and involuntary servitude with the ratification of the Thirteenth Amendment to the Constitution.

SECOND WAVE: 1820–1880

More than seven million newcomers, mostly from Western and Northern Europe, entered the United States during this period: about a third were Irish, many of whom were fleeing from their country's disastrous potato famine. Another third were German, who in general arrived with more wealth, and ventured to the Midwest in search of farmland. The California Gold Rush that began in 1849 and the building of the First Transcontinental Railroad from 1863 to 1869 brought migrants from around the world, including the first substantial Chinese population in the United States. The large pool of Chinese workers later turned to Californian agriculture, but rising xenophobia in California and elsewhere culminated in the Chinese Exclusion Act of 1882, which effectively ended this labor flow.[41]

THIRD WAVE: 1880–1920

Over roughly four decades, more than 24 million so-called "new immigrants" entered the United States from Southern and Eastern Europe. As agriculture rapidly transformed into a large-scale industry, the need for farming labor increased and the United States began importing Asian (predominantly Chinese, Japanese, and Filipino) labor as African Americans moved into other industries. By the time of the 1910 census, foreign-born residents accounted for nearly 15 percent of the U.S. population and about 24 percent of the U.S. labor force.[42] The 1917 Immigration Act, the nation's first set of widely restrictive immigration rules, established the "Asiatic Barred Zone," which banned immigrants from most Asian and Pacific island nations save Japan and the Philippines. As historian Mae Ngai notes, this geographical parameter "codified the principle of racial exclusion into the main body of American immigration and naturalization law."[43]

An immigration pause occurred in 1915 as the First World War spread across Europe. As immigration flows began again in the 1920s, the Immigration Act of 1924 introduced strict numerical limits, or "quotas," based on national origin in an attempt to curtail the migration of "undesirable races." The severe economic depression of the 1930s further discouraged more foreigners from moving to the United States. In order to compensate for the loss of farm labor to military enlistment during the Second World War, the Bracero Program (1942 through 1964) brought in more than 4.5 million Mexican farmworkers who were granted temporary U.S. guest worker status.

FOURTH WAVE: 1965–PRESENT

The national origins quota system was phased out with the passage of the Hart-Celler Act of 1965, replaced by a skills-based preference system, and for the first time since the colonial period, immigration became dominated by non-Europeans. In response to the 9/11 terrorist attacks, post-2001 immigration enforcement amplified the significance of migrant "illegality," resulting in an increase in deportations and border security expenditures. Today, the vast majority of U.S. agricultural workers come from Central and Latin America, with an estimated 75 percent being undocumented. Underpinned by their political vulnerability, undocumented migrant farmworkers continue to be exposed to dangerous working conditions, labor violations, and low pay.[44]

"immigrant labor subsidy" transferred billions of dollars in value to the sector, increased agricultural land values, and turned the Second World War into an agricultural boom placing the United States at the forefront of global agricultural markets.

After the war, the large manufacturing facilities producing wartime nitrates (for bombs) and toxic chemicals (for poison gas) were refitted to produce fertilizers and pesticides.[45] Since the U.S. mainland had not suffered any war damage to its productive infrastructure—on the contrary, it had expanded—heavy industry quickly converted to peacetime production, pushing out tractors and combines in place of jeeps and tanks. The U.S. banks were flush with recently printed war dollars. They eagerly lent money to farmers to buy chemicals and machinery. Petroleum, cheap and abundant, fueled the modernization of agriculture. More land was brought into production and farms got a lot bigger. Production soared, bringing down food prices. Huge food surpluses built up. For a while, the government offloaded this food in Europe as food aid. But when U.S. farmers could no longer absorb all the fertilizers, pesticides, and new machinery being produced in the United States, companies began selling these inputs to Europe as part of the U.S.'s Marshall Plan for European reconstruction. Pretty soon, Europe didn't need more food or inputs from U.S. companies, either. Europe began to overproduce food.

Instead of cutting back on production, Northern governments used combinations of subsidies, price supports, and quotas to ensure a continuous oversupply. Why? On the one hand, this lowered the price of grains for powerful grain traders. On the other, these cheap surpluses could be channeled into food aid and dumped into overseas markets. Overproduction in the North was used as a battering ram to open up grain markets in the Global South (and to hook Southern consumers on U.S. products), to the detriment of the unsubsidized farmers in the South who could not compete. In India, the United States used food aid as a political weapon to force the Indian government to accept U.S. fertilizers and hybrid seeds.[46] The U.S. price supports to farmers were lowered yearly. Overproduction increased year after year, and farms got bigger in order to stay financially viable, forcing smaller farms out of business.

Most of the benefits of government support to agriculture are captured by large corporations that revel in the cheap grain, and by seed, machinery, and fertilizer suppliers. Although public support for the food system is vital, the way that subsidies and market-price supports have been used in the United States and Europe exacerbated oversupply, leading to international dumping driving family farmers bankrupt. These farmers sold out to larger, more capitalized operations, leading to corporate concentration in the food system. [47]

In part, this was a Cold War strategy. Western governments were trying very hard to steer what they began calling "underdeveloped" countries (former colonies) away from the Soviet Union. Governments in the Global South received food aid, then sold the food at low prices in national currency. This provided them with revenues for public works (when not siphoned off through corruption). It also undermined their capacity for local food production, however, because farmers could not compete with food from the Global North that was sold at prices below the costs of production. Squeezed between plantation agriculture and cheap food, smallholders—those growing most of the locally consumed food—became more and more impoverished. The result was to reverse the South-North flow of food. Former colonies went from supplying the North with food to becoming dependent on the North for their food.[48] This simply confirmed the Western notion that poor countries needed to be "developed." Agriculture was to play a central role.

The Green Revolution: Exporting the U.S. Industrial Model

In 1970 Norman Borlaug, a crop scientist from Iowa, won the Nobel Prize for developing high-yielding dwarf hybrids of Mexican wheat, which were later introduced to India and Pakistan. Borlaug is widely credited for "saving a billion people from hunger." The application of Borlaug's breeding techniques to rice and maize and the general spread of hybrids, irrigation, fertilizers, and pesticides from the United States to the developing world became known as the *Green Revolution*. The term was specifically selected to counter the communist-inspired "Red revolutions" that swept poor countries in Asia, Africa, and Latin America during the 1960s. Modern agriculture was capitalism's bulwark against rebellion.

The Green Revolution (1960–1990) was a campaign to spread capitalist agriculture—itself an extension of the industrial North's economic model—into the countries of the Global South. Though routinely credited for saving the world from hunger, the Green Revolution also produced as many hungry people as it saved.[49]

On the one hand, the spread of high-yielding hybrids displaced thousands of local varieties of wheat, maize, and rice, leading to a 90 percent reduction of *in situ* agrobiodiversity. Because Green Revolution hybrids would only produce high yields with heavy applications of fertilizer, irrigation, and pesticides, industrial agriculture quickly became a major contributor of pollutants and greenhouse gases.

On the other hand, because the Green Revolution required capital input, it primarily benefited middle- and large-scale farmers who could afford to pay for them.[50] Smallholders went bankrupt, resulting in the massive displacement of the peasantry, who fled to the cities in search of work or migrated to the fragile hillsides and forest frontiers to grow subsistence crops. During this period vast slums began to ring the major cities of the Global South creating, as Mike Davis described it, a "planet of slums."[51]

As a technological centerpiece, the Green Revolution was similar to the English high farming that sought to replace peasant agriculture during the agrarian transition of the seventeenth and eighteenth centuries. The rationale of capitalist development—that people should leave the countryside to work in manufacturing and industry—concentrated the best agricultural land in fewer, larger, and richer holdings. The enclosures of the Green Revolution affected not only peasant land but peasant seeds. Green Revolution hybrids essentially privatized the genetic material developed by the peasantry over millennia. Though this material was free to the seed industry, hybrids do not "breed true" (when seeds were saved and replanted, the plants tended to express regressive genetic traits). Farmers were obliged to buy these new seeds every year. Similar to the first agrarian transition, industrial agriculture under the Green Revolution also depended on the peasantry for cheap labor. Known as "functional dualism," the Green Revolution's dependence on the peasantry was largely masked by capitalism's celebratory claims of technical superiority.[52]

The persistence of the peasantry throughout the Green Revolution was not only due to the ability of these family farmers to self-exploit. Because there weren't enough jobs in the cities, large sections of the peasantry steadily opened up new areas of tropical forest and fragile hillsides to farming, using slash-and-burn techniques. After a few years weeds, declining fertility, and pressure from cattle ranchers obliged peasant farmers to move on.

When the large, highly capitalized farms could no longer absorb more hybrid seeds and chemical inputs from the Green Revolution, governments lent money to peasant farmers so they could buy these products. The combination of Green Revolution practices and inputs on the best land, the increase in area of agricultural lands, and the application of chemicals on the peasant farms of the hillsides and forest frontiers produced a glut of basic grains worldwide that would last for decades. Unfortunately, the use of chemicals and hybrid seeds on these fragile soils was not sustainable. After initial increases in productivity, much of this land quickly degraded, leading the peasantry to abandon farming or push even deeper into the agricultural frontier. Though yields were increased using new technology, sometimes dramatically, much of the credit for "saving the world from hunger" claimed by the Green Revolution is due to the displacement and vast expansion of peasant agriculture.

The story of Gabriel Sanchez, a peasant farmer in the state of Tlaxcala, Mexico, is an example. In the 1960s, Gabriel married and obtained two hectares of hilly, rain-fed land to farm. In good years, Gabriel and his budding family produced enough maize, beans, and squash to feed themselves and sell a bit on the market. Over time they accumulated a cow, two mules, and a few sheep and goats that they grazed on communal land. Like most of their neighbors, they had a pig that ate kitchen scraps. A dozen or so of their chickens and turkeys foraged around the yard. These typically ended up prepared in a delicious chocolate-chili *mole* that I was lucky enough to taste on festive occasions. The family saved their seed for planting from one year to the next and always kept a grain reserve on hand for poor harvest years. When he could, Gabriel worked for wages nearby on large farms.

In the early 1970s the Mexican government offered peasant farmers credit to buy the Green Revolution's hybrid seeds and synthetic fertilizer. Gabriel was one of the first in the village to sign up—an "early adopter" in development parlance. (His father advised against it; he didn't believe in going into debt.) The government contract obliged him to grow his maize as a monoculture, eliminating the beans (which added nitrogen to the soil and were a staple of the family's diet) and the squash (which helped conserve moisture and fed his animals). This meant he had to buy beans to feed his family and feed to maintain his animals, but the yields and price he got from the new maize were high enough to cover these costs. Everything went well for the first couple of harvests. Then, since fewer and fewer farmers were growing beans, the price went up. Since more and more farmers were growing hybrid maize, the price of corn fell. At the same time, because the organic matter in the thin hillside soils of his farm was not being replaced, despite the new fertilizer, Gabriel's yields began to drop. Gabriel rented some more land, took out more credit, and applied more fertilizer in an effort to maintain his income. But the hybrid maize did not stand up to pests very well. He had to buy pesticides, further increasing his production costs. Hybrid maize didn't store well, either, so Gabriel had to sell most of his crop soon after harvest when prices were lowest. Months later, when he had to buy maize to feed his family, the price was much higher. One year a drought hit. The hybrid maize, unlike local varieties that had been selected over millennia to withstand severe weather events, withered away. To make matters worse, his youngest daughter fell gravely ill. Gabriel sold most of his family's animals to pay the medical expenses and cover his farm debt. He went to work in Mexico City on a construction site. His wife and oldest son grew maize, beans, and squash on as much of the family plot as they could manage that year and left the rest to be cultivated by relatives. Unfortunately, the soil had lost most of its fertility. The harvest was poor. The family was determined to hang on to the farm, but knew that another year of debt, drought, or illness would ruin them.[53]

Gabriel's story is typical of the second stage of the Green Revolution when government banks extended credit to peasants so they could buy high-yielding varieties and synthetic chemical fertilizers. Although official accounts of the Green Revolution profile the successful farmers who became bigger and more productive, they rarely mention the millions who went bankrupt and were driven out of farming. The agrarian transition in which some small farmers become large operators and the rest are forced to work for wages—a standard feature of capitalist agriculture—is often presented as a natural occurrence or as an inevitable process of modernization that invariably has winners and losers. In fact, the process is still hotly contested and continues to be the subject of much debate.

The difference between the first and the second agrarian transitions was marked by intensity: what took two centuries during the Industrial Revolution took less than fifty years under the Green Revolution. What made the difference? In a word: *capital.* Whereas capital was largely funneled into industry during the first transition, the Green Revolution funneled significant amounts into agriculture during the second.

The Corporate Food Regime

Today's corporate food regime—thus named to reflect the rise of the global corporations controlling our food supply from farm to fork—was built on the food regimes that preceded it. The Vietnam War and the 1972 oil crisis were the catalysts that introduced the new regime. In 1972 oil-producing Arab nations formed a cartel, restricting production and raising the price of petroleum. Banks filled up with "petrodollars" at the same time that money printed by the U.S. Treasury to pay for the Vietnam War began to make its way into the international banking system.[54] Because they had to pay interest on all this cash, private banks were eager to invest, and loaned this money generously with favorable terms to developing countries in the Global South. The United States and European governments encouraged heavy borrowing, in large part so that Third World countries would buy Northern technology and hire Northern expertise for their economic development.

The modernization of agriculture was a big part of this development strategy. The Green Revolution pushed high-yielding hybrid seeds, synthetic fertilizers, and pesticides, irrigation, and farm machinery with the help of the international agricultural research centers of the Consultative Group on International Agricultural Research (CGIAR). Legions of consultants and experts from the United Nations Food and Agriculture Organization (FAO), the U.S. Agency for International Development (USAID), and private development agencies worked under lucrative contracts in the development industry. The billions of dollars in development aid spent during the heyday of the Green Revolution (1960-1980) succeeded in opening vast markets for Northern agricultural technologies—and in flooding the global market with food. The oversupply of food drove prices steadily downward.

Then, in a move to stem the nagging inflation left over from the Vietnam War, in 1979 the U.S. Federal Reserve tightened the money supply. With less cash available, interest rates rose as high as 20 percent. High interest rates slowed the economy, creating a recession. People bought fewer goods on the world market. High interest rates also meant higher payments for borrowers. This squeezed borrowing countries that had counted on high prices in global markets to pay back their development loans. Starting with Mexico in 1982, countries began defaulting on their loans, sending the Global South into a profound economic crisis and creating an unpayable foreign debt.[55]

Because commercial banks refused to extend further credit, the World Bank and the International Monetary Fund (IMF) moved to fill the gap. The bank loaned (public) money to debtor countries so they could keep up their payments to private banks in the Global North, doing so on the condition that these countries institute structural adjustment policies (SAPs). The IMF and the World Bank then used the SAPs to force countries of the South to open up their economies to international markets by removing controls on international finance capital, privatizing state-held industries and services, and deregulating labor markets.[56] The bank also pushed debtor countries to dismantle their grain reserves, stop growing food and instead grow "non-traditional" export products, which would fetch dollars on the world market to pay back the banks. This was supposed to get prices right and provide cheaper food through global trade. Coincidentally, what the SAPs also did was to make the Global South dependent on food from the Global North. The Northern banks not only got their money back, they locked developing countries into endless payments. The SAPs were the first salvo in a global agenda known as the "Washington Consensus," which steadily imposed neoliberal economic policies around the globe.

In 1995, following the Uruguay Round of GATT negotiations (General Agreement on Trade and Tariffs, 1986–94), the World Trade Organization (WTO) was formed and agriculture and trade-related aspects of intellectual property rights (TRIPs) were officially added to the trade agenda. The inclusion of the TRIPs was essential for the rapid global expansion of genetically modified maize and soybeans. Unless developing countries could be kept from reproducing the North's new GMOs, the chemical-*cum*-seed companies like Bayer and Monsanto were not going to do business in the Global South. The WTO enshrined the structural adjustment policies of the 1980s and early 1990s into international treaties (where, coincidentally, citizens cannot rescind them) called Free Trade Agreements (FTAs). The stated purpose of the WTO was to reduce trade barriers and establish non-discriminatory mechanisms to enforce global trade rules. In practice, the WTO has protected the markets and subsidies of the United States and Europe while at the same time lowering tariffs in the Global South.

The United States and other countries have also signed bilateral and regional FTAs that are enforced by the WTO. The 1994 North American Free Trade Agreement (NAFTA) and the 2004 Central America–Dominican Republic–United States Free Trade Agreement (CAFTA–DR) are among fourteen different FTAs signed with the United States. The FTAs have been widely opposed by farmers in the Global South because they sanction Northern dumping (selling subsidized grains from the North at below their costs of production in the South). They are also rejected by many concerned citizens who oppose the loss of jobs and the lax labor and environmental regulations that are part and parcel of the free trade agenda. Indeed, citizen outrage against the FTAs is driving much of the rise of neo-fascism in the United States and Europe. At the time of this writing, The Trans-Pacific Partnership (TPP) and the Trans-Atlantic Trade and Investment Partnership (TTIP)—negotiated under strict corporate secrecy—are politically on hold.

The construction of the corporate food regime has been rife with painful contradictions. The Global South went from a billion dollars in yearly food exports in the 1970s to importing 11 billion dollars a year in food by 2001. The environmental costs of the neoliberalization of the global food system have been devastating. Industrial agriculture has destroyed up to 75 percent of the world's agrobiodiversity, uses up to 80 percent of the planet's freshwater, and produces up to 20 percent of the world's greenhouse gas emissions. Millions of peasants have lost their livelihoods and been forced to migrate across hostile borders and dangerous seas in search of work. In 2008 and again in 2011 when food price inflation sent a billion people into the ranks of the hungry, the world was producing record harvests. At the same time, giant agribusiness and agrifoods corporations were making record profits, as were major financial houses speculating with food commodities.[57]

The corporate food regime is characterized by the monopoly market power and mega-profits of agrifood corporations, globalized meat production, the emergence of agrofuels, and the devastating expansion of palm and soy plantations. Virtually all the world's food systems are tied in to today's regime, controlled by a far-flung agrifood industrial complex, made up of huge monopolies like Monsanto, Syngenta, and Bayer (all in the process of different mergers), and ADM, Cargill, Yara, Coca-Cola, Tesco, Carrefour, Walmart and even on-line giant Amazon (which recently acquired Whole Foods). Together, these corporations are powerful enough to dominate the governments and the multilateral organizations that make and enforce the regime's rules for trade, labor, property and technology. This political-economic partnership is supported by public institutions like the World Bank and the International Monetary Fund, the World Food Program, USAID, the USDA, the World Trade Organization, and private fortunes like the Bill and Melinda Gates Foundation.

Liberalization and Reform

Like the larger capitalist system of which they are a part, global food regimes alternate between periods of liberalization, characterized by unregulated markets, corporate privatization, and massive concentrations of wealth, and periods of devastating financial busts (like the Roaring Twenties and the stock market crash of 1929). When these busts provoke widespread social unrest—threatening profits and governability—governments usher in reformist periods in which markets, supply, and consumption are reregulated to rein in the crisis and restore stability to the regime. Infinitely unregulated markets would eventually destroy both society and the natural resources that the regime depends on for profits. Therefore, while the "mission" of reform is to mitigate the social and environmental externalities of the corporate food regime, its "job" is identical to that of the liberal trend: the perpetuation of the corporate control of the food system. Though liberalization and reform may appear politically distinct, they are actually two sides of the same system.

Reformists dominated the global food regime from the Great Depression of the 1930s until Ronald Reagan and Margaret Thatcher ushered in our current era of neoliberal "globalization" in the 1980s, characterized by deregulation, privatization, and the growth and consolidation of corporate monopoly power in food systems around the globe. With the global food and financial crises of 2007–2010, desperate calls for reform have sprung up worldwide. However, few substantive reforms have been forthcoming, and most government and multilateral solutions simply call for more of the same policies that brought about the crisis to begin with: extending liberal (free) markets, privatizing common resources (like forests and the atmosphere), and protecting monopoly concentration while mediating the regime's collateral damage to community food systems and the environment. Unless there is strong pressure from society, reformists will not likely affect, much less reverse, the present neoliberal direction of the corporate food regime.

Conclusion: Food and the Logic of Capital

The role of agriculture in the rise of capitalism and the role of capitalism in the food system spans several centuries. Understanding this history is essential in understanding the food system because as a capitalist food system it is going to work the way capitalism does. Food—from seed to plate—is organized in a way that generates the highest possible global cash flows, regardless of the consequences.[58] The history of capitalism illustrates a typical trajectory, in which the system shifts from liberal market periods characterized by deregulation, privatization, "free trade," and corporate dominance, to reformist periods in which supply and trade are regulated, the government invests in the economy, and the public sphere is dominant. Our food system, as this exploration of the three global food regimes demonstrates, is central to this process.

In her book *This Changes Everything: Capitalism vs. the Climate*, Naomi Klein points out that the present neoliberal form of capitalism, a form that simply shows the nature of capitalism as a system, is incompatible with reversing climate change.[59] It is also incompatible with a healthy, equitable, and sustainable food system.

The tendency of capitalism is to constantly grow and expand; to concentrate more and more monopoly power in the hands of a few firms; to pass off capital's social and environmental costs to society (or turn them into a market) and to experience cyclical crises of overproduction and economic boom-busts. That is also the nature of the capitalist food system.

This is why calls to "fix a broken food system" are misplaced. To call the system broken is to believe it once worked well for people, the economy, and the environment. This would mean ignoring the three centuries of violence and destruction characterizing global food systems since the first food regime. The food system is not broken; rather, it is working precisely as a capitalist food system is supposed to work. That is the first thing we need to realize if we want to change it.

— 2 —

Food, a Special Commodity

Commodities are so central to capitalism that Karl Marx started his multivolume opus *Capital* with an explanation of them:

> A commodity is, in the first place, an object outside us, a thing that by its properties satisfies human wants of some sort or another. The nature of such wants, whether for instance they spring from the stomach or from folly makes no difference.[1]

That's right, under the capitalist mode of production food is a commodity, just like any other. It doesn't matter if the food is fresh organic arugula or a Big Mac, teff from the highlands of Ethiopia, or Cheez Whiz from Walmart. It doesn't matter whether you need it or not, whether it is good or bad for you, whether it is locally produced or traveled from afar, or whether it was corralled, caged, free range, or led a happy life. If enough people *want* it and have the money to buy it, someone will turn it into a commodity and sell it. And, of course, even if people don't know they want it, companies will do their best through the wonders of advertising to try to convince them to buy it, in effect creating a market for a new (or even a slightly changed) food product.

Marx's writings provide perhaps the most exhaustive examination of what capitalism is and why it works the way it does. We are not going to present Marx's inquiry into capitalism here (For those interested in it, there are excellent online classes and companion guides.)[2] However, here we are going to draw on some of Marx's key concepts from *Capital* in order to explain why and how the capitalist food system works as it does. Like Marx, we'll start with the commodity.

Because it satisfies the basic human need to eat, food is at the core of any society. Without food, capitalism or any other economic system would grind to a halt. We incorporate it into our bodies and can't live very long without it. Food is clearly a special commodity, with essential properties that make it unlike all others. Food's difference is important, though in capitalism, it is just another product that is bought and sold.[3]

As a commodity, food—like shirts, automobiles, or smartphones—is produced to be sold in a market. The production and sale of food commodities responds to market demand, which is different from need. If you have enough money you can buy as much food as you like. Those who need food but can't afford it must produce it themselves, barter for it, steal it, or rely on charity. Or they can go hungry, as do over one billion people around the world.

Like all commodities, food embodies different forms of value (which is explored later in this chapter). Because food is indispensable to human labor, and since human labor is a part of the value of all commodities, the value of food permeates the entire economic system. Just how is the value of food determined? And how does food's value affect its price? Why is organic food more expensive than conventional food?[4] Why is food from large-scale, industrial monocultures and confined animal feedlot operations cheaper than food from small, sustainable family farms? How does food's value affect our health and the environment?

Partial answers to these questions can be found in the laws of supply and demand. For example, when affluent consumers in Europe and the United States suddenly discovered quinoa, they were willing to pay high prices for the relatively limited supply of this ancient

Andean staple. The "poor people's food" quickly became too expensive for the poor, forcing them to look to cheap imported bread and pastas for nourishment. On the production side, traditional quinoa farmers were pushed out of the market as the crop was moved from the terraced hillsides, where it was part of a complex cropping and animal husbandry rotation system, to the bottomland pastures where it is now cultivated as a monocrop in large, mechanized fields. These fragile grazing areas, which have sustained llamas for millennia, are disappearing under the quinoa boom, resulting in erosion, dust storms, and hardship for traditional communities.[5]

Another reason is economies of scale. Large farms, even though they frequently produce less per acre than small farms, have more market power in buying and selling than small farms, can leverage more capital (and usually pay lower interest rates), and usually benefit from more direct and indirect subsidies than do small farms. Large industrial farms are made possible by cheap petroleum and natural gas, as well as internal combustion engines that allow farmers to work larger and larger plots of land without increasing labor costs. Because of mechanization, large farms have lower labor costs per acre of land or per amount of food produced than small farms. They also replace nitrogen-fixing cover crops, legume hay crops, and bulky animal manure with concentrated synthetic fertilizers. Large monoculture production allows for the mass standardization of cultivation, processing, distribution and sale, all of which lower market transaction costs for each ton of food produced. This increases the *labor productivity* of the industrial farm in relation to other farms. Thus, fewer farmers can produce more food by cultivating more land. The average area of land cultivated by a farmer in the United States is fifty times the world average.[6]

Of course, the advantages in labor productivity also come at a high energy cost, the true price of which is not paid for by industrial agriculture.[7] Nor does "mass food" pay for any of the social and environmental costs caused by the industrial model of food production, such as pollution, greenhouse gas emissions, food contamination, antibiotic resistant bacteria, diet-related diseases, poverty, dispossession, and displacement.

Small farms, organic or not, are less like these standardized "factories in the field" and more like intensively complex, knowledge-based systems that demand lots of expertise, thus keeping labor costs high relative to conventional products. In addition, the social and environmental benefits of many of these farms, for example, soil and water conservation, high agrobiodiversity and species richness, and rural employment are not recognized by the market nor remunerated by society.[8]

There are many ways we can look at food—as particular parts of a culture, the amount of energy used to produce it, access to land, the phenomenon of hunger amid plenty, and so on. But most critical for understanding food in a capitalist food system is the fact that food is a commodity, valued not just as sustenance but as potential capital. Food has a *use value* (to feed people) and an *exchange value* (as a commodity). But before the market even kicks in, the amount of *socially necessary labor time* has defined the parameters of food's price.

Use Value, Exchange Value, and Socially Necessary Labor Time

Use value is a measure of the usefulness of a thing. The usefulness of food is that it sustains us, can be pleasurable to consume, and provides us the energy and nutrients we need to live, work, play, and reproduce. The use value of food, a commodity we eat every day, is fundamentally different from the use value of a shirt, an automobile, or a smartphone. But all commodities must be traded in a marketplace on the basis of some kind of common measure. Money is the medium through which this exchange occurs and thus *price is the measure of food's exchange value*. The exchange value of a commodity is roughly equal to the cost of its production plus profit. But if commodities have different use values, what makes the exchange value for a certain amount of food commensurate with the exchange value of a car or a smartphone? This issue is confounded even more by the vast differences in wealth and income in our society. Food to hungry people has a huge use value, but they don't have enough money to purchase it. The price of food doesn't (and can't) take into account the needs of people with low ability to pay, what the economists call a lack of *effective demand.*

What value is common to all commodities? All commodities, including food, are the products of human labor. Even honey, made by the planet's beleaguered bees, needs to be collected and processed by human labor. Wild mushrooms still need to be gathered; salt needs to be mined or produced in evaporating ponds; and wild fish must be caught. Even the new, fully automated parlors for milking cows need human labor to make and maintain the milking machines and care for the animals. One way or another, human labor—physical and mental—is common to all commodities and directly or indirectly embeds the value of labor into everything we buy and sell.

The value of labor within our food isn't easily perceived. As David Harvey says, "When you go to the supermarket you can see the exchange values [prices] but you can't see or measure the human labor embodied in the commodities directly. [The] embodiment of human labor has a phantom-like presence on the supermarket shelves. Think of that next time you are in a supermarket surrounded by these phantoms!"[9] In addition to not knowing the amount of labor it took to get a particular product to the supermarket shelf (including its packaging, an important part of corporate sales efforts) different products might have different markups, or rates of profit. Thus the price of a product, its exchange value, supplies little information about the labor needed for its production.

One reason the labor in commodities is phantom-like is because it is abstract. The societal value of labor can't be calculated by simply adding up the amount of labor time expended in producing a pound of broccoli in California's coastal valleys, but depends on the amount of *socially necessary labor time* needed for its production. The value of labor in a commodity is based on the *average levels of worker productivity* in a given society. This is why we don't pay more for the exact same product that took more labor time to produce than the one with less labor time. If you took your home-cultivated broccoli to the supermarket, it would sell at close to the same price as its industrial cousins, unless the store could distinguish it in some way from them.

Here's how the average levels of worker productivity works:

Let's compare two hypothetical farms in the United States, one organic and one conventional. The ten-acre organic farm grows vegetables 10 months of the year and employs an average of 10 people. It produces 10 tons (T) of vegetables per acre each year for a total of 100 T/yr. That means each person's labor produces the equivalent of 10 T/yr., or a ton a month. So, each ton of produce "embodies" one month of a worker's labor. Now look at the neighboring 100-acre conventional farm, also employing an average of 10 people over 10 months. Assuming yields are the same at 10T/acre (in the United States, they are typically from 9 to 20 percent more) total production is 1,000 tons. Each of these tons contains just 1/10 of one month of a worker's labor.

Even though certified organic produce is often two or three times more expensive than conventional produce, by a straight-line labor calculation in our example it should cost 10 times more, which of course it does not. That is because the value of labor in the commodity—organic or conventional—is primarily determined by average level of *socially necessary labor time* (social within the framework of a capitalist system of production, not in terms of what would be best for society as a whole), which in this case is the labor time needed to produce conventional food. The amount and the cost of socially necessary labor depends on how much it costs to produce labor power in a society; that is, how many years and resources it takes to raise and train a worker to a needed level of skills, how much it costs to feed, clothe, house, and maintain her or him, the costs of health care and retirement, and more. This is referred to as the cost of *reproduction* of the worker's labor.

Once the value of the socially necessary labor time is established for the commodity, a lot of other market factors come into play—like a person's willingness and ability to pay more for organic, the high costs of machinery and chemical inputs of conventional farms, lower transaction costs for large farms, the willingness of small-scale farmers to work below the minimum wage, the possibility of direct marketing and certified organic "premiums," among other things. Regardless, the difference in price between the two is still a fraction

Figure 2.1: Socially Necessary Labor Time

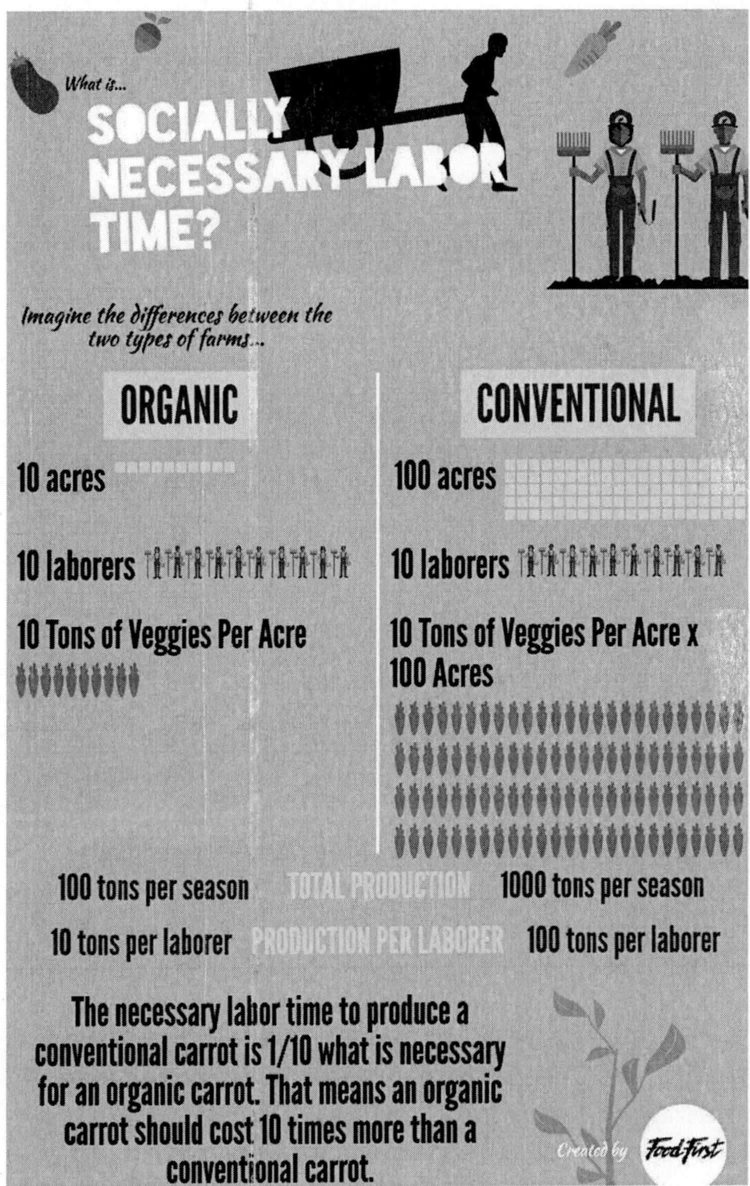

Source: Alyshia Silva, Food First.

of the difference in labor input because the commodity's value is not determined by individual labor but by socially necessary labor time.

But, you say, an organic carrot is not the same product as a conventional carrot! The organic carrot has no pesticide residue, did not use synthetic fertilizers, and did not release toxins into the environment! Well, fair enough, but isn't it interesting that organic farmers must charge *more* for a product that uses *less* external inputs? The reason is that the price of the extra labor power used in organic production is not determined by the organic production process itself but by the cost of socially necessary labor in agriculture, generally. And because so much agricultural production is highly mechanized, the socially necessary labor time to produce a carrot, a potato, or a chicken has been reduced to a very low amount.

When we inquire into the commodity's value (rather than just the price) the question "Why is organic so expensive?" becomes "Why isn't organic more expensive?" The answer is that once an organic good becomes a commodity, its exchange value will be largely determined by the amount of socially necessary labor time to produce a similar conventional product. It appears that mechanization of conventional agriculture is the reason for the low value of socially necessary labor. But this is only half the story. The other half is that labor is also *exploited* in the food system. Its value is actually much higher than its cost in the labor marketplace. The evidence for this is the abject poverty of farmworkers and foodworkers. It is fair to say that they are super-exploited, being paid wages too low to support themselves and their families at an average standard of living.

Ever since peasants were pushed off the land and made dependent on wages, agricultural labor has been paid far less than its social value (what it costs to reproduce a farmworker's capacity to work), much less what it adds to the price (exchange value) of food products. Today agriculture and food processing in the United States and Western Europe largely depend on undocumented labor. Undocumented workers—without whose labor power the food system would collapse—are criminalized by definition. This status makes it extremely difficult for them to demand living wages or basic

Coalition of Immokalee Workers

The small farm town of Immokalee, Florida, located forty miles inland from the Gulf of Mexico, is the epicenter of Florida's $650 million fresh tomato industry and home to the state's largest farmworker community. The Coalition of Immokalee Workers (CIW), a worker-based human rights organization, has organized for the labor rights of tomato pickers since the early 1990s. Built on a foundation of farmworker community organizing and bolstered by a national network of churches, students, and consumer activists, the CIW has fought to address the precarious conditions faced by Florida's agricultural workers: their poverty, occupational hazards, vulnerability to unemployment, and subjection to slavery and irregular immigration status.[10] The organization's work encompasses three broad and overlapping campaigns: the Fair Food Program (FFP), the Anti-Slavery Campaign, and the Campaign for Fair Food, which builds alliances between farmworkers and consumers to demand major corporate buyers sign on to the Fair Food Program. Signatories to the CIW's Fair Food Program (FFP) make a commitment to a wage premium in their supply chain in the form of a "penny per pound" of harvested tomatoes, compliance with the Fair Food Code of Conduct, the provision of worker-to-worker education sessions, a worker-triggered complaint resolution mechanism, and the establishment of health and safety committees on every participating farm.[11] To date, fourteen major food retailers have signed FFP agreements, including Walmart, McDonald's, Subway, Taco Bell, Burger King, and Whole Foods. Placing workers' agency at the center of the campaign is key to the FFP's success. The Fair Food Program is a workers' rights program designed, monitored, and enforced by the workers themselves.[12] Direct agreements with food retailers and growers serve to shape a new geopolitics of food production and labor, one that is worker-driven and not

> dependent on the good will of corporations to bring justice to Florida's fields.
>
> The CIW's Anti-Slavery Program has uncovered, investigated, and assisted in the prosecution of numerous multi-state, multi-worker farm slavery operations across the Southeastern United States, helping liberate over 1,200 workers held against their will. The U.S. Department of State credits the CIW with "pioneering" the worker-centered and multi-sectoral approach to prosecutions, and hails the CIW's work on some of the earliest cases as the "spark" that ignited today's national anti-slavery movement.[13]

labor rights. Further, the cost of what it takes to feed, raise, care for and educate a worker from birth to working age (the costs of reproduction) are assumed by the immigrants' countries of origin and is free to their employers in the rich nations, such as the United States and the nations of Western Europe. The low cost of immigrant labor works like a tremendous subsidy, imparting value to crops and agricultural land. This value is captured by capitalists across the food chain, but not by the worker. It is also captured by governments, for example, through taxes and Social Security, which immigrant workers pay, but get little or no benefit from. The effect of criminalizing immigrant labor is to drive down its cost while passing the value of immigrant labor power up the food chain.

This helps explain why the tendency in organic farming is to shift from small, diversified labor and knowledge-intensive farms to large, capital-intensive organic monocultures. These are the farms that giant supermarket chains like Walmart, Tesco, and Carrefour buy from, not just because transaction costs are lower with large economies of scale, but because Walmart can pay less for products from large industrial organic farms, which will be delivered on familiar, standardized pallets on a fixed schedule. The downward pressure of socially necessary labor time on wages also helps explain the growing conflict between small to medium and large-scale organic farms and between indigenous peasant farmers and new mechanized farms producing ancient crops like quinoa for trendy commodity markets. The combination of mechanization, quantity buyers, and regulations that favor large-scale production for large-scale distribution lowers the value of socially necessary labor time (that is, it lowers the average amount of labor needed to produce a commodity) and favor large farms—organic and otherwise.

The commodity nature of food leads to the differentiation of the agricultural sector. Large farms get bigger as they buy out mid-size farms. Small conventional farms get even smaller and off-farm income becomes more and more important to livelihoods. The "disappearing middle" of the U.S. farm sector is a reflection of capitalist differentiation in agriculture. Large mega-farms are growing a larger and larger share of our food.[14] Even though the number of very small farms is growing in the United States (especially those operated by women and farmers of color), they aim mainly to sell in niche markets and their percentage of total food production is small.[15] The same trend applies to organic farms.

Notice that nothing about large-scale industrial farming and low values of socially necessary labor time (on conventional or organic farms) has anything to do with sustainability, which encompasses environmental and social considerations. Large organic farms generally use procedures best described as "input substitution," using large amounts of products that have been approved by the U.S. Department of Agriculture's National Organic Standards Board. Large, mechanized organic farms use copious amounts of petroleum, over-apply organic pesticides and fertilizers, and ship their produce thousands of miles in plastic containers to supply uniform organic winter vegetables in Northern climates. This kind of industrialized organic farming can't be considered "sustainable," no matter how green the label.

So how do small commercial farms—organic or otherwise—compete with large, capital-intensive farms? The simple answer is, most don't.

Most of the world's 1.5 billion small-scale and peasant farmers find a niche market where they do not compete with industrial agriculture. Examples are community-supported agriculture (CSA), such as farmers' markets or farms that sell directly to local restaurants, or farmers who produce primarily for family consumption and barter, selling only a small part of their production on the market. They also economize by using unpaid family labor, cut costs by using on-farm agroecological methods to maintain fertility and manage pests, and supplement farm income with off-farm employment. Most small farmers don't make much money. That doesn't mean that they all live poorly—though many do—but that they operate outside the circuits of capital and do not commodify their products or all of their labor. This kind of livelihood strategy is based on use values rather than exchange values, growing food for people not profits.

Of course, there are many small-scale farmers who do manage to make a decent living despite the small size of their operations. They do this by carefully combining different *forms* of production and exchange (like agroecological, organic, non-organic, market-oriented, self-provision, and barter) into particular *farming styles* that lower costs and reduce their exposure to market risk.[16] For these strategies to be effective within the larger capitalist economy, it usually requires specific geographic and regulatory conditions that are favorable (or less adversarial) to small farmers, as well as savvy farmers. Small-scale co-op dairy farmers in Norway have a protective monopoly on milk and cheese production that provides them with a high income (subsidized largely by oil revenues). Small-scale Asian-American farmers in the Sacramento Delta region of California own small plots of rich agricultural land and produce locally for tightly managed ethnic markets in Sacramento and San Francisco. They bought small, low-lying farms cheaply because their area was prone to seasonal flooding. Then, when the Delta levee system was extended, they found themselves in possession of prime agricultural land in close proximity to major urban centers where Asian communities were eager to buy Asian products.

One way or another, these farmers change the relation between the use value and exchange value of food, defying the logic of the commodity markets that would put them out of business. In doing so, they are producing vast amounts of use value that either circulate as goods rather than commodities or that have established a commodity market that is protected from global circuits of commodity capital. This is one reason why their farms are generally vilified by corporations and institutions in the corporate food regime.

Food's use values and exchange values are interdependent. Socially necessary labor time must be expended to produce a commodity that we can consume in order for it to be exchanged as a commodity. Break any link in this chain of relations and we can no longer talk of a commodity but of a "good" that is traded outside of normal commodity markets. If you grow your own vegetables for self-consumption or give some to your neighbor, you eliminate exchange value. Produce a product that does not fulfill any wants or needs, and it has no use value. Sit around idly instead of expending socially necessary labor time, and you won't have a commodity to sell (unless you work on Wall Street or have a lot of money to invest, but that's another story).

So What?

Why is it important to understand value in our food system?

Because the production, appropriation, and accumulation of value determines the system itself. Unless we change the underlying value relations of our food system—the contradiction between food as essential for human life and food as a commodity—we will be working on the margins of a system that is structurally designed for profit rather than need, speculation rather than equity, and extraction rather than resilience. This doesn't mean that the many social innovations challenging the inequities and externalities of the corporate food regime around the world are not worth implementing. On the contrary, our food system needs innovation. But for these hopeful alternatives to have a chance of becoming the norm rather than the alternative within a food system that is structurally favorable to large-scale industrial agriculture, we will need to know what structural parts of the system need changing.

Much of the global food movement is concerned with the intrinsic usefulness and importance of good, healthy food (its use value).

The food justice movement fights for affordable healthy food (use value and exchange value). Farmworkers and food workers are on the other side of the equation; they want living wages and decent working conditions. These are aspects that are not recognized by a system designed for profit above all else and in which a) labor time of the most labor-efficient operations governs the worth of labor in less efficient operations; and b) labor is purchased as cheaply as possible and laborers work under conditions to increase their efficiency to the limit (socially necessary labor time). Family farmers are also concerned about socially necessary labor time (of the farmworkers they hire and of their own labor) and exchange value (price paid to the farmer). Certain crops and management styles impart ecological services to the farm and society (use values aside from food). Not all of these can or should be turned into exchange values (such as carbon sequestration in soil, pollination, better water quality, or genetic diversity).

With capitalism, value is only recognized when it is embodied in a marketable commodity. The commodification of food, labor, and agriculture has not given us an equitable, healthy, and resilient food system. The relationship between use value and exchange value—and the social relationships embedded in socially necessary labor time—have implications for the food movement and the strategies chosen for the transformation of the food system. Though we are not likely to lose the commodity form of products any time soon, we can work to change the relation between use and exchange values, and we can change the terms of socially necessary labor time (and working conditions) to make a more sustainable and equitable food system that reduces the exploitation of workers and does not pass off onto society the social costs (the externalities) that the producers ought to bear.

For example, small-scale family farmers tend to self-exploit by working long hours that when added up don't equal a minimum wage. It is not uncommon for these farmers to make less hourly than the seasonal workers they hire. They may not be able to save much for their children's education or their own retirement. It is in their objective interest to ally with farmworkers to raise the minimum wage and improve working conditions on all farms—large and small. This is because raising the value (the wage income) of socially necessary labor in food commodities would indirectly raise the value of the farmer's own labor within the commodity itself. If *all* farmworkers received living wages and basic social benefits, it would help to level the playing field between large-scale industrial operations and small-scale production, ultimately benefiting farms that use family labor. Of course, it would help, but it clearly wouldn't fix the system. Because the large-scale producers use much less labor per acre or per pound of product, the increase in wages won't affect them as much as the small-scale farmers where labor is a much larger portion of their budget.

Another example and fashionable notion for changing the food system—one that fits nicely with ideas of freedom, choice, and personal agency—is to "vote with your fork" by boycotting cheap junk food or buying fresh, local, organic food. In effect, this strategy selectively engages with the exchange value of the food system to send the market a signal of what kind of use values—healthy, non-processed, GMO-free, high-fructose corn syrup free, organic, sustainable, local, fair trade—conscious eaters prefer.

Though most people in the world simply cannot afford to eat according to their values, it is important for those who can to do so. But again, this doesn't change the basic commodity relations of value in the food system. Nor does it resolve the issue of large-scale intensive "organic" producers making it hard for smaller scale, more environmentally sound farmers to make a living.

A "local" label on a food commodity at the supermarket may or may not make it cost more than other similar food products, may or may not mean passing higher prices on to the producer, and may or may not mean the food comes from close by, depending on the interpretation of "local" by the retailer. Certified organic and fair trade products like fruits and vegetables, coffee, and bananas are commodities that attempt to extract a price premium in the marketplace by raising the exchange value of these commodities. A higher price to consumers pays for programs that are supposed to help the environment, use fewer pesticides, and pay more to small-scale farmers. There are many documented social and environmental benefits to certified organic and fair trade markets, the least of which has been the possibility for family farmers—those upon whom both the organic and fair trade systems were built—to get a better price for their product. However, the steady entry of large-scale producers into both organic and fair trade markets is driving down the value of socially necessary labor time for these products. This is welcomed by large retailers because higher volumes mean that lower prices can be paid to farmers and also that sales and profits are higher. Unfortunately, this process will eventually squeeze out all but the largest producers.

From the perspective of value, there are different measures that could protect small- and medium-sized producers. One option is to peg the organic and fair trade premiums to the costs of production rather than to the conventional price, which is the current practice. Since labor is the biggest (rising) cost for producers in this market, this will increase the value of labor in these products, benefiting small and medium producers. However, this will only work if certification is denied to large-scale farms.

Agroecology—working together with, and relying on, ecological functions to raise crops and animals sustainably—is one way farmers are staying in business despite the downward trend in prices. In Costa Rica, many farmers producing for the Fair Trade coffee market have been steadily converting their coffee farms to pasture because labor and organic fertilizer and pesticide costs have risen dramatically while coffee prices have plummeted, reducing revenues by much more than the compensation they received from Fair Trade premiums. However, those farmers that employ agroecological practices continue to produce coffee because they do not use as much organic fertilizer or pesticide.[17] Although its volume is much lower and it is difficult for small farmers to accomplish, direct marketing of coffee (that does not go through a fair trade distribution system but is sold directly from producer to consumer) can also provide a much higher premium to farmers.

The undervaluing of labor, due to both below-subsistence wages of many workers and the higher level of mechanization in conventional food commodities, is a heavy leveler and helps explain why organic and fair trade products have failed to raise the bar in the mainstream food industry. When voting with our fork, we should remember that the freedom to buy food according to our values does not in and of itself change the power of commodities in our food system. If we want to change the power of commodities in the food system, we will have to change the way we value the labor in our food as well.

The Value of Value

When most people consider value in a capitalist sense, they think about the price of something. This led Oscar Wilde to deliver the powerful observation that most people know "the price of everything and the value of nothing."[18] Values take on multiple forms, varying across time and space from generation to generation, culture to culture. People may consider something to have value simply because they hold it dear, like a beautiful sunset. This is often labeled intrinsic value. Then there are personal values, things people consider important that make up the moral principles they strive to uphold, such as honesty, fairness, loyalty, and compassion. The ingenuity of capitalism is that it has been able to convert these intangible values into exchange values that can be bought and sold in the marketplace. Marketers trying to sell anything from food and beverages to cars and housing developments utilize this highly profitable strategy to cultivate desire for their products and brands by imbuing them with intangible, yet emotionally powerful "values" such as health, hope, happiness, even the betterment of the human soul.[19] But beyond using subliminal value-messaging to sell products, capital also sells intangible values directly. Fairness and health, once simply considered values to live by, can now be purchased through fair trade and organic labeling. Values have been appropriated and utilized by corporations as marketing differentiators for their products—products for which they'll charge a premium.

The contradiction between the use and exchange values of food commodities is not easily resolved. Stopgap measures like certified organic and fair trade do not favor low-income consumers. As both of these labels enter mainstream supermarkets, the returns to farmers shrink, favoring big agriculture rather than small and medium farmers. Immigrant farm labor—criminalized under present immigration law—is another key contradiction in the food system, one that is not resolved through guest worker programs (which keep wages low) or through amnesty programs (because workers immediately leave farm work). Living wages for farmworkers and parity prices for farmers that cover costs and provide for a decent living would invariably drive up the price of food, meaning that the rest of society would require a living wage in order to buy good food. Agroecology provides farmers with some protection from the upstream side of the "cost–price squeeze" of the capitalist food system, as do direct marketing arrangements for the downstream side. Some farmers and some consumers can protect themselves from the ravages of commodification in these ways. But if these hopeful alternatives are to move from the margins to the mainstream, the basic structural conditions of use value, exchange value, the value of labor power, and socially necessary labor time will have to be transformed.

A Slightly Nerdy Explanation of Surplus Value, the Holy Grail of Capitalism

Many people commonly confuse capital, value, and money. Money is a measure of exchange value and as such can be used to represent capital and facilitate buying and selling. One way of thinking about capital is as "value in search of more value." A person or a firm that has accumulated some measure of wealth, usually cash as well as stocks, bonds, and various financial instruments that can be easily converted to money when needed and uses this to produce or obtain more wealth. Under capitalism, money is normally used in the process. Capital emerges when money is put into circulation to make more money.[20]

Suppose "M" represents money and "C" represents a commodity, like grain, kale, or gardening rakes. Someone takes money, produces a commodity with it, and then sells the commodity for money: M-C-M. Actually, the point is to sell the commodity for more money than what one invested in it, so we have M-C-M′, in which M′ represents the original amount of money invested plus profit. This money is capital that will be reinvested, after using some portion for the capitalist's higher living standards.

So isn't capital just profit? Not exactly. Capital refers to the entire process and to the things in the process, including the commodity that is bought and sold, the labor embodied in the commodity, and to the social relationships between the workers, machines, and owners of the capital being produced. Capital always embodies a social relation. In any case, at the core of capital lives the Holy Grail of capitalism: profits. There is no end point to the system; those who own the capital try to continually accumulate more and more capital. The term Marx used to describe what most would call profits was *surplus value*.

Let's look at our equation again:

If M-C-M′ and M′ represents the original money invested plus profit, where did the extra value of M′ come from? The original money-capital "M" was used to hire workers who would then use the means of production (machines, raw materials) to produce a commodity "C" that when sold rendered M′, that is, the original capital invested plus the increase in capital. How did the capital change? Money was used to pay for raw materials, machinery, and labor. But when these were transformed into a commodity by workers, extra value was created. This extra value is surplus value.

The question is, where did the surplus value come from? Labor-power and the means of production were all paid for with M, right? Did their combination magically create extra value? Some people like to think so. But capitalism is definitely not about magical thinking.

When the capitalist pays the worker for his or her labor-power, it is as if the capitalist rented a generator for its power. (If this was slavery, the capitalist would own the generator.) Imagine that the capitalist pays for four hours of power but the generator actually runs for eight hours. The extra four hours of labor-power are a "surplus" of power that in the production of the commodity infuse it with surplus value. To whom should this extra value belong? In a capitalist system, it belongs to the capitalist. He or she owns the means of production and bought the labor-power, precisely to generate surplus value. And the capitalist justifies receiving the surplus value by figuring it is a "return" for use of his capital. But let's say that a capitalist borrows money to start the business (not uncommon) and hires a manager (also not uncommon). In this case, the capitalist did not use any of their own money nor provide production oversight. The interest was paid on the loan, the manager received a salary, the workers received wages, all the raw materials were paid for, and so on. So how do the profits miraculously arise in this situation? Every input cost was paid for. But it was the workers who took the machinery, raw materials, and power and converted it into a salable commodity. In other words, they added more value during the production process than they were paid for. Another way to look at it is that they worked longer than they needed in order to produce the quantity of commodities that would have been sufficient *if* workers had been paid the full amount of money that represented the value they added. So, workers labor longer than the time it would take to produce the commodities they need to maintain their subsistence. Their wage embodies less labor time than the hours they are compelled to labor. Compelled because they themselves own no means of production, no capital, but cannot live without access to it.

As a commodity itself, labor-power has a clear use value and an exchange value: exchange value is the worker's wage, the use value (to the capitalist) is its ability to create surplus value. The workers are allowed to keep the exchange value of their labor. But they must give up the use value to the owner of the means of production. As Karl Marx explained in the second volume of *Capital*, "The purchase of labor-power is a contract of sale which determines that a greater quantity of labor is provided than is necessary to replace the price of labor-power, the wage."[21]

The separation of workers from both the use value and the product of their labor is known as "alienation" and is the seed of class conflict. Of course, capitalists believe that they have every right to appropriate surplus value. After all, they deserve a rate of return for the use of their money (assuming it is not borrowed) and their willingness to assume risk. The laborers sold their labor-power of their own free will and knew full well what the capitalist was going to do with it. Besides, the capitalist provided employment, isn't that a good thing? Well, yes, that's one way to think about it. But there are a few more things to consider.

First, let's dispense with the fiction that laborers sell their labor-power of their own free will. Long ago, the enclosures dashed the possibility for huge numbers of peasants to feed, clothe, and house themselves and their families. Nothing remained for them but their ability to work for wages. And the British Poor Laws (that criminalized the unemployed) tried to make sure that they would be willing to sell their labor to capitalists. Given a real choice, including other more pleasant occupations, most people would not have gone to work in England's "Satanic Mills" that worked people to death to produce textiles. Ever since then, ensuring that workers are dependent upon wages is pretty central to capitalism; so for most people, this is not a choice but a condition.

Second, though it is true that capitalists put their own capital into the project of production (or borrow capital), it is also true that this capital had to come from somewhere: it too originates in surplus value. It is a tautology to claim rights over more surplus value because one has had rights to previously appropriated surplus value!

Third, let's think about production, value, and exchange. In mainstream economic theory, goods are traded between people until all parties are satisfied and trading stops. This is called "Pareto optimality," a point at which no one can gain without at least one person losing. So, just imagine that farmers producing potatoes in Idaho want iPhones made in Beijing, and that workers producing iPhones want potatoes. Farmers and workers start trading. When all the farmers in Idaho have iPhones, and all the workers in Beijing have all the potatoes they need, both parties are satisfied and the value of potatoes equals the value of iPhones. Now imagine a system in which all goods produced are traded among actual producers all around the world until Pareto optimality is reached. Everyone is satisfied—except for the capitalist. Why? Because in this system there is no *profit*. Goods are traded on the basis of their use value until everyone has what they need to use. All the use values even out. Clearly, this is not what happens under capitalism, in which all goods are commodities and money is the intermediary of all trading. At the end of the day, when trading stops, some people have gotten much richer.

Where did this extra wealth come from? It came from surplus value. Who, then, decides how wealth will be extracted and to whom it will belong? Is it the consumer? No. Is it the worker? No. It is the capitalist. That's why the system is called capitalism and not "laborism" or "workerism."

The quest for surplus value is at the core of capitalism. It is the moving force for the whole system, propelling it ever outward. Squeezing out more and more surplus value from commodity production—the motor force behind capitalism—drives the system to exploit both labor and the environment, which is called "efficiency." Although individual businesspersons (capitalists) may have more complex and varied motivations, in the role of owner or manager of a large business that must compete with other like businesses, these individuals must be concerned almost exclusively with the bottom line.

One way to make the bottom line higher is to *increase absolute surplus value* by extending the workday while paying the same wages for labor-power. We can see this in the berry fields of Washington State, in which the piece rate paid to immigrant labor for the harvested basket drops, thus making farmworkers harvest more boxes and work longer hours for the same pay.

Another method entails an increase in *relative surplus value* by introducing technological innovation or organizational changes to shorten socially necessary labor time in the production process, thus improving productivity. Increasing the line speed in meat processing plants is an example of increasing relative surplus value. One of the business mantras during the Great Recession of 2007–2009 as people were fired in huge numbers was that the remaining workers needed to "do more with less." Indeed, while unemployment ballooned, so did productivity as workers labored harder and harder to keep from losing their jobs.

Increasing relative surplus value is also achieved in capitalist livestock production through "biological speed-up." For example, selective breeding, genetic engineering, and the use of antibiotics and growth hormones has drastically reduced the growing time of animals on factory farms and shortened the lactation time and the number of lactations of dairy cows, even as each cow produces more milk per lactation. Cows produce more milk than ever before, but live much shorter lives, burning out in just a few years. Poultry farms can now grow chickens from chicks to broilers in eight weeks. The negative biological and environmental consequences of biological speed-up are well documented; cows are biologically exhausted after three lactations and are then "beefed"—most becoming hamburger. The manure ponds of confined animal feeding operations (CAFOs) have become environmental hazards; hormones and antibiotics used in animal production disrupt human hormonal development and endocrine functions, and create resistant bacterial strains. But since these costs are borne by society rather than the livestock and dairy industries, they do not affect the increase in relative surplus value.

Biological speed-up is not restricted to land-based livestock. Salmon production has steadily moved from intensified sea harvest to intensive caged farming of genetically modified, inland farmed fish. The patented AquAdvantage salmon combines genes from the Chinook and Atlantic salmon with the ocean pout, a fast-growing eel-like fish, reducing production time "from egg to plate" from three years to eighteen months. Far from an environmental breakthrough, the genetically engineered "salmon" will still be grown largely on fish meal and grown in ponds in Panama before being shipped around the world.[22]

Like capital, our food is a *social relation* that embodies the labor, value, ownership, expertise, biology, and power relationships of the capitalist system. This logic of capital—rather than the logic of fairness, compassion, ecology, conservation, or health—governs our food. Our attempts to change or transform the food system hinge on changing the social relation embedded in our food. Because food is both a commodity and an existential necessity, and because our food system impacts all other aspects of our social and economic system because we all eat, the social relation of food is pivotal in terms of human well-being. The firms controlling our food system understand this perfectly, exploiting the public use value of food to extract exchange values for corporate profit. Substantive changes to the food system will affect the entire economic system. Perhaps this is precisely what we need.

The Inhumane Treatment of Animals

FRED MAGDOFF

The raising of animals in large factory farms is done under inhumane conditions. Chickens for meat (broilers) are raised in barns of tens of thousands of birds.[23] The chickens have been bred to gain weight rapidly—this, of course, means more rapid turnover and more profits—and have large breasts because of the preference for white meat. They are less active because so much of the energy they consume is converted into growth and thus they spend most of their lives sitting on the floor—even as the manure accumulates during a growing cycle—usually losing feathers on their breasts and developing sores as well because of the almost constant contact with manure. The barns are only cleaned out after the chickens have been shipped but the litter (manure) may be left for the next group of chickens by placing a thin layer of fresh litter such as wood chips on top of the old manure. Raised mostly in dim light (companies may forbid natural lighting), they live a short six- to eight-week life entirely in the barn. They are fed a diet laced with questionable additives such as antibiotics that enhance growth, but many die under the crowded conditions, and one of the jobs in this operation is to go through the barn regularly and remove dead birds or those with deformities. The incredibly rapid growth of meat birds—from 0.002

to 8.8 pounds in eight weeks, analogous to a baby that weighed 6.6 pounds at birth growing around 660 pounds in two months—produces abnormal birds. There is no question that chickens grow faster than humans, but the extra-rapid growth caused by "improved" genetics and optimal feeding has created a most unfortunate animal. Because the birds have been bred to grow so rapidly their legs may not be able to support them, so there are always lame ones, unable to walk; these are usually euthanized. *New York Times* columnist Nicholas Kristof commented on the treatment of meat birds: "Torture a single chicken and you risk arrest. Abuse hundreds of thousands of chickens for their entire lives? That's agribusiness." Chickens in caged layers may have it even worse, with little room and their entire lives within the small cage and no ability to even peck at the ground.

These problems are not confined to poultry. Hog gestation—with sows in crates in which they cannot turn around so as to make it "more efficient" for them to feed their piglets—is difficult to look at even in photos. Beef cows, which are ruminants, have evolved to be able to gain their entire energy diet from grasslands, with cellulose—a structural element of plants that we cannot digest—providing most of their energy as a result of the activity of microorganisms in their rumens. In order to get them to gain weight rapidly, beef cows on feedlots, with thousands of animals, are fed diets high in corn grain, and soy to provide protein. (Growing corn and soybeans requires high rates of pesticides and fertilizers that would not be needed if cows were on pasture, where pests pose less of a problem and most of the nutrients are directly recycled into the land as manure and urine.) Again, antibiotics and hormones are part of the system to produce the most "efficient" weight gains.

Thus, because the pursuit of profit is the goal of raising these farm animals under industrial conditions, the only issue considered is how to do so as rapidly and cheaply as possible.

— 3 —

Land and Property

The law locks up the man or woman
Who steals the goose from off the common
But leaves the greater villain loose
Who steals the common from the goose.
—SEVENTEENTH-CENTURY ENGLISH FOLK POEM

On Earth Day of 2012, two hundred students and community residents occupied the Gill Tract, a 26-acre agricultural research station owned by the University of California, Berkeley.[1] Inspired by Brazil's Landless Workers Movement (MST), the group planted over 1,500 vegetable seedlings, set up an encampment, and demanded the UC's Office of Capital Projects halt a plan to sell the Gill Tract for private urban development. Among other housing and recreation projects, the university hoped to sell a portion of the Gill Tract to the Whole Foods supermarket chain. The "Occupy the Farm" movement called on the university to instead establish an urban community farm to serve the public interests of the growing urban agriculture movement in California and the San Francisco Bay Area. Throughout the 23-day occupation, teams of protesters cleared, planted, and cultivated the farm. Rather than negotiate, UC Berkeley cut off the Gill Tract's water supply. Neighbors provided water for a massive bucket brigade. The university finally sent riot police to drive occupiers from the research station. A year of organizing, a community referendum, legal battles, threats of a boycott (leading Whole Foods to pull out of the project), and another brief land occupation followed. In the spring of 2014 the university announced it was halting the sale of the Gill Tract for at least ten years. Occupy the Farm had succeeded in stopping the sale of the last large piece of prime agricultural land in San Francisco's urban East Bay region.

The Gill Tract occupation is emblematic of the calls for *land justice* and *land sovereignty* sweeping the globe. Though the term is often associated with the massive land occupations of the MST in Brazil and with peasant resistance to extractive industries and land grabs in Africa, Asia, and Latin America, and to growing pressure for popular control over agricultural land everywhere, the fact that a movement of well-fed, relatively affluent, and predominantly white urban protesters challenged the sale of publicly owned land for the purpose of growing food indicates just how widespread people's rejection of the privatization of public resources and the corporatization of our food has become.

Food and Property

Capitalism would be pointless if individuals and corporations were not able to appropriate the value of things for their exclusive benefit. Private property confers monopoly ownership rights to both use values and exchange values of commodities. Though it can't exist without public and common forms of property, private property is the basis for capitalist wealth accumulation. Private property dominates modern food systems. Other forms of ownership include cooperatives, traditional uses, and collective ownership. Each of these prohibits, restricts, or redistributes exchange values and can allow for shared use values, sometimes by taking land, labor, or capital off the market, essentially "de-commodify" them.

"Who owns what?" is the first of four key questions in political economy.[2] The private ownership of land (and increasingly, fisheries) is foundational to capitalist food systems, in which the tendency is to commodify everything by turning it into private property to be bought, used, and sold as the owners see fit. While capital will go to great *regulatory* lengths to turn everything into private property (for example, land, seeds, water, genetic information, carbon emissions, knowledge), once a thing becomes a commodity capitalists may seek to *de-regulate* capital so that it can be traded without impediments such as tariffs, labor laws, or policies for environmental protection.

The objective of private property is the appropriation of surplus value for the accumulation of wealth. Period. This requires the hand of the state to enforce property rights, print money, and ensure the free flow of capital. But this doesn't lead to a sustainable or equitable food system. In fact, because the tendency of capitalist markets is toward concentration of ownership and constant growth, without strong regulation and control from society, exactly the opposite happens. The gap grows between rich and poor and the environment is destroyed.[3]

Our capitalist food system has concentrated the wealth of the six-trillion-dollar-a-year industry in a handful of oligopolies, from Monsanto, Bayer, and Syngenta on the farm input side, to huge grain and livestock companies like Cargill and Smithfield, and the global grocery giants Walmart and Carrefour on the output side. It has also led to massive deforestation, desertification, and pollution.[4] At the same time, the existing food system leaves many people hungry and malnourished, leading to widespread protests and social struggles for equity, sustainability, and the right to food itself. Sooner or later—because of the nature of capitalism—land and property are drawn into the epicenter of this resistance.

Private, Public, and Common Property

Most of us have an idea of the difference between public, private, and common property: Public belongs to all citizens and private belongs to me. Common property is owned by a community—like a cooperative. Open-access resources are not property at all, rather they are elements like the air, the high seas, and outer space that no one owns, at least not yet. These simple definitions describe the different ways we treat resources under property regimes, but property was not always understood in this way. Indeed, despite some continuities, the rules regarding property are constantly being modified. The main issue with regard to private property isn't really about whether individuals and families can own furniture, utensils, or grooming products. The real issue is the private ownership of the means of producing goods and services we all need to live.

Modern-day conflicts over the patenting of life (known as genome property), corporate personhood, privatized water, and land grabs have their roots in centuries-long processes of wealth accumulation, state-making, and imperial expansion. The struggles over resources have been accompanied by heated debates over the social, economic, and ethical justification of private property. These historical arguments go to the core of political and economic power.

Property and the State

In the fourth century BCE, the Greek philosopher Plato extolled the virtues of common property because he believed it would encourage cooperation and avoid divisiveness. After his death, his pupil Aristotle argued against the Commons because he thought it encouraged free riders. He favored private property because he thought it bred prudence and responsibility. Property was the basis for citizenship and freedom. Freedom was contingent on owning one's self, rather than being owned (as a slave). Citizenship depended on owning property (land or slaves). But the problem was, if things and people could be privately owned, who or what would enforce the rights of private property? The answer was government. Both philosophers placed property at the center of a powerful state. The problem for governments ever since has been that the power of the state does not depend only on the rights of property owners but on a combination of coercion and consent of *all* of the governed—even the propertyless.

So, the protection of private property depends in no small degree on the existence of public property—in other words, the State. Establishing and maintaining public property is not easy; the governed have to consent to be governed, pay taxes, and serve in the military. If the state is not providing them with any benefits, why should they? Coercion will work for a while, but unless there is a *social contract*, force is unsustainable in the long run. So the question was—and still is—how can the state reconcile the private ownership of the production of essential goods and services with the public good?

> [Private] property is continually in need of public justification—first, because it empowers individuals to make decisions about the use of scarce resource in a way that is not necessarily sensitive to others' needs or the public good; and second, because it does not merely permit that but deploys public force at public expense to uphold it.[5]

Without the power of the state, individuals and corporations could not enforce their exclusive claims to property's uses and benefits. It is still the *sine qua non* for private property. Public property, which theoretically belongs to all citizens, also requires the power of the state to ensure that public officials can administer access to parks, schools, roads, forests, and other resources. This means there is a balance of Plato and Aristotle in all capitalist property regimes.

The Romans developed a complex legal system to rule the extensive properties of their empire, dividing property into *res publicae, res privatae*, and *res communes*: state, private, and Commons. Those properties that couldn't be possessed and were available to all (open access) were *extra patrimonium.*[6] The Romans saw pretty clearly that the combination of private property and government was not sufficient to extract resources from their minions, the subjects of whom depended on the Commons for their survival. They left common property to unpropertied people because otherwise the empire would not have been able to rule over or extract wealth from them, despite the power of the Roman legions. For thousands of years, the

Commons ensured for the community the food security that private property and government wouldn't or couldn't provide. In many ways and in many places around the world, the Commons still does.[7]

Private property has been the cornerstone for the *liberal nation-state* that merges democratic political systems with capitalist economic systems. The "father of Classic liberalism," philosopher John Locke (1632–1704), famously claimed private property was part of a natural order in which ownership belonged to whoever added labor to a natural object—especially land. This theory was used by the landed gentry of the eighteenth century to rationalize the dispossession of church, crown, and common property. It was used by the founders of the United States to support their struggle for independence from England, and later elaborated upon to justify "Manifest Destiny," the supposed divine right of the United States to appropriate the lands of the North American continent. (Conveniently forgotten in the drive to accumulate new real estate was Locke's proviso that the appropriation of property through labor did not give an individual the right to encroach on common land or dispossess already inhabited land.)

The role of public goods in capitalist systems was first addressed by utilitarian thinker John Stuart Mill (1806–1873), who thought that "humane capitalism" (a combination of public spending and liberal markets) could best meet the needs of individuals. But it was English economist John Maynard Keynes (1883–1946) who probably did more than anyone else to support the notion of public property in capitalist economic systems. To bring the United States and Europe out of the Great Depression, Keynes argued for the strong intervention of the state in the economy, including taxing the rich, public deficit spending, job programs, and control of interest rates. Though this did not address the issue of land and property directly, Keynes's economic theories gave a prominent role for public goods and to the state in public life. Keynes probably believed in the power of the public purse more than the need for public land, but Keynesianism and its later iterations provide the rationale for public property's economic role in capitalist systems.

The Commons and the Tragedy of Commodification

Who argued for the Commons? In *The Great Transformation,* Karl Polanyi (1944) called for social control over the market (which is, after all, a social institution) and for the de-commodification of capital, labor, and land. In an historical analysis that spanned centuries, he made a case for the rational and compassionate allocation of resources through the *public sphere,* the social, cultural, and institutional space of democratic, civic engagement where the problems and the projects of the community are discussed and decided upon. Though not arguing against property *per se,* he argued against its unregulated commodification and in favor of preserving the social institutions—like the Commons—that protected people and communities from the ravages of unregulated markets.

Polanyi was part of a long and significant tradition, from anarchist Pierre Proudhon's "Property Is Theft"[8] on to Elinor Ostrom's "Governing the Commons,"[9] which sought solutions to the challenges of production and distribution centered within the decision-making space of the public sphere, rather than the market. Proudhon rejected legal claims to land as property and held that property, "to be just and possible, must necessarily have equality for its condition."[10] He argued in favor of an individual's right to land access and to the product of his or her labor. As far as he was concerned, no one could lay claim to the product of anyone else's labor. Elinor Ostrom won the 2009 Nobel Prize in Economics (the only woman to do so) for her work on the Commons and "Common Pool Resources."[11] Her fieldwork with traditional societies convinced her that natural resources held in common could be sustainably managed without regulation from government. She also believed that collective action and reciprocity were critical components to human survival and for solving social dilemmas in which individual short-term self-interest undermines the greater good.[12] Ostrom's framework for common pool resources still serves as the most comprehensive, functional definition of the Commons.[13]

When a resource is neither public nor private nor commonly owned it is called "open access" (*extra patrimonium*). Ecologist

Garrett Hardin notoriously confused open-access resources with the Commons in his article "The Tragedy of the Commons."[14] Concerned with overpopulation, Hardin claimed that the unrestricted use of the world's resources would lead to ecological and civilizational collapse. He used a simple metaphor taken from an obscure 1833 economics pamphlet that described an open pasture in which self-interested, individual herdsmen each added animals to their flocks in an effort to increase their individual material gain. This "rational choice" on the part of individual herders eventually led to the degradation and collapse of the common pasture and the demise of the herders:

> Therein is the tragedy. Each man is locked into a system that compels him to increase his herd without limit—in a world that is limited. Ruin is the destination toward which all men rush, each pursuing his own best interest in a society that believes in the freedom of the Commons. Freedom in a Commons brings ruin to all.

It was a powerful, masculine metaphor that struck fear into the hearts of environmentalists. Capitalists, on the other hand, rejoiced. They used the Tragedy of the Commons to push for the privatization of both common lands and public lands. Ironically, Hardin, who was a staunch Malthusian with strong racial overtones to his assumptions, was actually arguing against the free-market capitalists, who took him for their standard bearer:

> We can make little progress in working toward optimum population size until we explicitly exorcize the spirit of Adam Smith in the field of practical demography. In economic affairs, *The Wealth of Nations* (1776) popularized the "invisible hand," the idea that an individual who "intends only his own gain," is, as it were, "led by an invisible hand to promote . . . the public interest." Adam Smith did not assert that this was invariably true, and perhaps neither did any of his followers. But he contributed to a dominant tendency of thought that has ever since interfered with positive

> action based on rational analysis, namely, the tendency to assume that decisions reached individually will, in fact, be the best decisions for an entire society.

Hardin had never actually seen a Commons or taken the time to study them. He assumed it referred to any area that was not privately owned. He was rigorously challenged by a number of anthropologists and historians and soundly disproven by Ostrom. Nonetheless, Hardin's central thesis—that too many people using common resources are the cause of environmental collapse—is still used to justify everything from the privatization of fishing grounds to enclosures of indigenous lands for nature reserves. This notion has persisted, especially among the large conservation organizations, despite ample evidence that the "tragedy" was not too many people chasing after limited resources but rather the unregulated capitalist exploitation of open-access resources in search of profits. For example, the real problem in the decline of fisheries isn't overfishing by large numbers of fishermen but rather the huge industrial trawlers in search of global profits that overfish with nets that damage the sea floor.

Under capitalism, what is politely termed "open access" is actually a *frontier*. A frontier is a territory in which resources are in dispute. The "agricultural frontier" in Central America is a classic example. One of the effects of the Green Revolution was the displacement of millions of peasants by larger-scale farmers. To keep them from coming to the cities, governments encouraged them to colonize the rainforests with vague promises of land titles. Destitute farmers slashed and burned ancient trees in a desperate attempt to access land and nutrients for food. After a couple of years, weeds choked their fields, driving them to chop down more trees. Big cattle ranchers, encouraged by the lucrative markets of the "hamburger revolution" in the United States, quickly moved in to grab the new pasture, pushing peasant farmers deeper into the rainforest. Land titles, given on the basis of "improvements"—that is, clearing the forest—were expensive to process and thus steadily accrued to the large landholders. The rainforest was hard to access but full of precious hardwoods, gold, and other resources for whomever could reach them. A free-for-all ensued throughout the 1980s and 1990s as industrial carpetbaggers from around the world jumped to grab resources in the open-access regime of Central America's rainforests.[15] Because the forest was first cleared by poor, dispossessed peasants, the name "agricultural frontier" was given to the process of the rainforest destruction.

The process is playing out today in open-access frontiers in which the resources are in dispute, being grabbed, privatized, commodified, traded, and speculated on in world markets. The remaining rainforests in Indonesia, the oil in the North Pole, the carbon in the air, the fish in the sea, even the genes in our bodies have become part of an open-access frontier and thus the first step in their ownership by capital. The tragedy is not of the Commons but of the commodification of nature and the unregulated, private exploitation of its resources.[16, 17]

Land, Labor, Capital, and Markets

Markets have been around a long time, but before the nineteenth century did not organize society as they do today. Throughout feudalism and mercantile capitalism, markets served as one more complement to social life. Under mercantilism the market was firmly under the control of a centralized state administration. These arrangements spread around the world through imperial licenses and charters like the British and Dutch East India companies, the Massachusetts Bay Colony, and the Hudson Bay Company, or the vast Spanish land grants in what is now Mexico, the U.S. Southwest, and California. As Karl Polanyi pointed out, "Regulation and markets, in effect, grew up together."[18] The concept of a "free" market was not only unknown, it ran counter to reality.

With the emergence of the market economy, or "self-regulating market," everything was assigned a price. Ideally, a perfect, self-regulating market provides everyone—producers, landowners, workers, bankers, and traders—with sufficient income to buy all the goods that are produced. In a perfect market economy all commodities, including money, people's labor power, and the land, are bought and sold in the market.[19] Rent is the price of land; wages are the price of labor; and interest is the price of money. But are these really commodities?

A commodity is something that is produced for the purpose of sale in a market for more than the cost of producing it. But land can't be produced for the market; it is simply part of nature. Labor is really people, who are not "produced" to be traded on the market but are born and raised to live life. Money is not technically produced as a market good either, and only has value as a medium of exchange to facilitate the circulation of goods (it also has use value). As Karl Polanyi put it:

> Labor is only another name for a human activity which goes with life itself, which in its turn is not produced for sale but for entirely different reasons, nor can that activity be detached from the rest of life, be stored or mobilized; land is only another name for nature, which is not produced by man; actual money, finally, is merely a token of purchasing power which, as a rule, is not produced at all, but comes into being through the mechanism of banking or state finance. None of them is produced for sale. The commodity description of labor, land, and money is entirely fictitious.[20]

The same can be said of resource deposits, like gold, oil, or uranium. They are not commodities, but commodities are produced as the resource is exploited. With agricultural land, there is the possibility—if managed wisely—for it to retain its productive capacity forever. But in a market economy, all are treated as commodities. Land, labor and money, all essential to agriculture and the food system, are considered "false commodities."[21] This is because none of these are actually manufactured for consumption. Until recently, none were regularly bought and sold on the market, either.

Over time, economies dominated by market relations produce market societies, market cultures, and a market ideology. Today, the logic of the market penetrates all other forms of production, exchange, politics, and everyday life. Agricultural land, once a measure of wealth and power and a means by which to produce value,

Land and Labor: A Farmworker's Perspective

ROSALINDA GUILLÉN, farmworker, organizer, ecofeminist

Living in the labor camp, nothing there was ours. Nothing! We were landless. In Mexico, we had our place. The first thing we realized when we got to the labor camp was that nothing was ours. We couldn't go anywhere, do anything, touch anything. It was made very clear that nothing belonged to us. That's a very dislocating feeling. You're nowhere. That had a huge impact on me. Being taken away from our land in Mexico was huge. My mother went into a deep depression and we, as children, were stunned. We refused to accept that the labor camp was a reality.

Farmworkers in the United States are the largest landless workforce in the food system. We're not just landless in that we don't own the land we're working—we don't even own our own homes. The biggest issue for many farmworkers is that people expect us to live in farm labor camps. Labor camps are like a slap in the face—throwing in our faces how really landless we are, how little we count for in every way. When you live in a labor camp, the people in town know that you live there. Therefore you're something less than everybody else in the community, because you don't have a place. Some of these other workers own their homes. When you go into rural towns there are parks named after somebody, buildings named after somebody. That's like a recognition that you're a human being that owns something in the community. For farmworkers, we're nowhere. We're not seen anywhere. We are so invisible, except for the value we bring to some landowner.

You have to have land to produce food. You have to have land to package it. You have to own the land where you put the coolers. Some landowner is receiving the value of your work. What you're getting is the opportunity to give him value, and that's it.

> As farmworkers that happens over and over again everywhere, in every community where you go. The value of what we bring to a community is blatantly waved aside. We're invisible. Our contributions are invisible. That's part of the capitalist culture in this country. We are like the dregs of slavery in this country. They're holding on to that slave mentality to try to get value from the cheapest labor they can get. If they keep us landless, if we do not have the opportunity to root ourselves into the communities in the way we want, then it's easy to get more value out of us with less investment in us.
>
> We need to look at farmworkers in this country owning land, where we can produce. That is the dynamic change we need in the food system.[22]

is now a financial asset, its value atomized and repackaged, bought, sold, and circulated in global markets at the speed of a keystroke. The land, of course, never moves, but its ownership changes rapidly. Rents produce a steady income stream for non-farmer owners, something that doesn't happen if one owns gold or silver.

What does this mean for our food system?

It means that farmland is prohibitively expensive for young, beginning farmers. It also means that farmers are getting older. The average age of a farmer in the United States is fifty-eight. Over a third of the farmers in the European Union are over sixty-five. Many of these farmers lament that there are no farmers left to work the land anymore, even though they are often surrounded by farmworkers from the Global South who used to be farmers. The other side of the ageing of the farm sector is reflected in many villages in the Global South populated by old people and young children. There are many, many young people around the world who still want to farm but can't because the price of land is too high and the returns to production too low for them to enter farming. What has happened? Why is farmland becoming so expensive, and why is it so hard to be a farmer?

From Land Rent to Land Grabs

From a market perspective, the reason farmland prices have risen is because the price of food has gone up, thus making farmland more valuable. Urban sprawl and population growth also push farmland prices up. When the price of farmland increases, it attracts financial speculators who engage in "arbitrage" by buying low and selling high. But there are deeper, structural reasons why this is possible.

When land is commodified, it is taken out of traditional, common public holdings or reserves in order to be owned, rented, or traded in the market. Even areas of public land can be commodified through leases and licenses. Land value is partially reflected in its market price (exchange value), which is influenced by market demand. But the use value of land also influences its market price. Part of this use value is called "land rent." Though the term originally referred to the part of the harvest that landless peasants turned over to landlords, in the classic definition land rent refers to the income derived from land as a productive asset.

Location, natural fertility, surrounding resources, the availability of labor, technology, and changing use can all affect land rent, making some plots of land more valuable than others because of their capacity to produce more wealth. The land rent of a piece of property is always valued at its highest potential. However, this is not always the same as its market price.

Ideally, in a market economy the price of a plot of land faithfully reflects the value of its land rent. But under capitalism this can fluctuate wildly. Sometimes the price of land in the marketplace drops far below the value of the land rent. This can happen when production is undervalued; for example, during a glut when commodity prices drop below the costs of production. If this happens for too long, the market price of the land will also drop because working the land doesn't turn a profit. In the United States and the European Union, taxpayers provide subsidies to grain farmers so that they can stay in business even when prices fall due to overproduction. These subsidies can keep the price of land in line with the land rent, though too many subsidies can inflate the price of land beyond the rent as well. Sometimes the price of land is much higher than its land rent. This can happen when agricultural prices are artificially increased through subsidies, hoarding, or speculation, creating a financial "bubble" that inflates the price of land. One example is the land-price bubble in the Midwest due to U.S. government subsidies for corn-based ethanol production. Under this scenario, land is worth more as a financial asset than as a productive asset: you can make more money buying and selling land than by farming it. This is the case for much of the agricultural land in the United States today.

With a few notable spikes due to war and oil crises over most of the last half-century, the chronic overproduction of food has steadily

Biofuels

Biofuels invoke an image of renewable abundance that allows industry, politicians, the World Bank, the United Nations, and even the Intergovernmental Panel on Climate Change to present fuel extracted from corn, sugarcane, soy, and other crops as a "clean and green" transition from peak oil to a renewable fuel economy. Myths of sustainability and abundance divert attention away from powerful economic interests that benefit from this biofuel transition, avoiding discussion of the multiple ripple effects and trade-offs between food, feed, energy, and the environment that come with the expansion of biofuel production. These trade-offs are multidimensional, with both local and global implications. In the United States today, biofuels are mainly produced from corn and soybeans grown on existing agricultural land However, there is increasing concern that biofuel production expansion could bring some 10 million acres of fragile land protected by the government's Conservation Reserve Program into production.[23] There are also indirect land-use effects in other countries. Experts have long been concerned that by affecting prices, biofuel mandates will have impacts on land use far beyond the countries in which they operate, particularly in the conversion of pasture and forest land.[24] This is already occurring in countries such as Brazil, Indonesia, and Malaysia, where forests are being slashed to expand soy, sugarcane, and oil-palm plantations for biofuel production. One of the most pertinent effects has been the massive appreciation in U.S. agricultural land values. "The average price of U.S. farmland increased 74 percent between 2000 and 2007 to a record $4,700 per hectare. In Iowa—a leading maize-producing state—farmland values rose by roughly $2,470 per hectare between 2003 and 2007 to more than $7,900 per hectare."[25] Rapid growth in biofuel markets has resulted in equally rapid capitalization and concentration of power among a handful of corporate partnerships in grain, oil, and genetic engineering—primarily Cargill, Archer Daniels Midland, and Monsanto. The convergence of these powerful industries has far-reaching effects that will transform both food systems and rural economies worldwide.

driven down food prices and kept agricultural land prices more or less indexed to the land rent. The food price spikes of 2007–2008 and 2011 changed all that. Food is now more expensive and commodity prices are fluctuating wildly. Land values are climbing. Financial investors who have ignored farmland for decades now see it as a good investment. According to agrarian sociologist Madeleine Fairbairn:

> Although some insurance companies have had farmland holdings for years, most financial investors found farmland, and agricultural investment in general, unappealing compared to the much higher returns to be made in financial markets. However, this began to shift around 2007 as the prices of agricultural commodities started to climb and land prices followed suit. The recession that began with the bursting of the U.S. housing bubble in 2008 caused investor interest to suffer a momentary dip but also added fuel to the fire, as investors sought alternative, and more secure, places to put their money.[26]

At least a quarter of farmland acquisitions are a result of financial speculation and hedging. In fact, land is becoming as or more important as a non-farm financial asset than a farm-based productive asset. Called "financialization," this phenomenon attracts billionaires and institutional investing, from pension funds, hedge funds, university endowments, private foundations, and sovereign wealth funds to the $8.4 trillion market in farmland. Investors already own up to $40 billion in farmland assets. Farmland is consolidating, both because of

Land Rents in the U.S. Heartland

Most issues in the farm sector are connected to land ownership and tenure. An owner of productive agricultural land may not necessarily be a farmer or have any interest in farming (termed a non-operating landlord). Or they may be a farmer that farms only part of their land and leases the rest (part-owners). Or they may be full-owners who own 100 percent of the land they farm. Over the past three decades, shifts in ownership and increases in farm size have seen more renters (farmers who rent 100 percent of the land they farm) and part-owners farming a growing number of acres, especially in the agriculturally productive Midwestern United States.[27]

In 2012, agricultural producers rented and farmed nearly 354 million acres of farmland, nearly 40 percent of total U.S. farmland, according to the results of the USDA's Tenure, Ownership, and Transition of Agricultural Land (TOTAL) survey. Of this rented land, individual farmers own 20 percent, while the remaining 80 percent is rented out by non-farming landlords, either as individuals or participants in differing ownership arrangements.

The percentage of rented farmland is increasing across the Midwestern United States, with a larger portion of farmland being managed by renters rather than owners.

In Iowa, the leading state for corn production, 53% of farmland (16 million acres) was farmed by renters in 2012, up from 48% in 1982. Meanwhile, the average farm size for part-owners and tenants has nearly doubled. The 2007 Census found that there are nearly 1500 part-owner and tenant operators who each farm more than 2000 acres in Iowa: a steep increase from the 238 part-owners and tenants who farmed over 2000 acres in 1982. Conversely, full-owners are farming fewer acres. This farm size increase for part-owners and tenants is also a national trend, with part-owners and tenants operating 78% of farms over 2000 acres nationally.[28]

There is no singular causal factor for this trend, but rather a confluence of factors: (1) increased production via an expansion in acreage is increasingly occurring due to the need of U.S. farmers to cover mounting costs for equipment and other expensive inputs; (2) high commodity prices are likely to be driving renters to farm more land in order to maintain profit; (3) ever-increasing land sales prices serve as barriers to entry for new farmers, leaving rent as their only viable option.[29]

When farmland is rented, particularly from non-operating landlords, a short-term, bottom-line approach to farming may more often be applied, an approach that stands in contrast to the long-term management processes required for more sustainable production systems. Non-operating landlords are less likely to be enrolled in the USDA's Conservation or Wetlands Reserve Programs, while intense competition for cropland—as farmers try to outbid each other to offer the highest rents—often leaves only the largest operators, those with more liquid capital, able to compete for rented land. Power inequalities between tenant and landlord are extremely difficult to dismantle given the inherent unequal nature of land tenure, in which one owns the other's means to production. And with fierce competition for farmland, as is the case in Iowa and generally across the Midwest, this asymmetry is only exacerbated.[30]

land grabs and a scalar change in the forms of production that favor big land—and big investments.

Institutions like the World Bank welcome this, arguing that big land deals bring agricultural investment. But as farmland concentrates in the hands of fewer and fewer owners interested in short-term financial profit, farmland becomes disconnected from those who actually cultivate it.

The financialization of farmland is different than other forms of real estate speculation because farmland is a productive asset. When farmland's exchange value is worth more than its use value, the logic governing how it is used changes dramatically. The investment time horizon for speculative sale and purchase of land as a financial asset is fractions of a second as bits and pieces of the property's value change hands in global financial markets. Compare this to the time horizon of a family farmer who plans on farming the land productively and sustainably for generations. When farmers become operators and managers on land owned by international investors, there is no incentive to invest in soil fertility, reforestation, conservation, and other sustainable practices that require generational stewardship. The only incentive is to pump out more production, whatever the environmental cost, to ensure rising returns to investors.

The increase in farmland's value on financial markets is far above farmland's land rent, its value as a productive asset. This situation is not permanent, but it is damaging and can be dangerous for farming, the environment, and the national economy. How did it come about?

The Land Fix to the Crisis of Over-Accumulation

Since the 1980s the United States Federal Reserve has kept interest rates on loans to private banks very low, making it easy for investors to borrow money. Banking regulations have been relaxed to facilitate financial investments.[31] But behind the neoliberal regulations lurks a familiar crisis peculiar to capitalism: over-accumulation.

This kind of farmland investment—and outright land grabs—are a quick fix for an age-old capitalist problem that has taken on global proportions. In a recession, purchasing power is reduced because of unemployment and underemployment. Goods pile up unsold. Banks fill with cash because there are no attractive outlets for productive investment. During the Great Recession of 2007–2009, many large businesses cut costs drastically, fired workers, and worked the remaining employees harder. Doing more with less increased productivity for business but reduced the overall purchasing power of the working class, leading to an over-accumulation of goods. Investors are reluctant to invest in productive activities if no one will buy their products. Global corporations are sitting on mountains of cash. There are literally trillions of excess dollars sloshing around the world's banks waiting for profitable investments. With interest rates near zero, money is cheap. Nonetheless, banks are reluctant to lend because they don't think they will get a return on the investment.

When this happens, land becomes a good refuge for excess capital. As Mark Twain purportedly said, "Buy land, they're not making any more of it." There is no point in holding wealth as money (which is losing value) when one can hold wealth in land, which can potentially gain in value. Investors count on buying land at low prices, then selling high when the recession is over. The current rush to buy land has driven up prices worldwide. Today the price of agricultural land is rising so fast that its financial value is outpacing its productive value: land is worth more in terms of what it can sell for than for what it can produce. Susan Payne, global land speculator and CEO of Emergent Asset Management, once bragged:

> In South Africa and sub-Saharan Africa the cost of agriland, arable, good agriland that we're buying, is one-seventh of the price of similar land in Argentina, Brazil, and America. That alone is an arbitrage opportunity. We could be moronic and not grow anything and we think we will still make money over the next decade.[32]

What Ms. Payne is referring to is that the price of land in South Africa and sub-Saharan Africa is so low in relation to its land rent (what it is worth for what it can produce) that the capture of the difference (arbitrage) between low price and high land rent will provide investors with a handsome profit. Any benefits from actually growing crops are secondary to the deal. This is why the ability to capture value without having to produce anything is often referred to as "rent-seeking behavior" or "neo-rentism."

With the fall in value of almost all global currencies, former drivers of land inflation like gold mining and mineral extraction have also returned in force. "Green grabbing" of land to access carbon markets, set aside nature reserves, and to plant agrofuels is also on the rise. But relatively few land grabs actually result in productive projects, leading many observers to ask if the land rush is not just one gigantic speculative bubble.

Land Grabs

A convergence of global crises across financial, environmental, energy, and food sectors in recent years has seen powerful transnational and economic actors—from corporations to governments to private equity funds—rush to gain access and control of land. This is occurring globally, but there are clear North-South (and increasingly even South-South) demarcations that echo the land grabs of colonial times.[33] There are various mechanisms through which land grabbing occurs, including straightforward private-private purchases of large tracts of land, and public-private long-term leases through which investors hope to build, maintain, or extend large-scale agro-industrial and extractive enterprises. National governments in "finance-rich, resource-poor" countries are looking to "finance-poor, resource-rich" countries to help secure their own food and, especially, energy needs into the future. Three key factors underpin the recent momentum in global land grabs: 1) increased demand for food, feed, pulp, and other industrial raw materials, driven by global population and income

> growth; 2) increased demand for biofuel crops as a result of policies and mandates in key consuming countries and regions, such as the United States and European Union; and 3) shifts of agricultural production from regions already operating at their productivity frontier (such as the United States and China) to land-abundant regions where the price of land is relatively cheap, namely Latin America, Africa, and Asia. In many cases, private investors, including large investment funds, have acquired land and cleared it of local inhabitants and users for merely speculative motives, in the hopes that the price of arable land will continue to rise in the future. Land grabs do not happen overnight. Markets must be deregulated (or created), national laws must be changed (or broken), and infrastructure must be developed. This is the drilling down of investment capital in which land grabs, whatever their form, are simply one part of a larger reconfiguration of rules, markets, and landscapes. The "grab" is one link in a long chain of larger political and economic transformations called "territorial restructuring."[34]

Territorial Restructuring: Colonizing Places and Spaces for Capitalist Development

Land, while viewed by the market as a tradable commodity, is the social space where economic and community decisions are made. It is the place of neighborhood, culture, and livelihoods. For indigenous peoples, it is their territory. It is home.

Land arbitrage opportunities come about by bringing new land—with an attractive land rent—into the global land market where rents can actually be capitalized. While capitalism has a natural tendency to seek out rents, such rents are not always so easy to capture, that is, bring to the market for sale. Other people or communities might already have possession of the land; infrastructure may be deficient; land might be regulated to restrict use or protected from sale by law, treaty, trusts, or reserves. Once purchased, speculative (rent-seeking) capital may face difficulties in raising the price for resale. Established land markets might not exist or may have been destroyed by economic collapse, war, or corruption. People and communities might resist the commodification of their land.

The capture of land value (rents) and the extraction of profits (surplus) from a given area requires a series of physical and political conditions that favor capitalist investment. If these conditions do not exist, the private sector needs the state to create them. If the state is weak or unwilling, the private sector can turn to multilateral development organizations for help.

The World Bank, Inter-American Development Bank, Asian Development Bank, African Development Bank, and European Development Bank were all created to facilitate the development of capitalism. The development banks can work individually, with each other, or with other multilateral institutions, governments, and transnational corporations to create the conditions for capitalist development, rent capture, and surplus extraction in a given region, country, or territory. This process is called *territorial restructuring.*[35]

Territorial restructuring follows a "logic of territory" and "logic of capital."[36] The first logic includes activities such as privatization, environmental enclosures (like nature reserves), and land titling programs that convert traditional or communal landholdings into individual, private ownership. The second logic utilizes the instruments of finance, investment, market liberalization, and environmental deregulation. The former is concerned with the physical *places* capital is interested in exploiting for profit, the latter with the social *spaces* in which the political decisions are made over these resources to allow businesses to profit.

Because of the weak planning and regulatory capacity of many countries, infrastructure—roads, electricity, or power generation—is also a means for territorial restructuring. If territorial restructuring takes place where people already live, it can completely transform communities, for better or for worse. If it takes place in sparsely populated areas, it can facilitate colonization, also for better or for worse. Land reform and land titling programs are often a part of territorial restructuring. Once formal titles to the land are given to original inhabitants, or more likely, to owners taking control following dispossession, it can become a saleable commodity. Depending on the political objective, territorial restructuring projects can either be regressive or redistributive.

For example, the World Bank worked diligently to restructure the Guatemalan Highlands in order to open it up to gold extraction by Northern mining companies. Reviving the sector was a remote possibility until 2001–2004 when the international price for gold jumped from $277 to over $400 an ounce.[37] Old, low-grade, mined-out or hard-to-reach mines around the world suddenly became potentially profitable. In Guatemala, gold deposits are found in the Western Highlands, home to most of the country's impoverished indigenous population.

For decades during the country's civil war, the Highlands was the theater for widespread and grisly episodes of government and paramilitary human rights abuses. After the signing of the Peace Accords in 1996, the World Bank quickly advised the Arzú government to modernize the nation's mining sector. This led to one of the most imperialist mining codes since Guatemala's independence from Spain in 1821. Under the new mining law, companies could be 100 percent foreign owned, 6 percent mandatory royalty levels were replaced with a mere 1 percent, and the 58 percent tax on profits was reduced to 31 percent. In a country where poor consumers pay up to $140 a month for water, the substantial quantities of it needed for processing gold ore became free to mining companies. Licensing was streamlined, and though some environmental regulations were strengthened, no provisions were made to increase the regulatory capacity of the ministries of Mining and Environment, thus making these improvements effectively symbolic.

In 1997, the World Bank introduced a $13 million project designed to prepare conditions for the privatization of the state-owned telephone company, roads, and ports. This was quickly followed by three projects totaling over $133 million, all in the same year. In all, from 1997 to 2005, the bank introduced twenty-four separate projects totaling $859 million, loaning more to Guatemala in nine years than it had in the past forty. The bank's post-accords suite of projects included seven project investments from the bank's private sector lending arm, the International Finance Corporation (IFC), totaling $139 million. The largest of these projects—$45 million—went to Glamis Gold Corporation of Canada to reactivate the Marlin Mine in the predominantly indigenous municipality of San Marcos.

Nearly one-third of the bank's project lending since the Peace Accords went directly or indirectly to the Western Highlands for a wide array of projects that both redirected the flow of wealth and mitigated the social and environmental consequences of mineral extraction: reconstruction, land titling, and roads. A large, natural resources management project was particularly deceptive. A natural resources audit carried out by the bank had determined that the best prospect for generating revenues for indigenous communities in the Western Highlands was through reforestation. The project sought to work with communities to formalize private land titles so that they could take advantage of potential carbon markets. These carbon markets never materialized. The bank's audit did not mention that gold was an important natural resource in the region. Nor did it mention that sharing just a fraction of the profits from the gold lying underneath the ground within these communities would increase their wealth many times more than carbon markets. The fictitious market for environmental services was a ruse to divert attention from the real profits at stake.

The Marlin mine was strongly opposed by the indigenous residents in surrounding communities, who carried out a widespread public consultation in which 99 percent of those interviewed voted against it. Delegations of indigenous leaders traveled to Washington to file a complaint with the IFC and implore the World Bank to stop funding the project. Though they were not aware of the legal and physical restructuring that would transform the Western Highlands in the interests of foreign mineral extraction, they knew that the influx of workers and the contamination from open-pit cyanide mining would overrun their lands.

The indigenous communities lost their fight against the Marlin mine. By the time they realized that the mine was coming, their territory was already deep in the throes of a capitalist restructuring. The mining concession was actually the last step in a series of projects and agreements designed to open the area to foreign mining interests. The land where they had grown food and lived for centuries had become part of another logic, one in which they were in the way.[38]

The Real Tragedy: The Loss of the Commons and the Public Sphere

For three centuries, capital has waged war to appropriate the Commons and open-access areas for free exploitation. In times of market expansion, it has also sought to privatize all forms of public ownership and to subjugate the power of public decision to the needs of capital. Given the steady march of capital into land, markets, and politics, it is remarkable that today, following a quarter-century of neoliberal privatization and deregulation, there is any public sphere of or Commons left to appropriate.

Although it is true that much of the decision-making spaces of the public sphere worldwide have been destroyed by neoliberalism, large parts of the world's food systems still follow a community rather than a private market logic. Some countries must import a significant amount of their food from abroad and their populations are quickly affected by changes in prices on international markets. However, in total, only about 15 percent of food crosses international borders and well over half of the world's food is produced by small farmers and peasants. The 86 million acres of land currently being grabbed by speculators and producers of agrofuels have given rise to widespread resistance, indicating that people around the world are stubbornly hanging on to land and livelihoods outside the logic of capital. Moreover, seemingly against all odds, people are working to reestablish the Commons as a means of resisting the capitalist food system.

One of the largest examples of this resistance is the *ejido* system of Mexico. Ejidos are collectively managed tracts of land that are usually divided into family parcels. The Mexican ejido system, established by the Mexican Constitution in 1917, has its roots in the Aztec *calpulli* and in the collective land management of seventeenth-century Spain. Mexican ejidos replaced the *hacienda* system (a feudal arrangement), left over from the days of Spanish colonialism. Ejidos provided land to the peasantry, who fought a bloody revolution against the landed oligarchy. Members of an ejido have rights to farm the land but no private title. The *asamblea ejidal* or ejido assembly to which all *ejidatarios* belong is the highest authority regarding the use and management of the ejido, and its authorities are elected democratically by ejido members. For over seventy years the vast ejido system of Mexico ensured peasant access to land, food, and livelihoods. It was the backbone of the Mexican food system, far outproducing its industrial food sector, even after the introduction of the Green Revolution in the 1960s. Large land interests in Mexico never gave up hoping that one day they could take back the land lost in the Mexican Revolution, particularly the vast extensions of land distributed during the presidency of pro-poor reformer Lázaro Cárdenas (1934–1940).

In 1991, in preparation for the signing of the North American Free Trade Agreement (NAFTA) between the United States, Canada, and Mexico, Mexican president Carlos Salinas de Gortari constitutionally abolished the ejido and gave individual property titles to its farmers, effectively privatizing millions of acres of what had been public land. A neoliberal modernizer who did his graduate studies at Harvard and the Kennedy School of Government in the United States, Salinas de Gortari was eager to send a strong signal to Northern investors that Mexico's economy was open for business—starting with peasant farms. The hope was that the *ejidatarios* would sell their land to Mexican and North American agribusiness concerns, paving the way for the development of capitalist farms and the incorporation of Mexican agriculture into the globalized food regime. Although the neoliberal policies of the scandal-ridden Salinas de Gortari presidency led to the crash of the Mexican economy in 1994, they did not lead to the widespread sale of ejido land. Though the small farmers of the ejidos were effectively abandoned with the privatization of agricultural services, and though NAFTA did drive several million farmers into bankruptcy (leading to waves of migration to the United States in search of work), most ejido farmers have not sold their farms. One strong factor in this was the refusal of women to part with the land. Alicia Sarmientos, an *ejidataria,* states:

> We discovered that we had rights to land because if we are married and our husbands want to sell the ejido, they can't do it without our consent. . . . We realized that we had this power. This has been great because many women have not permitted their husbands to sell the ejido. The men have migrated to work, okay, because of economic need. They have wanted to sell the land, but no! We women are defending ourselves now. We can work the land.[39]

Restructuring Land and Property; Rebuilding the Public Sphere

Because of global capital's need to constantly expand, because of its tendency to store excess profits in land, and because of the current expansion of the financial sector, land and resource struggles are occurring in both rural and urban food systems of the Global North and the Global South. Private property relations dominate the corporate food regime, but private property cannot exist without the public sector: multilateral banks, police forces, infrastructure, and the power of public government to enforce and ensure private accumulation. Similarly, many of the world's food producers cannot survive without common property, and none can survive without the public sphere. Open-access resources can be converted into public, private, or common property (this is precisely why they are usually in dispute). The interplay of different property forms under capitalism is complex and fluid and reflects different class interests that can be part of class domination or part of different forms of resistance.

The Commons can supplement the food, fiber, and other resource needs of small-scale farmers, pastoralists, and fishermen, lowering their livelihood costs and allowing them to sell their products cheaply, and thus help them compete with large-scale, capitalized production.

Brazil's Landless Workers Movement—MST [40, 41]

Few issues have been as contentious in contemporary Brazilian politics as land reform. Born out of resistance to the economic plans imposed by Brazil's military governments during the 1970s and 1980s, an array of popular movements pressed the Brazilian state for reforms. A strong convergence of movements came together in 1984 to form the Brazilian Landless Workers' Movement (Movimento dos Trabalhadores Rurais Sem Terra, or MST). Taking advantage of the 1964 Land Statute, in which land must serve a "social purpose," the MST began by occupying idle and socially unproductive lands belonging to the latifundios (large landed estates). With its roots in socialist activism, Liberation Theology, and the popular education theories of Paulo Freire, the MST is now at the forefront of social action for agrarian reform. The MST identifies and occupies underutilized or empty lands to gain legal title and bring them into productive use by employing agroecology. Once underused land is successfully occupied by families organized by the MST, schools, cooperatives, and credit unions are set up and the land is farmed to grow fruits, vegetables, grains, coffee, and livestock. Present in 23 of Brazil's 25 states and with over 1 million members, the movement has ratified over 2,000 settlements, settling over 370,000 families with an estimated 80,000 more awaiting settlement, established a network of approximately 2,000 primary and secondary schools, partnered with 13 public universities, 160 rural cooperatives, 4 credit unions, and started food processing plants, and retail outlets. In recent years, the MST has established itself as an influential voice in international advocacy networks such as the World Social Forum and Via Campesina.

However, this "subsidy" from the Commons can cut both ways. If the Commons is used to produce goods for market rather than for subsistence, low prices in the market can lead to the overexploitation of the Commons. Also, when small-scale producers or their family members work for industrial wages, the Commons can allow industry to obtain labor power more cheaply, essentially allowing industry to appropriate the subsidy of the Commons. So, under certain conditions, the market and the private sector may indirectly benefit from the Commons. In recessionary or deflationary times, capital may seek to privatize the Commons in order to put its wealth in land rather than hold it as money. If capital wants land or needs labor, it can use the power of the state to enclose the Commons and force smallholders to sell their land and enter the labor market. So even though the Commons is a historic refuge for non-capitalist relations in the food system, it does not always escape manipulation by capital.

Capitalism has the same fluid, opportunistic relation with public goods. In order to access, appropriate, or steal resources, the private sector needs the economic and coercive power of the state. In times of capitalist crisis—for example, the lack of profitable investment opportunities—the private sector calls upon the state to eliminate regulations in order to provide capital with more flexibility and opportunities to profit. And when financial crashes occur, the state is recruited to bail out the large "too big to fail and too big for jail" companies with taxpayer money. Even in good times the private sector relies on state subsidies (for example, the U.S. Farm Bill, with most of the benefits going to agrifoods businesses), the privatization of public goods (research at public universities), and the complicity of public regulatory bodies (like the U.S. Food and Drug Administration) to ensure the privatization and unregulated circulation of goods. The private sector also relies extensively on public property in the form of infrastructure to do business.

Open-access resources are sometimes left as such—in which case they are often subject to dispute between different users—or can be brought under the control of the state, to be privatized or placed in the public domain. Opening the North Pole to oil rigs, the buying and selling of carbon credits, and the vast "uninhabited lands" of the Sahara and equatorial rainforests are examples of this. In some cases, capital prefers the free-for-all of open access in order to extract wealth without having to pay for externalities or be subjected to regulation. Sometimes capital needs the resources and regulatory power of the state to facilitate access.

Under private property relations of the liberal capitalist state, all economic actors have *equal rights* to do business. With public property relations, all actors have an *equal vote*. In common property relations all actors have *equal power*. This goes a long way toward explaining the persistence of the Commons, even under capitalism.

The mechanism for exchanging (buying and selling) private property is the market. The mechanism for deciding what happens to both public property and the Commons is the public sphere. Without a market, private property would wither and die. Without a public sphere both public property and the Commons eventually disappear, leaving the future of society to whatever corporations have the most market power. The last three decades of neoliberal privatization have not just seen the transfer of trillions of dollars in public and common property resources to the corporate-dominated private sector, they have also seen the steady erosion of the public sphere—the basis for community survival. Gone are the *ejido* assemblies of Mexico where villagers came together to manage their land-based resources; gone are the parent-teacher associations that engaged the community in their children's education; gone are the community health committees that addressed issues of environmental health and much, much more.

Property is not just a reflection of social relations, it *is* a social relation. Any project for the reconstruction of public and common property must necessarily work to recapture and strengthen the public sphere. Any effort to rebuild our civic life must also restructure property.

— 4 —

Capitalism, Food, and Agriculture

For one who gained riches by mining,
Perceiving that hundreds grew poor,
I made up my mind to try farming,
The only pursuit that was sure!

—"LAY OF THE OLD SETTLER," NORTHWEST UNITED STATES FOLK SONG BY FRANCIS D. HENRY, CIRCA 1874

Two hundred years after capitalism emerged in Europe, the term "capitalist agriculture" was still largely an oxymoron. With the exception of wool and the colonial trade in hides, cotton, tobacco, coffee, tea, and sugar, there was very little direct capitalist investment in farming. Food was something to be bought cheaply—and farmland something to be leased at a high price—but farming *per se* was not considered a wise investment for the burgeoning capitalist classes. In many parts of the world today, and in many ways, capitalist agriculture is still a contradiction in terms. This is because while the business of selling inputs (seeds, tools, machinery, and fertilizer) to farmers and trading in farm products can be quite lucrative, farming itself presents certain obstacles to capitalist investment.

On one hand, this tension between agriculture and capitalism has produced an irrational capitalist agriculture rife with intractable social and environmental problems.[1] On the other hand, it has resulted in the "persistence of the peasantry" and of petty commodity production worldwide.[2] Today, despite centuries of capitalism, large-scale capitalist agriculture produces less than a third of the world's food supply, made possible in large part by multibillion-dollar subsidies and insurance programs. Peasants and smallholders still feed most people in the world, though they cultivate less than a quarter of the arable land.[3]

Obstacles to Capitalist Investment in Agriculture

Farming is a risky business. Environmental factors like droughts, floods, freezes, and pest outbreaks make agriculture a bad bet. Farmers must buy expensive, industrialized products (machinery, chemicals, and genetically modified seeds) in order to produce cheap raw materials, typically resulting in low margins of profit. Agriculture under capitalism has a tendency to overproduce; for the last half century the world has produced 1.5 times more than enough food to feed every man, woman, and child on the planet. Overproduction in the Global North has led to a steady decline in the price of agricultural commodities. Commodities in most industries are manipulated by a handful of monopolistic corporations that try to avoid "price wars" between each other. There are far too many farmers in agriculture to engage in this inter-firm behavior and no single farmer or group of farmers controls enough of the food supply to influence price by increasing or reducing supply. Farmers must take the prices they are given. Individual farmers have to cover their fixed costs and can't, on their own, hold back production to raise prices. Unless government programs or marketing boards limit production in times of falling commodity prices, farmers will do exactly the opposite: producing more in an attempt to cover their fixed costs. When farmers try to "farm their way out" of low prices, the result is even lower prices.

To keep commodity prices stable, capitalist governments implement price supports and supply management programs. These can take the form of "set-asides" to take land out of production, grain reserves, and marketing boards and commodity agreements to manage market supply. Governments can buy up excess grain, taking it off the market. This helps to sop up oversupply, raising prices to farmers. Tariffs and subsidies are also used to manage prices. Subsidies are especially liked by grain companies and processors because these allow them to buy up product cheaply, letting the taxpayer pick up the bill in the form of direct payments to farmers.

Subsidies are often criticized by some environmental groups, which claim that they drive overproduction of cheap food and are given primarily to large farmers. The reality is that low prices drive overproduction, which results in subsidies. Eliminating subsidies (without other major structural changes to supply and price) would likely drive small and midsize farmers out of business, thus contributing to further farm consolidation into larger and larger farms. All of these measures have fallen in and out of favor and have been replaced with others, such as crop insurance, that basically attempt to resolve the same contradiction. Without some form of supply and price management, farmers typically increase their production, thus bringing down commodity prices even more. Then, if they can, they switch to higher-value crops and start the boom-bust cycle all over again.

Can farm programs ensure a stable, fair income for farmers and a healthy, affordable food supply? Of course they can. Unfortunately, capital is not invested in ensuring a fair income for farmers but in profiting from agriculture. Banks give loans; seed and chemical companies sell hybrids, GMOs, fertilizers, and pesticides; grain companies buy and process corn, wheat, and soy. All of this without having to worry about an individual farmer's crop failure. But, you say, fortunes are made by capitalists who take risks! True perhaps, but in farming, risks prevail and fortunes are rare.

One reason capital generally avoids investing directly in farming is the "fixity" of land-based production. Farmers are tied to the land through their soil, fences, barns, farmsteads, and local knowledge. If a farm is losing money, it can't just cut its losses and move to an overseas "free enterprise zone" like a sweat shop. Another big difficulty is contracting skilled seasonal labor on a timely basis. Few people have the combination of quickness and stamina needed to harvest crops efficiently, all day long, all season long, year after year.[4] Also, farmers are price-takers rather than price-makers; because of the perishability of most agricultural crops, they can't withhold their products from the market to drive up the price but must take whatever comes along, even if it means losing money. All of these factors act as disincentives to direct investment by capital.

But there is an even bigger deal-breaker for capital. At the core of agriculture's production process is a troublesome disjuncture between labor and production time:

> Working time is always production time; that is to say, time during which capital is held fast in the sphere of production. But vice versa, not all time during which capital is engaged in the process of production is necessarily working time.[5]

What this means for farming is that labor and capital are invested "up front" to prepare the soil and plant the crop, and then only intermittently to irrigate, cultivate, fumigate, etc. The sum of all activities in which labor is needed is "labor time." But to bring a crop to harvest takes a lot longer than the sum of the labor time because agricultural production also depends on slow natural processes like water and nutrient uptake and photosynthesis. Livestock takes time to grow to market weight. So the full agricultural production time is much longer than the amount of labor time invested in producing a crop.

These time-consuming natural processes are a necessary part of agricultural production. During this period, however, capital is immobile, tied up in the production process. Unlike a factory that can speed up or slow down production on an hourly or daily basis, a farm can't fine-tune its operations to constantly respond to price signals. Adjusting labor and input costs to respond to market changes is difficult or impossible within the agricultural year. But even more basic is that surplus value—the "holy grail" of capitalism—*is only created when labor is being absorbed into the commodity.* This happens when farmers and laborers perform work, either by hand or using tools and machines (that were made with labor sometime in the past). When labor is not being employed in the production process, capital is essentially dormant.

Capitalist agriculture does all it can to make farms work like factories, from eliminating labor and expertise with machines to standardizing crop phenotypes for easy harvest, even ripening, and long shelflife. But the core objective of capitalist agriculture is to shorten production time in relation to labor time. In their seminal article "Obstacles to the Development of Capitalist Agriculture," Susan Mann and James Dickenson explain how this has led to very specific forms of large-scale, highly capitalized production on one hand, and the persistence of small-scale, "petty commodity production" on the other:

> [The] capitalization of agriculture progresses most rapidly in those spheres where production time can be successfully reduced. Conversely . . . those spheres of production characterized by a more or less rigid non-identity of production and labour time are likely to prove unattractive to capital on a large scale and thus are left more or less in the hands of the petty producer.[6]

For example, capitalist livestock operations have greatly reduced the days to maturity of poultry, pork, and beef through selective breeding, antibiotics, and hormones. Traditional livestock breeds and heirloom crop varieties may be tastier but take much longer to mature than industrialized animals and cultivars. The new GMO salmon doesn't taste better (nor is it better for the environment), but was developed because the fish grow to market size in half the time of wild salmon.

The flip side of the disjuncture between labor and production time is, as Mann and Dickenson point out, the persistence of the "petty producer": peasants, smallholders, and family farms that farm on the margins of capitalist agriculture. These farming units *can* be more productive (kilo per hectare and pounds per acre) than industrial farms, because smallholders have to make the most they can on very small plots of land.[7] These farmers intensify productivity because unlike in industrial agriculture they can't increase overall production by farming larger and larger areas. They use family labor and cut costs by using low-external input, agroecological methods. They have a knack for finding market niches. But the existence of nearly 1.5 billion small undercapitalized farms in the world (plenty of which are *less* productive than industrial farms) also reflects the fact that because of the disjuncture between labor and production time, capital has simply been invested elsewhere, at least for now.

Capital's avoidance of actual farming and the technological development of agriculture have also resulted in a large family farm sector that is fully engaged in commodity production. Ninety-seven percent of farms in the United States are family-owned and a full 87 percent rely mostly on family labor. Of the 3 percent of non-family corporate farms, most are tightly held by just a few partners.[8]

Smallholders today in the Global North as well as the Global South interact with capitalist markets by selling part or all of their crop as a commodity. However, in the South—and increasingly in the North—they also try to avoid global markets where they are unable to compete with industrial agriculture. Rather, they sell in locally or regionally constructed markets, barter, or seek to process their product on a small scale to add value. Many also seek to lower costs and risk by avoiding capitalization schemes and industrial intensification. This gives rise to many farming styles that may have a lower market output but can provide higher farm incomes, and is reflected in the tremendous heterogeneity of practices.[9] These petty commodity producers making up the majority of the farmers in the world have been around since the dawn of capitalist agriculture. Though their proportion of overall production has diminished, there are about as many smallholders in the world today as there were a century ago.

The Agricultural Treadmill

Over the past hundred years, farmers have been continually offered new technologies from land-grant universities, the USDA, and large agribusiness firms with the inherent promise of increased profits. Willard Cochrane saw the continual application of new technologies resulting in a "technology treadmill" that the farmers had to jump on if they expected to survive.[10] Professor John Ikerd summed up the inner workings of the treadmill in his presentation at the 2002 Missouri Farmers' Union Annual Conference: "Invariable [sic], these technologies require more capital, but reduce labor and management, allowing each farmer to reduce per- unit costs of production while increasing total production. However, as more and more farmers adopt these new technologies, the resulting increases in production cause prices to fall, eliminating the profits of the early adopters and driving those who refuse to adopt, or adopt too late, out of business. This 'technology treadmill' has resulted in chronically recurring overproduction and has been driving farmers off the land for decades."[11]

Increasingly advanced industrial technologies encourage farming on an ever-expanding scale. For farmers who choose to expand their operations, many incur large debts in order to finance the major capital investment required for new technologies. This investment in specialized machinery encourages the planting of monocultures and abandonment of crop rotations, as farmers attempt to get the greatest use out of their expensive equipment, designed to cut and gather uniform crops. Similar, and even inherent, to the technology treadmill is the "chemical treadmill."

Chemical pesticides in agriculture were at first embraced by many farmers with the promise (from chemical companies no less) of lower overall costs. Ultimately, the ongoing use of chemical pesticides and fertilizers increases costs, as pests become more chemical-resistant and fertilizers deplete the soil of vital nutrients. Secondary pest outbreaks (organisms that weren't formerly major pests but become so as their natural enemies are destroyed by targeted pesticide use) and changes in soil qualities from overuse of fertilizers leave crops more vulnerable to disease and damage. As "superbugs" and "superweeds" have developed in response to widespread and continuous use of chemicals, farmers are left little option but to purchase more and more pesticides each year just to keep crop losses at a standard rate.

Farmers, farmworkers, and rural residents end up being the bearers of the risks associated with new technologies and chemicals, be they economic, environmental, or health-related, with the financial benefits asymmetrically accruing to off-farm capital. Unlike farmers, the farm input supply sector receives a return when they sell their product or technology, regardless of the farmers' production outcome. Why not then just jump off the treadmill? Getting off the industrial agriculture treadmill is no simple task: the cost-price squeeze that encouraged farmers onto the treadmill in the first place has increased rather than decreased in intensity as small family farms are run out of business and production becomes increasingly concentrated on large commercial farms.

Opportunities for Investment—Not Farming

On the other hand, the obstacles to capitalist development in agriculture sooner or later become opportunities for capitalist development in the food system. The agrifoods sector is extraordinarily adept at inventing technologies or services to make profits without actually engaging in the risks and limitations of farming.[12] The land itself can be used to generate profits to capital without assuming the risks of agriculture through financialization, which allows investors and speculators opportunities to profit from the value of land and crops without actually having to farm.[13] Even the market risks of agriculture are an opportunity for capital. Commodity *futures* are promises from buyers to pay a certain price on the farmer's product. Farmers can lock in prices long before they harvest. Buyers of futures are speculating that the actual price of the agricultural commodity (like wheat, corn, or pork bellies) at time of sale will be higher than the price established when they bought the futures. This is a way of making (or losing) money on the difference in seasonal prices. There is even a market for betting for or against the rise or fall in the value of commodity futures. The value of this financialized market has increased exponentially since the 2008 global food crisis. The tremendous volatility in food commodities has driven this market opportunity.

The Financialization of Food

The global food crisis of 2007–2008 certainly elicited worldwide attention when rapid and extreme increases in food prices led to civil unrest and riots in almost thirty countries. The crisis sparked international debate among institutions, scholars, and activists about its underlying systemic causes. Analysts attributed the rising food prices to a "perfect storm" of converging factors, one of which was financial speculation in the agricultural commodity market. While the world food economy has had links dating back centuries to financial markets via agricultural commodities futures exchanges, an increasing trend toward "financialization" has occurred, whereby international financial institutions—banks, financial service firms, and large-scale institutional investors—have become involved in previously isolated commodities markets.

Agricultural futures markets developed in the United States over 150 years ago and have been under federal regulation since the 1920s (U.S. Commodities Future Trading Commission). The futures market developed to provide a vital link between two parties: sellers (farmers) and buyers (food processors and manufacturers, flour mills, meatpackers) that agree to buy and sell a specified product for delivery in the future at a fixed price. On the most basic level, the agricultural futures market allows farmers to avoid having to sell all their crops at harvest times, when the supply is high and the price is low.[14] Instead, both sellers and buyers can lock in a fixed price well in advance of the point of exchange, allowing both parties to hedge their bets and reduce risk from potential volatile prices and seasonal fluctuations.

The deregulation of commodity markets from the 1990s onward obscured the distinction between those with a physical interest in the commodity (farmers and food processors) and those with a financial interest in the commodity (purely speculative investment bankers and money managers), treating them as one and the same. For speculative investors, agricultural derivatives are not about the agricultural products they represent (they will never come in contact with the corn, beans, or wheat) but the financial opportunities they offer. Just prior to the global food crisis, a flood of new speculative investments from Wall Street not only increased the liquidity but also the volatility of the market. In the 2006–2008 period, average world prices for rice rose by 217 percent, wheat by 136 percent, maize by 125 percent, and soybeans by 107 percent, pushing millions of people worldwide into the ranks of the extremely poor and hungry.[15] In the United States, grocery store food prices rose by 6.6 percent and cereal and bakery prices rose by 11.7 percent in 2008, the biggest increase in almost three decades.[16]

Although the argument is not universally accepted, a number of significant global institutions, including FAO, UNCTAD, the G20, the EU, and the World Bank, either accept or at least acknowledge that financial speculation is a significant contributor to food price volatility, with the global poor, who spend up to three-quarters of their income on food, harmed the most.

Because of the disjuncture of labor and production time, the easiest ways for capital to penetrate agriculture is on the upstream and downstream sites of the production process through what is called *appropriationism* and *substitutionism*.[17] On the upstream (production) side, capital steadily *appropriates* on-farm labor processes by replacing agroecological management practices (like the use of green manures, cover crops, animal-based fertilization, biological and biodiverse forms of pest control, and farm-grown seed stock) with synthetic fertilizers, pesticides, and genetically engineered seeds.

On farming's downstream side (merchandising, processing, retail, and consumption), capital *substitutes* direct producer-consumer relations with a complex of buyers, wholesalers, carriers, commission merchants, packers, cooperatives, and grower-shippers who send farm products on to canners, bottlers, and packers before ending up on supermarket shelves, restaurant plates, and in fast-food cartons. Farm products are also broken down into basic ingredients (protein, carbohydrates, and oil) to be reassembled in industrial products like soft drinks, processed food or cosmetics. The tendency toward overproduction in the farm sector means that new markets must be developed for the ever-increasing volume of production. As Richard Walker's landmark study on California agriculture points out, the profitability of substitutionism depends on acquiring good quality crops cheaply and dependably, moving products along the pipeline efficiently, and adding value through processing in factories and restaurants.[18] Those firms able to vertically integrate along either side of agriculture's complex value chain are rewarded with greater capital efficiencies.

The downstream process of substitution *explodes* farm products from a direct relation of producer-product-consumer into an array of basic ingredients for a vast array of food products sold by the powerful supermarket sector. Upstream, appropriation does the opposite by *imploding* the complex farm labor process into fewer and fewer inputs. Monsanto's GMO seeds, for example, have introduced *Bacillus thurengensis* (Bt) genes and a gene that is tolerant to glyphosate (a powerful herbicide) into their seeds. The Bt genes replace pesticides and the glyphosate-tolerant genes allow the cultivar to withstand applications of herbicide (that is, at least until insects develop a tolerance to Bt and weeds develop a tolerance to glyphosate). Even the ostensibly humanitarian effort to *biofortify* crops like "Golden Rice" or the "GM banana" that attempt to insert vitamins into crops are a substitute for a diversified diet—and a diversified farming system. This results in fewer and fewer vitamin-rich cultivars in the field, and a loss of diversity in diet as well. The drive to introduce more "stacked" seeds (with multiple introduced characteristics) through genetic engineering that controls pests and weeds, incorporates vitamins, and resists drought is a classic example of how appropriationism replaces diverse farming systems and complex farm, labor, and management processes, collapsing them into a single seed commodity.

The concentration of capital in the agribusiness and agrifoods sectors has given rise to multibillion-dollar oligopolies that control credit, farm inputs, services, processing, distribution, and retail. The incessant expansion of these corporations has steadily shaped agriculture's labor and production processes to conform to the capitalist logic of appropriation and substitution, and increasingly, global finance capital. This has resulted in the steady decline of the farmer's share in the value of agricultural production. U.S. farmers received over 40 percent of the food dollar in 1910, but by 1990 they received under 10 percent.[19]

Contract Farming

One way that capital profits from agriculture without engaging in the risks of farming is through the system of contract farming. A modern version of sharecropping and tenant farming, contract farming is a fixed-term agreement in which the farmers give exclusive rights to a firm to buy their product. Though a *market-specification contract,* the firm guarantees the producer a buyer, based on agreements regarding price and quality, and with a *resource-providing contract* the firm also provides production inputs (like fertilizer, hatchlings, or technical assistance). If the firm provides all the inputs and buys all of the product, it essentially controls the production process while the farmer basically provides land and labor:

> Contract farming is a form of vertical integration within agricultural commodity chains, such that the firm has greater control over the production process, as well as the quantity, quality, characteristics, and the timing of what is produced. Contract farming,

Contract Livestock and Poultry Production

Poultry producers often get into the business by obtaining a contract that guarantees the delivery of chickens for a few years. Based on that contract they obtain large loans, often backed by the federal government, to build poultry houses on their own land. The poultry company delivers chickens and feed and tells the farmer how to raise the chickens.

In exchange, the farmers have to dispose of the chickens' waste, compete against neighbors in a "tournament" system in which high-producing farmers are paid more per pound, and lower producing farmers are paid less,[20] and work to pay off the debt they took on to get into the chicken farming business. The farmers are generally on flock-by-flock contracts, with no guarantee of future bird deliveries. Well before the loans for the buildings are paid off, they could lose the contract. This gives the companies great leverage over the farmers, since the chicken houses are basically useless other than to raise chickens, and the farm has a construction loan that needs to be paid off.

These challenges don't just impact poultry farmers; they are also seen in the pork industry, but the issues are most acute with poultry because chicken production has operated under the integrated system the longest. In fact, many refer to what is happening with hogs as the "chickenization" of the pork industry. Signs of similar changes are beginning to occur in cattle markets.[21]

> in its various forms, allows a degree of control over the production process and the product without the firm directly entering into production.[22]

Pineapple in India, passion fruit in Brazil, asparagus in Thailand, cow-calf operations in Canada—around the world grains, vegetables, almonds, chocolate, sugarcane, palm oil, cattle, poultry, and hogs are farmed under contract, often between family farmers or "petty producers" and large corporate food processors like Pepsi, Cadbury, Del Monte, Purdue, and Tyson. There are many different types of arrangements regarding credit, installations, inputs, quantity, quality, and price.

Two things are common to all contract farming. First, the farmer takes full risk on the product. If the crop is poor or fails, or the flock underperforms or dies, the farmer, not the firm, assumes the loss. Second, whereas the farmer has long- and medium-term investments in land, installations, and equipment, the firm only invests seasonally (in seedlings, fertilizer, or chicks). This means that farmers are often "locked in" to contracts for many seasons while they pay off their long-term investments, regardless of the price they receive.

Contract farming is usually presented as a "win-win" arrangement that ensures supply to the buyer and a buyer to the farmer. In the United States, contract farming dominates the poultry industry. The World Bank considers contract farming to be the primary means for linking peasant farmers to the global market and promotes it widely in Asia, Latin America, and Africa.[23]

The downsides of contract farming are few—for the buyer. Sometimes farmers will find ways to hold back their product or sell it elsewhere at a better price. But since the farmer is the most leveraged partner, the pitfalls can be many: the buyer can stop renewing the contract and buy elsewhere, provide substandard inputs, make unreasonable demands regarding quality or installation upgrades, or reduce the price or keep it fixed even as the price of inputs soars. All of this can lock the farmer into a sort of debt bondage that is all too reminiscent of sharecropping and tenant farming.

The Metabolic Rift

Like Adam Smith and David Ricardo before him, Karl Marx followed the early development of capitalism and its relationship to agriculture very closely. He witnessed the early capitalization of agriculture, so he wasn't suggesting it couldn't exist. Rather, he believed that capitalist agriculture was biologically and socially irrational, stemming from the "metabolic rift" created by capitalism as it drove people from the countryside into the cities. Urban concentration led to a one-way flow of nutrients out of the countryside and into the city, where they were consumed as food and goods. These nutrients were not returned to the countryside, but were sloughed into the rivers and oceans as waste. Marx saw both the flow of nutrients and the flow of people as an essential—but destructive and exploitative—part of capitalism:

> Capitalist production collects the population together in great centers, and causes the urban population to achieve an ever-growing preponderance. This has two results. On the one hand, it concentrates the historical motive force of society; on the other hand, it disturbs the metabolic interaction between man and the earth, i.e. it prevents the return to the soil of its constituent elements consumed by man in the form of food and clothing; hence it hinders the operation of the eternal natural condition for the lasting fertility of the soil. . . . All progress in capitalist agriculture is a progress in the art, not only of robbing the worker but of robbing the soil; all progress in increasing the fertility of the soil for a given time is a progress toward ruining the more long-lasting sources of that fertility. . . . Capitalist production, therefore, only develops the techniques and the degree of combination of the social process of production by simultaneously undermining the original sources of all wealth—the soil and the worker.[24]

Early capitalist agriculture addressed the declining fertility of agricultural soils caused by the metabolic rift by digging up graveyards and mining old battlefield sites from the Napoleonic wars for bones to use as fertilizer. New lands were conquered. The colonies provided a bounty of natural resources and nutrients. When guano was discovered, European empires annexed hundreds of islands and mined thousands of tons of the nitrate-rich fertilizer. These measures postponed the impoverishment of the world's agricultural soils, but did nothing to resolve the metabolic rift. They did succeed in further contaminating major rivers, aquifers, and streams.

The problem of falling fertility of agricultural soils in capitalist economies—from the wheat fields of Ukraine to the tobacco fields of the Americas—resulted in environmental problems and ways of thinking about agriculture, population, and wealth that are still with us today. David Ricardo and Thomas Robert Malthus believed that poor fertility not only put a permanent premium on naturally fertile lands (land rent) but required population control to avoid mass starvation. These views were challenged by Scottish agronomist-farmer James Anderson, who insisted that farmers could build and maintain soil fertility—even on poor soils—with manure, drainage, conservation, and careful cultivation practices. This didn't happen, not because of a lack of manure or a lack of knowledge, but because the landed gentry had no interest in making these investments, preferring instead to live off the rents from the poor farmers who worked their lands. Farmers cultivating rented land had no incentive to invest in building the soils of the owner's land. In this view, private property, not overpopulation and limited fertility, was the problem facing agriculture and society. Land reform, a focus on keeping people in the countryside, and the recycling of human and animal manure was the solution to pollution and the metabolic rift. The invention of synthetic fertilizer and colonization of other lands, however, allowed European capitalism to avoid land reform.

In 1840, German chemist Justus von Liebig's *Organic Chemistry and Its Applications to Agriculture and Physiology* identified nitrogen, phosphorous, and potassium as the basic elements for plant growth. This led to the production of soluble "superphosphate" that gave poor soils an initial boost in productivity—until potassium and nitrogen became limiting to production. While phosphorous and potassium could be mined—and guano was high in both nitrogen and phosphorous—it would be seventy more years until synthetic nitrogen fertilizer was invented, eventually leading to the emergence of the commercial fertilizer industry.

Most political economists, chemists, and agronomists welcomed the introduction of synthetic fertilizers but did not consider them to be a solution to soil fertility. Despite being considered the father of synthetic fertilizers, Liebig argued for the recycling of nutrients. "Rational agriculture," he claimed, would give "back to the fields the conditions of their fertility." Following Liebig and Marx, Karl Kautsky foresaw the science of agroecology when he referred to "advances in cultivation" without synthetic fertilizers:

> Supplementary fertilizers . . . allow the reduction in soil fertility to be avoided, but the necessity of using them in larger and larger amounts simply adds a further burden to agriculture. . . . [They] would then, at most, have the task of enriching the soil, not staving off its impoverishment. Advances in cultivation would signify an increase in the amount of soluble nutrients in the soil without the need to add artificial fertilizers.[25]

For nearly a half-century since the use of synthetic agricultural inputs became widespread after the Second World War, the problem of urbanization and the metabolic rift was largely forgotten. Today, capitalist agriculture is inconceivable without synthetic fertilizer. However, as the hypoxic "dead zone" in the Gulf of Mexico attests, not only has capitalism's metabolic rift led to urban-based pollution, capitalist agriculture is now a major source of rural and marine pollution as well. But pollution is only one of the manifestations of capitalist agriculture's irrationality. The wholesale reliance on synthetic fertilizers—and the inability to confront the metabolic rift— have led to the spread of monocultures, the concentration of agricultural land in large holdings, and a host of social and environmental externalities. Why?

The ability to apply nitrogen, phosphorous and potassium to agricultural soils eliminated the practices of cover cropping, inter-cropping, and relay-cropping with legumes. This separated grain cultivation from livestock production, leading to monocultures and feedlots. It also eliminated the use of animal manure as a soil conditioner and supplementary source of nutrients, especially important micro-nutrients that helped plants resist damage from insects and disease. Pesticides were introduced and as insects' resistance to them grew, their use steadily increased. Livestock operations concentrated near processing plants that tended to locate in economically depressed areas with little or no environmental and labor regulations. As big seed and chemical suppliers, grain companies, and livestock processors in the United States became even bigger, control concentrated in the hands of a few oligopolies that dominated certain geographic regions. The southern Great Plains holds gigantic confined animal feedlot operations (CAFOs), while Delaware, Maryland, and Virginia specialize in poultry. Hog production is concentrated in parts of the Midwest and in North Carolina. The net metabolic effect of capitalism on agriculture has been first to separate humans from agriculture, then to separate animals from plants, severing nutrient cycling between primary and secondary producers and consumers.[26] (See Figure 5.1)

The separation between humans, animals, and plants have in turn created more lucrative opportunities for capital investment both upstream and downstream in the farming process (appropriation and substitution). Using grain production in the U.S. Midwest as an example, Fred Magdoff points out that it has been disastrous for the environment (and many farmers):

1. The first decision to concentrate on one or two crops automatically means that a more ecologically sound and complex rotation of crops is not possible.
2. Planting corn after corn or alternating between corn and soy leaves the soil without living vegetation for more than half of the year.
3. Because per acre (per hectare) profits are low for these crops, more land is needed to produce sufficient total farm profits to maintain a family at current economic standards.

Figure 5.1: Changes in the Spatial Relationships of Plants, Animals, and Humans

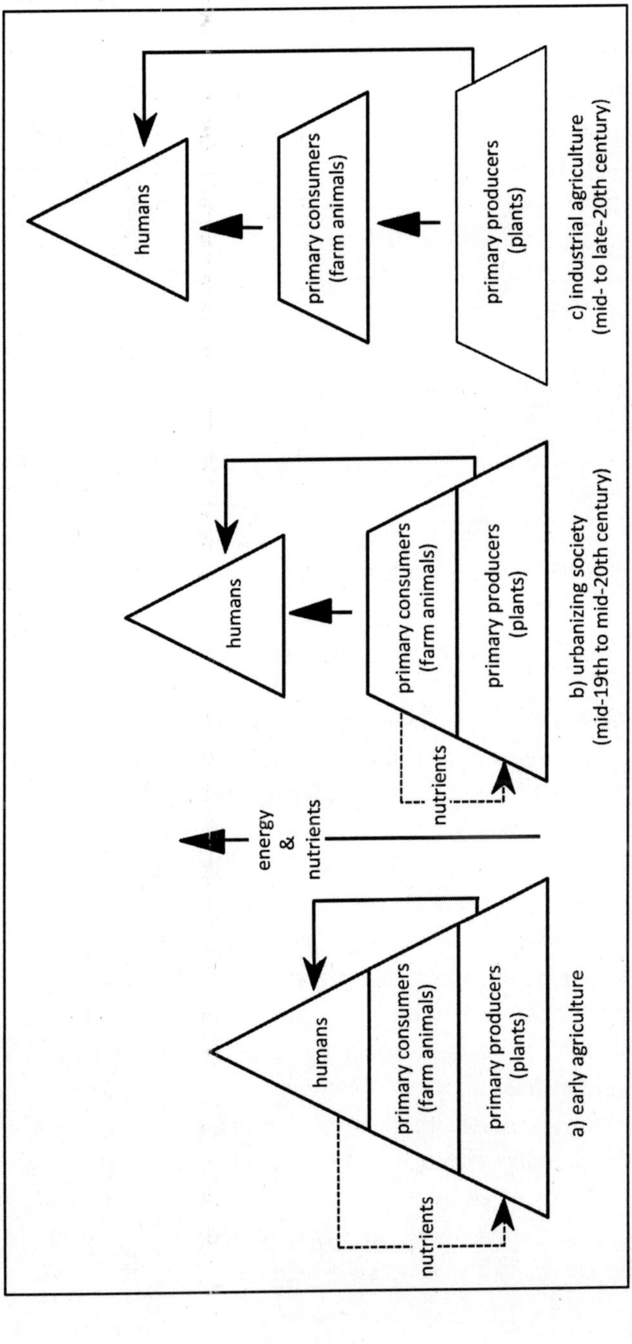

Source: Modified from Fred Magdoff, Les Lanyon, and Bill Liebhardt, "Nutrient Cycling, Transformation and Flows: Implications for a More Sustainable Agriculture," *Advances in Agronomy* 60:1–73 (1997).

4. A larger farm means that larger machinery is needed in order to cover the larger area.
5. Specialization in corn and soybeans leads to more pesticide use.
6. Specialization in corn and soybeans leads to more fertilizer use than would be needed in a more complex rotation or on integrated farms raising both animals and crops. The two-crop, corn-soybean system is particularly "leaky," with elevated levels of nitrates routinely reaching ground and surface waters.
7. Because larger areas are being farmed, anything that simplifies the system is attractive to farmers and allows them to farm even larger areas. And this is where GM seeds come in.
8. A new dimension has been added over the last decade with on-the-go electronic information gathering as farmers go over fields for preparation, planting, and harvesting. These costly additions to field equipment mean that the full suite of these is primarily of use to very large farms.[27]

Global Warming

The classical political economists who studied agriculture and capitalism could not have predicted what may be the most irreversible consequence of the metabolic rift: global warming.

Agriculture, livestock, and other related land uses (such as deforestation) are responsible for just under a quarter of global greenhouse gas emissions.[28] But not all agriculture systems are created equal. While *industrial* agriculture represents the majority of emissions from global agriculture, ecologically based practices, used primarily by small-scale farmers, not only contribute fewer emissions, but also sequester more carbon and other greenhouse gases.[29] Nonetheless, the capitalist incentives to double down on large-scale, energy-intensive monocultures far outweigh the incentives to diversify agriculture and conserve natural resources. Crop losses due to the effects of climate change, such as more intense droughts and floods, hit small farmers the hardest, threatening their hold on the land. Climate change also affects livestock and fisheries through, for example, the reduction of quality forage and changes in marine life due to increased water temperatures.[30] However, many investors view climate change as an opportunity. With increased climatic instability, land degradation, and water scarcity come the potential for soaring profits. As celebrity investor Jeremy Grantham observes, "Good land, in short supply, will rise in price to the benefit of the landowners."[31]

A Rational Agriculture

Fred Magdoff describes rational agriculture, the antithesis of capitalist agriculture today:

> A rational agriculture would be carried out by individual farmers or farmer associations (cooperatives) and have as its purpose to supply the entire population with a sufficient quantity, quality, and variety of food while managing farms and fields in ways that are humane to animals and minimize ecological disturbances. There would be no exploitation of labor—anyone working on the farm would be like all the others, a farmer. If an individual farmer working alone needed help, then there might be a transition to a multi-person farm. The actual production of food on the land would be accomplished by working with and guiding agricultural ecosystems (instead of dominating them) in order to build the strengths of unmanaged natural systems into the farms and their surroundings.[32]

Rational agriculture *reverses* appropriationism and substitutionism by bringing these production, distribution, and market functions back to the farm and the community, and *intensifies* production time rather than shortening it by inter-planting, companion planting, cover cropping, relay cropping, and other agroecological methods. A rational agriculture also reduces or reverses the metabolic rift by recycling and conserving nutrients, conserving water and fixing carbon. Proposals for rational agriculture imply a de-concentration of large industrial plantations and repopulating (rather than depopulating) the countryside.

Agroecology

Agroecology is the science and practice of sustainable agriculture. Agroecological farmers work with and enhance on-farm ecological functions (rather than replacing them with the chemical inputs of appropriationism). With agroecology, farmers primarily use animal manures, legumes, and cover crops to provide nutrients. Weeds are controlled by cultivating, cover-cropping, inter-cropping, and mulches (live or dry). Pests are managed by attracting predators with companion planting, interrupting pest cycles and vectors with crop rotations, alley cropping (in which annual crops are grown with rows of perennial trees and bushes), and the use of trap crops and repellant crops. Though these are just a sample of different agroecological management practices, they give an indication why agroecology is anathema to capitalist agriculture: agroecology is knowledge intensive (rather than capital intensive) and thus doesn't provide an opportunity for the appropriation of profits by agribusiness.

Agroecology was first developed as a science when ecologists and anthropologists made careful observations of peasant farming systems, some of which had been sustainably producing food for millennia.[33] They observed that farmers' vast knowledge of soils, plants, organisms, weather patterns, and microclimates allowed them to manage farm ecosystem processes (water cycle, mineral cycle, energy flow, and community dynamics between the organisms of an ecosystem). This gave their farming systems tremendous environmental resiliency and allowed them to produce a surplus, recycle nutrients, and conserve water and resources. Many of these systems formed part of inter-regional nomadic, pastoral, and trading networks that not only traded goods but recycled nutrients.

In the wake of the well-documented ecological destruction of the Green Revolution, the practice of agroecology spread steadily among peasant farmers as a way to restore productivity and ecosystem functions to hundreds of thousands of hectares of degraded farmland.[34] Though some of these practices require more labor (especially in the transition period before they are well established), many also reduce labor or spread labor out more evenly over the agricultural year.

Today, agroecology is taught in many universities and is the subject of a number of scientific journals. It is the preferred agricultural method for many rural development projects and has been widely adopted by smallholders around the world. Commonly referred to as the "science of sustainable agriculture," agroecology has been endorsed by the International Agricultural Assessment on Science, Knowledge and Technology for Development[35] and the former United Nations Rapporteur on the Right to Food[36] as the best agricultural method to end hunger, eliminate poverty, and address climate change. Indeed, this is because agroecology is, in human and ecological terms, a "rational agriculture."

But agroecology is not part of the agricultural development programs of the U.S. Agency for International Development, the Consultative Group on International Agricultural Research (CGIAR), the Alliance for a Green Revolution in Africa, the Department for International Development (DFID), the World Bank, or the plans for agricultural development of the African, Asian, or Inter-American Development banks. Funding for agroecological research in the National Science Foundation (NSF) in the United States represents less than 1 percent of the funding dedicated to conventional agriculture.

If agroecology is so great, why don't agricultural development institutions support it? The simple answer is because the objective of these institutions is the development of *capitalist* agriculture. This is accomplished by expanding the opportunities for capitalist investment through appropriationism. Since agroecology reduces the ways that capital can appropriate agriculture's labor process, it works at cross purposes to capitalist agriculture.

But what about substitutionism, the downstream side of agricultural production?

The long, global food value chains of substitutionism have led to a "supermarket revolution" in which a handful of retail oligopolies (like Walmart, Tesco, and Carrefour) dominate the global food market. In the United States, some 3 million farmers produce over 7,000 farm products. These are processed by 28,000 manufacturers, then sold through 35,000 wholesalers to 150,000 stores where they reach *300 million consumers.*[37] The power over the trillions of food dollars flowing from farmer to consumer is concentrated with the processors, wholesalers, and retailers. The interest of these firms is to extend and control the substitution side of the food value chain in order to capture a higher percentage of the food dollar.

Moral Economy

Like agroecology, a *moral economy* pushes back against capitalism. The concept of moral economy comes from historian E. P. Thompson's studies of the emergence of capitalism in Britain. In the first instance, moral economy was defined in relation to widespread protests over what was seen as the reprehensible trend of grain hoarding and price gouging during food crises.

> My own usage [of "moral economy"] has in general been confined to confrontations in the marketplace over access (or entitlement) to "necessities"—essentially food. It is not only that there is an identifiable bundle of beliefs, usages and forms associated with the marketing of food in time of dearth, which it is convenient to bind together in a common term, but the deep emotions stirred by dearth, the claims which the crowd made upon the authorities in such crises and the outrage provoked by profiteering in life-threatening emergencies, imparted a particular "moral" charge to protest. All of this, taken together, is what I understand by moral economy.[38]

Thompson argued that the periodic food rebellions that dogged the emergence of capitalism in the eighteenth and nineteenth centuries found their social justification when capitalism breached long-standing social agreements regarding the price, control and distribution of food, land, and labor.

Different from political economy, which studies the relationships between capital, resources, markets, and power, *moral economy* tries to understand the ways that communities make decisions based on normative principles. The underlying logic of the moral economy is the overall resiliency of the community. Thus there is not just one moral economy, rather, the term is used to describe an arena of social interaction that is deeper and broader than the political and economic systems in which communities are embedded.

A moral economy approach has been applied by agrarian scholars in an attempt to understand why peasant societies rebel,[39] and by development scholars trying to understand the management of the Commons, smallholder decision making, and villagers' actions and interactions not explained by economic rationality such as overexploitation, mutual aid, and market aversion.

More recently, moral economy has been used to describe an array of approaches and activities that prioritize socially regulated relations of reciprocity over commodity (market) relations, such as value-based cooperatives, farmers' markets, community-supported agriculture associations (CSAs), "Food Commons," in which food is treated not as a commodity but as a common good,[40] "civic agriculture," which puts citizens rather than corporations in charge of agriculture,[41] and other intentional approaches to the food system. In this regard, the new moral economy pushes back against the wholesale privatization of social institutions and "the market" as the organizing principle of society. The moral economy puts people before profits.

Farming Styles

An appreciation of the moral economy is essential to understanding the heterogeneity of today's food and agricultural systems. Indeed, many of the market failures described by conventional economists—and the long-standing tendency for farmers and communities to seek out alternatives to the capitalist food system—are a reflection of the moral economy.

As agrarian scholar Jan Douwe van der Ploeg explains, though the moral economy is governed by different rules than political economy, it is not external to it,

> In everyday life, complexities . . . are governed through cultural repertoires (consisting of values, norms, shared beliefs and experiences, collective memory, rules of thumb, etc.) that specify recommended responses to different situations. . . . The moral economy is not external to the "economic machine": it is essential to the "machine's" performance.[42]

Van der Ploeg has observed different farming styles he describes as "capitalist," "entrepreneurial," and "peasant." Around the globe, we find that these styles operate alongside one another, though with very different logics and often very different results. *Capitalist farms* both produce and rely completely on commodities; land, water, labor, energy, and inputs are all bought on the market and all farm products are sold as commodities. Capitalist farms tend to be large and rely on relatively little manual labor. *Entrepreneurial farms* are more midsized. They are also "commodified" but use more family labor. *Peasant farms* (or small family farms operating on a peasant logic), reduce their reliance on commodity inputs like fertilizer and big tractors, by using on-farm inputs (manures, animal traction, etc.) and family labor. A significant part of the agricultural product is consumed on the farm or traded outside commodity markets. All three farming styles are embedded in a larger capitalist food system, but the farming styles reflect very different forms of engagement and very different strategies of dealing with environmental and market risks. Because peasant-style farming usually takes place on smaller farms, the total output is less than capitalist or entrepreneurial farms. However, their total output *per unit* of land (tons/hectare; bushels/acre) tends to be higher.[43] This is why, as capitalist agriculture converts peasant-style farms to entrepreneurial and capitalist farms, there is often a drop in productivity, even though individual farm production increases as a result of larger size.[44]

Different farming styles also show different degrees of environmental and financial resilience in the face of extreme weather events and market volatility. In the Netherlands, a rise in input prices and a fall in milk prices led to bankruptcy (and government bailouts) for many capitalist and entrepreneurial farms whereas peasant-style farms were less affected. In general, these smaller, less capitalized producers had higher margins than producers using other farming styles.[45] In Central America, peasant farms using agroecological practices suffered fewer losses after Hurricane Mitch than did the entrepreneurial family farms that practiced conventional agriculture (pesticides, fertilizers, hybrid seeds). Many conventional farmers never recovered from the massive disaster.[46]

Beyond the Dead End of Capitalist Agriculture

Far from the pastoral, "feed the world" narratives that often depict agriculture, a brief dive into the political economy of capitalist agriculture reveals that it is and has always been a terrain of conflict, struggle, and resistance. The immense power of capitalist agriculture can easily obscure its shortcomings and weaknesses, giving the impression that it is invincible, or at least "too big to fail."

The upcoming trends in capitalist agriculture are not at all encouraging. If the current iteration of the agrarian transition is allowed to continue, we would expect the final depopulation of the countryside and the consolidation of agricultural production into the hands of 50,000 or so mega-farms, worldwide. These might be able to supply the planet with industrial food, but they will not provide employment for the 2.5 billion peasants, small farmers, and their families presently living in the countryside. These people make up a third of humanity. There is no new Industrial Revolution to provide employment to this many people. If rural communities are displaced, they will be pushed to the city slums. The global economy would have to grow at a rate of 7 percent over the next half-century to absorb just a third all this labor. This is impossible. The capitalist agrarian transition not only condemns a third of humanity to dispossession, unemployment, and misery, but most likely means global chaos.[47]

Won't the laws of supply and demand in agriculture eventually work things out? The notion that capitalist agriculture will somehow self-correct flies in the face of three hundred years of agrarian history. Reforms to the food system are desperately needed. The spread of alternative food systems outside the existing global food system will be essential not only to demonstrate that "another agriculture is possible" but to build political will within the food regime for deep, transformative reforms. Clearly, there aren't enough farmers in the United States to create the political will in the legislatures and in the committees that insulate the U.S. Farm Bill. Changes to agriculture will have to be anchored in strong consumer-farmer-worker alliances with a clear understanding of capitalist agriculture and a compelling vision for a better farm future.

— 5 —

Power and Privilege in the Food System: Gender, Race, and Class

Classism, racism, and sexism predate capitalism, but they merged powerfully during the formative period of the colonial food regime and have been co-evolving ever since. Slavery, exploitation, and continent-wide dispossession of the land, labor, and products of women, the poor, and people of color are still foundational to the capitalist food system, as are hunger, malnutrition, diet-related disease, and exposure to toxic chemicals. Poor women of color and children, especially girls, bear the brunt of these inequities.

Many people think these injustices are unfortunate anomalies of our food system, or that they are pesky vestiges of prior stages of "underdevelopment." Some believe the high rates of hunger and malnutrition afflicting underserved communities to be market failures, correctable through better information, innovation, or entrepreneurship. One way of thinking believes that poor individual choices are what drive land loss, diet-related disease, unemployment, low wages, and the desperate migration of millions of peasant families out of the countryside. There is no doubt that good information, initiative, and good personal choices are necessary for building a better food system, but given the system's structures, these alone are woefully insufficient for ending hunger, poverty, and environmental destruction.

The global food system is not only stratified by class, it is racialized and gendered. These inequities influence access to land and productive resources; which people suffer from contaminated food, air, and water; working conditions in food and farm jobs; and who has access to healthy food. These inequities affect resiliency, the ability of communities and individuals to recover from disasters such as the floods and droughts of climate change. The skewed distribution of resources and the inequitable exposure to the food system's "externalities" are rooted in the inseparable histories of imperialism, colonialism, and patriarchy.

But each form of oppression brings forms of resistance from workers, peasants, women, and people of color. Far from disappearing over time, struggles for justice take on new strategies and tactics, produce new leaders, forge new alternatives, and create new conditions from which to survive, resist, and fight for human rights. Understanding the structural conditions of struggle for those who are most exploited and abused by today's capitalist food system is essential to understanding not only the need for profound change, but the paths to transformation.

Gender, Patriarchy, and the Capitalist Food System

During the 2009 global food and economic crisis, 1 to 2 baby boys per 1,000 births died who would have lived in a non-crisis economy. The figure for baby girls was 7 to 8 extra deaths per 1,000 births.[1] That in the twenty-first century baby girls die at four to eight times the rate as baby boys during times of crisis should be a wake-up call for anyone who thinks the world has reached gender equality. The drivers behind this sordid statistic include a host of gendered inequities that include access to food, health services, fair incomes, and ownership. These are also reflective of women's disproportionate exposure to violence and their exclusion from formal structures of political power. These are not just phenomena from developing countries. In the United States over 30 percent of women earn poverty wages compared to 24 percent for men, and women are paid just 78 cents for every dollar men make to do the same job. These statistics reflect deep structural injustices.

But it's not only that women need to "catch up" with men. The inequitable position of women in the food system is actually part of what makes the food system work. How? Patriarchy.

Patriarchy predates capitalism by millennia. The emergence of agriculture, social hierarchies, and male privilege together established some of the pillars of what became the capitalist food system. In short, agriculture (probably invented by women) and animal husbandry (largely controlled by men) not only produced a surplus of storable food and a population boom within hunter-gatherer societies during the early Neolithic Period, but also unleashed a social struggle over the ownership and control of the food surplus. This struggle began between men and women.

Early control over the agricultural surplus was a defining moment for human civilization. The politics of nomadic hunter-gatherer societies—as often matricentric as patricentic—revolved around the laws of "irreducible minimum," which meant that everyone in the community or clan had the same rights to its food, regardless of their sex, age, or ability.[2] Mutual aid and cooperation were the primary tools of survival. Private property was basically nonexistent. The sexual division of labor between men and women did not confer power of men over women, or women over men. The gradual incorporation of agriculture, and a shift to semi-nomadic and sedentary communities, introduced a new mode of production and a new division of labor.

Men mainly hunted big game, an activity that allowed them to specialize in weaponry. They ranged far from the settlements where women took charge of gathering, small-game hunting, farming, and the care of young children:

> In hunter-gatherer and horticultural societies, there was a sexual division of labor—rigidly defined sets of responsibilities for women and men. But both sexes were allowed a high degree of autonomy in performing those tasks. Moreover . . . in many

> cases, [women] provided most of the food [combining] motherhood and productive labor. . . . Women, in many cases, could carry small children with them while they gathered or planted, or leave the children behind with other adults for a few hours at a time. Likewise, many goods could be produced in the household. Because women were central to production in these pre-class societies, systematic inequality between the sexes was nonexistent, and elder women in particular enjoyed relatively high status.[3]

But the roles of production and reproduction began to shift as agriculture came to dominate community activities. Agriculture demanded more time and more labor. Whereas hunting societies tried to limit their numbers in order to adjust their population to limited supplies of game, agricultural societies sought to increase the number of able-bodied family members to meet the greater labor demands of field work. As men steadily dedicated more of their time to agriculture rather than hunting, women began to specialize in childcare and household activities.

Most early agricultural societies were polygynous or polyandrous and matrilineal. Children knew who their mother was, but not their father. This was not a problem for children. Men from the father's clan were all "fathers," and the aunts from their mother's clan were also treated as "mothers." When a man died, his accumulated agricultural wealth was passed on to children through the "mother-rights" of the woman's clan. What "wealth" did men have? Primarily livestock.

Men controlled much of the livestock and ranged far from the settlements to find forage. Livestock provided milk, blood, and an on-the-hoof surplus of meat. As men controlled more and more of the surplus they were faced with a problem: How could they pass their accumulated wealth on to their children if they didn't know exactly who their children were? Patriarchy and private property emerged as a way for men to control both the inter-generational and the *intra*-generational distribution of agricultural surplus. The destruction of women's "mother-right" ensured men's livestock were inherited by the male rather than the female clan. Relying on U.S. scholar Lewis

Henry Morgan's work with the Seneca communities of the Iroquois nation, Friedrick Engels wrote:

> Thus, on the one hand, in proportion as wealth increased it made the man's position in the family more important than the woman's, and on the other hand created an impulse to exploit this strengthened position in order to overthrow, in favor of his children, the traditional order of inheritance. . . . Mother-right, therefore, had to be overthrown, and overthrown it was. . . . The overthrow of mother-right was the world historical defeat of the female sex. The man took command in the home also; the woman was degraded and reduced to servitude; she became the slave of his lust and a mere instrument for the production of children.[4]

For many, the rest is history—of patriarchy, property, and capitalism. Patrilineal inheritance and ownership shifted from clan to individual men, and eventually to primogeniture (the eldest son) inheritance. Monogamy (for women) was enforced to ensure only biological progeny inherited the father's wealth. The foundation for capital accumulation, the state, and the nuclear patriarchal family was established. Trade in agricultural surplus increased, leading to an even greater accumulation of wealth. This led to more production for exchange. This required more labor, in the form of big families and slaves, both owned and controlled by men. Women were subjugated even further and their reproductive burden increased.

The Neolithic Agricultural Revolution, largely credited for an explosion in global populations, was a social and political revolution that laid the basis for the establishment of states and social hierarchies between men and women and between classes. The development of the state and class differentiation were accompanied by the formation of patriarchal societies. Of course, not all agricultural societies became patriarchal. The Iroquois Nation and many other indigenous societies provide examples that patriarchy is certainly not inevitable. However, all *capitalist* societies did establish the rule of patriarchy as the hierarchical basis for class rule.

Women's subjugated status did not end their participation in the food system, but it did devalue their work both inside and outside the home. This is readily evident today. Although women produce much of the world's food, cook most of our meals, and feed and care for nearly everyone, they have less access to land and the means of production than men and earn less working in the fields and factories than men.[5] That these inequities are a reflection of patriarchy seems obvious, but to understand the intersection of gender and class we need to ask: How does *capitalist patriarchy* work in the food system?

Production and Reproduction

Two processes sit at the heart of capitalism: *production* and *reproduction*. In a strict capitalist sense, production is about making commodities to sell at a profit and reproduction is about providing human labor-power for capital. Workers who produce commodities need food, clothing, and housing. The cost of these "goods and services" over the course of the workers' productive lives—the cost of reproducing the labor force—is the cost of reproduction.

But this way of understanding things treats workers as gifts of nature. Where did the workers come from? Who fed, clothed, and cared for them and raised them to working age? As adults, who cooks, cleans, and cares for them when they are sick, ensuring they can have long, productive lives? What are the conditions of these caregivers? What is their economic status, their role in society, and their contribution to culture? What is their potential for transforming the conditions of production and reproduction? Addressing these questions brings us to the realm of *social reproduction* because workers aren't simply being "produced." They come from societies that correspond to a particular mode of production. Societies dominated by the capitalist mode of production are profoundly differentiated by class, race, and gender.

The food system is an essential part of the social reproduction of capital because it produces food that everyone eats and engages more people in productive activities than any other economic sector. Women, domestic labor, sexuality, and procreation are central to production and reproduction in the food system; women work throughout it *and* care for most food system workers and their families.

During the beginning of the Industrial Revolution, the sphere of reproduction was practically ignored. The textile mills of eighteenth-century England ran on the labor of men, women, and children who were quite literally worked to death. Labor was treated as an inexhaustible and disposable resource. Capital made no investment in the reproduction of labor. As capitalism shifted to heavy industry and the running and maintenance of machines became more complicated, it required a more skilled, less disposable worker. Because these workers were in shorter supply, the reproduction of this labor force required greater investment (in training) on the part of the capitalists, raising the value of specialized labor. But it did not mean that the reproductive work carried out by women (housework, cooking, child bearing, child rearing, and family nurturing) was paid at its full value. On the contrary, just as with wage labor, most of the value of women's reproductive work was passed on to the capitalist through the appropriation of the surplus value of the worker. In other words, the unpaid work of women in raising children and doing other housework was for all practical purposes a subsidy for the bosses, contributed by the wives of male workers. Women's domestic work was part of a capitalist mode of production that required it to take a certain form, one that disciplined it to play a subservient role in the production process just as capital had disciplined the worker to give up the product of their labor for an hourly wage.

Silvia Federici describes this as the "shift from absolute to relative surplus value" in the nineteenth century. In the first instance, capitalists simply increased the length of the workday in order to increase their profits above and beyond the wages paid to the worker (*absolute surplus value*). Violent clashes between laborers and capitalists brought hours from 16 hours a day down to 8. This shifted the strategy of capitalist accumulation to one of extracting profits by increasing *relative surplus value*. This is accomplished either by increasing productivity (through mechanization or automation) or by lowering wages. To lower wages without starving workers, the cost of wage goods (food, clothing, and housing) must be reduced. But, barring breakthrough technological advancements, decreasing the prices of wage goods purchased by workers means decreasing the price of commodities, which would decrease profits. Where did capitalism find the savings necessary for a decrease in wages? *In the reproductive (domestic, care-giving) work of women.* The cleaning, feeding, and physical and emotional care-giving carried out by women has a value to capitalist production because it maintains the labor force—the source of labor power. While this was always free to capitalists, it became more important as competition and technological development drove firms to cut costs and find savings in their quest for profits. This largely explains the capitalist turn from the exploitation of women as factory workers to their exploitation as full-time housewives.[6]

Another century would pass until mechanization ushered in the shift from absolute to relative surplus value in agriculture. Rather, colonialism expanded agriculture to new, conquered land where the exploitation of rich soils and abundant resources provided a natural "subsidy" to capitalist food and fiber markets (in addition to the "subsidy" provided by workers earning at or below subsistence wages). As the natural subsidy to agriculture inevitably waned, fertilizers, pesticides, and machinery were introduced to intensify the production process. This was accompanied by a steady shift of women's activities out of the field and into domestic (reproductive) work.

In her seminal work *Patriarchy and Accumulation on a World Scale: Women in the International Division of Labor*, Maria Mies challenges the orthodox Marxist bias in understanding the social origins of the gender division of labor. Less interested in *when* this division of labor occurred, Mies is concerned with *why* it resulted in a hierarchical structure of patriarchal oppression. "This division," writes Mies, "cannot be attributed to some universal sexism of men as such, but is a consequence of the capitalist mode of production, which is only interested in those parts of the human body which can be directly used as instruments of labor or which can become an extension of the machine."[7]

Capitalism requires worker's heads, hands, legs, and backs as labor power in order to produce surplus value. While women's heads, hands, legs, and backs also enter the labor market, their life-giving wombs and mammary glands are not considered profit making. This determination by capital relegates women's reproductive functions to the *realm of nature*. The capitalist division between "human labor" and "natural activity" values men's physical labor power as productive, but devalues women's reproductive activity as not productive. "Productive" in this strict sense refers only to the production of surplus value. Valuing only the work that produces surplus value—rather than the reproductive activity that produces the worker—is at the heart of the gender bias in the capitalist system.

Maria Mies rejects this narrow interpretation of the productivity of labor and considers women's production of life as non-wage "subsistence" labor—that is, the amount of labor needed for the production of life. She links the exploitation of women with the exploitation of slavery, colonialism, and of primary food producers—peasants:

> [The] general production of life, or subsistence production—mainly performed through the non-wage labor of women and other non-wage labourers as slaves, contract workers and peasants in the colonies—constitutes the perennial basis upon which "capitalists' productive labour" can be built up and exploited. Without the ongoing "subsistence production" of non-wage labourers (mainly women), wage labour would not be "productive." In contrast to Marx, I consider the capitalist production process as one which comprises both: the *superexploitation* of non-wage labourers (women, colonies, peasants) upon which wage labour exploitation is then possible. I define their exploitation as superexploitation because it is not based on the appropriation (by the capitalist) of the time and labour over and above the "necessary" labour time, the surplus labour, but of the time and labour necessary for people's own survival or subsistence production. It is not compensated by a wage, the size of which is determined by the "necessary" reproductive costs

of the labourer, but is mainly determined by force or coercive institutions.[8]

Immigrant farm labor is another modern-day example of "super-exploitation." In the United States during the Second World War, the labor of white farmworkers largely disappeared as men went to war and women moved into the factories. Peasant farmers from Mexico were imported under the Bracero Program to pick the country's crops. Mexican farm women largely stayed behind, taking care of families. The farm labor workforce has been treated as disposable ever since, with increases in productivity coming from increases in hours and a relative decrease in pay. Because it is treated as inexhaustible, there is no thought to the reproduction of the immigrant labor force, even in the twenty-first century.

However, the last three decades of neoliberal globalization have steadily destroyed household and village economies in the Mexican countryside, driving women across the Northern border in search of work. The massive transition of both the productive and reproductive

Women Farmworkers

The agricultural sector has historically been and continues to be one of the largest employers of women worldwide. In developing and developed countries alike, women in agriculture have less access to productive resources and opportunities than men.[9] Female farmworkers in the United States suffer disproportionately from workplace discrimination and abuse as a result of their intersectional identity—as farmworkers, people of color, women, and immigrants, be they permanent, temporary, or undocumented. Female farmworkers (who make up 24 percent of the U.S. agricultural workforce) earn less than male workers for several reasons: they work fewer hours, are sometimes paid less than men for the same work, and are occupationally segregated into lower-paying "women's work" positions. Some employers refuse to hire or promote women, and others have refused to give women benefits offered to men, such as housing.

Childcare is virtually never an employment benefit of agricultural work, and thus farmworkers' children work in the fields, "play" around the fields while their parents work, or are cared for at home, usually by grandmothers, aunts, or siblings. Agricultural employers, like the employers of other transnational migrants, rely heavily on the unpaid caring labor of some women to make possible the wage work of other women and men. The few rights that female farmworkers do hold are often violated purely on the basis of gender. The Southern Poverty Law Center reports, for example, that some employers take advantage of women's marital status by illegally paying women on their spouse's paychecks instead of issuing individual payment.[10] This illegal practice allows employers to deny women the minimum wage and evade extra payments like Social Security.

Reproductive oppression persists to the extent that women's reproduction is affected by 1) poverty rooted in low wages, low benefits, and exploited labor, 2) the work of migration that adds significantly to women's unpaid domestic labor, 3) hazardous work conditions, including pesticide exposure and increased vulnerability to sexual violence, and 4) weak labor and safety regulations limiting those hazards. It is important to recognize that though work sites are not gender segregated, men make up the majority of farmworkers in the United States and hold most of the supervisory positions, allowing the agricultural industry to foster a culture of patriarchal dominance. Together, the labor/occupational conditions of farmwork, the state of U.S. healthcare for farmworkers, and pervasive and stigmatizing social relations interact to create a context that regulates, controls, and exploits women farmworkers. In short, women work in a context of reproductive oppression.

workforce from South to North has allowed segments of the U.S. food system to prosper, especially large corporate farms producing fresh fruits and vegetables, processing enterprises, and restaurants. Similar patterns have played out in other parts of Latin America, Asia, and Africa as impoverished men, women, and children flood into North America and Western Europe searching for work.[11]

The "globalization of exploitation" in the food system's productive and reproductive spheres has given rise to diverse and broad-based movements for social justice up and down the food value chain. For example, for every four or five farmworkers in the United States, one is a woman. The preponderance—and militancy—of women in these movements is striking and has shifted the agenda for social justice in ways that reflect their condition and their presence.

Food—Systems—Racism

Racism, the systemic mistreatment of people based on their ethnicity or skin color, affects all aspects of our society, including our food system.[12] Racism has no biological foundation, but the socioeconomic and political structures that dispossess and exploit people of color, coupled with widespread misinformation about race, cultures, and ethnic groups, along with potential competition with the white population for jobs and educational opportunities, make racism one of the more intractable injustices. Racism is not simply attitudinal prejudice or individual acts, it is a historical legacy, deeply embedded in our institutions, that privileges one group of people over others. Racism—individual, institutional, and structural—also impedes good-faith efforts to build a fair, sustainable food system.

Despite its pervasiveness, racism is almost never mentioned in international programs for food aid and agricultural development. Although anti-hunger and food security programs frequently cite the shocking statistics, racism is rarely identified as the cause of inordinately high rates of hunger, food insecurity, pesticide poisoning, and diet-related disease among people of color. Even the widely hailed "good food movement," with its plethora of projects for organic

People of the Earth

ROSALINDA GUILLÉN, farmworker, organizer, ecofeminist:

[My father] loved being a farmworker. . . . He loved growing food, growing plants. He talked to us about it and kept journals about it. In those journals he would write, "Today I sat out in the fields. I was getting ready to go out, and the smell of the soil was this way. The birds sounded this way . . . the clouds . . . the air. Touching the soil makes me feel happy. It makes me whole." He was a person of the earth. He said, "We are people of the earth. There's no getting around it. We are people of the earth and we have to be in it." My father was a self-educated man. . . . He would say, "You are children of people of the earth. You are farmworkers. Don't let anybody make you ashamed for being that."

Industrial agriculture has taken the farmworker's voice away, so we don't hear them identifying themselves as people of the earth. We have been identified as machines, as beasts of burden. It's convenient for people to identify us that way because then it's easy to exploit us. But if you're talking about a human being who can express herself or himself as a person of the earth, with this intellect and wisdom about the right way to grow food, then it's not as easy to exploit. A lot of the family farmers and growers know that the way they're growing food and treating the earth is wrong. They feel guilty, and want a buffer between them and the reality of what farmworkers will say if you give them the opportunity. You're looking at that human being every day, knowing that you are doing wrong.

My father would say, "This is special. What you do is a work of grace, because what you do will make somebody else healthy and whole. You are feeding humans, and nobody else is doing that except for the person growing the food or the animal." I have to say that when I was in the fields working, I liked it. My father would say when the soil was ploughed,

> "Just stand here, *mi hija*, and smell. Take a deep breath." And we would. And he would say, "This is the only time you can smell that smell." Then when you irrigate it's another different smell, but it's the same earth. It's nourishing itself. Every time is different. You know the smell of the plants when they grow and the different types of plants by touching, sitting in the fields. . . .
>
> When we drive up to the field, you hire us to work and we sit in the field. We watch the sun come up, and the mist comes out of the soil, and the smells change, and the breezes come up, and the earth comes alive. And you feel an energy. Nothing else can give you that energy. And you want to get to the hoeing or whatever it is you're doing. It makes you feel good—the beauty of the earth around you, with the birds flying and the bees buzzing. There is nothing like it in the world. You know it, and I want you to know that we know it and we feel it, too. And it's wrong that you will not recognize that we are the same as you. [13]

agriculture, permaculture, healthy food, community supported agriculture, farmers' markets, and corner store conversions, tends to address the issue of racism unevenly.[14]

Some organizations *are* committed to dismantling racism in the food system and make this central to their activities. Others are sympathetic but not active on the issue. Many organizations, however, see racism as too difficult to address, tangential to their work, or a divisive issue to be avoided. The hurt, anger, fear, guilt, grief, and hopelessness of racism are uneasily addressed in the food movement, if they are addressed at all.

Racial Caste

The term *racial caste* describes a "stigmatized racial group locked into an inferior position by law and custom."[15] Racial caste is one consequence of a hierarchical imbalance in economic, political, and social power (sexism and classism are others). In North America and much of Europe, this racial caste system privileges light-complexioned people of Northern European ancestry. (Although racial caste has some social similarities to the Hindu caste system, it is historically very different.)

Any country that has been subjected to Northern colonialism has been structured by a racial caste system in which "whiteness" grants social privileges. This system was originally developed to justify European colonialism and enable the economic exploitation of vast lands in the Americas, Africa, and Asia. Outright dispossession through genocidal military conquest and government treaties affected 15 million indigenous people throughout the period of U.S. westward expansion. Colonization was largely carried out by white planters and aspiring white smallholder-settlers.[16]

In the Americas, Europeans and people of European descent murdered and dispossessed indigenous populations for their natural resources, sometimes enslaving them—for example, the Spanish Catholic missions. People from West African regions were enslaved, forcibly shipped across the Atlantic Ocean, and sold as chattel to do backbreaking labor, primarily on sugar, tobacco, and cotton plantations. Although slaves acquired through war and trade had been part of many societies for thousands of years, widespread commerce in human beings did not appear until the advent of capitalism and the European conquest.

The superexploitation of enslaved human beings on plantations allowed slave systems to outcompete agrarian wage labor for over two hundred years. Under slavery, human beings were bought, sold, and mortgaged as property. The tremendous wealth generated from slavery was sent to Northern banks where it was used to finance military conquest, more plantations, and ultimately, the Industrial Revolution.[17]

The social justification for the commodification of human beings was the alleged biological inferiority of the people who were used as property, and the supposed divinely determined superiority of their owners. This division of power, ownership, and labor was held in place through violence and terrorism. It also required constant religious and scientific justification, constructed on the relatively new concept of "race." Although enslaved peoples came from ethnically and culturally different regions of West Africa, they were classified as *black*. Though slave owners came from different areas of Europe where they had been known by vague tribal names like Scythians, Celts, Gauls, and Germani, they were classified as *white*.

Slavery produced over a century of "scientific" misinformation that attempted to classify human beings on the basis of their physical traits. Eventually, people were racialized into three major categories: Mongoloid, Negroid, and Caucasoid, with Caucasians awarded superior intelligence, physical beauty, and moral character. Scientists argued over how to classify the many peoples that didn't fit into these categories, such as the Finns, Malays, and most of the indigenous people in the Americas. The messiness of the categories was unimportant to the political and economic objectives of racism. Systematically erasing the unique ethnic, tribal, and cultural backgrounds of the world's people while elevating a mythical Caucasian race was a shameful exercise in egregiously bad science, but it endured because it supported the control of the world's land, labor, and capital by a powerful elite.[18]

Slavery had a tremendous influence on food and labor systems around the world and was the central pillar of capitalism's racial caste system until it was widely abolished in the late nineteenth century. In the United States, after nearly three years of bloody civil war, the Emancipation Proclamation of 1863 released African Americans living in Confederate states from slavery, though it took nearly two more years of war before ex-slaves could freely leave their plantations.[19] The Thirteenth Amendment to the U.S. Constitution finally put a legal end to slavery in the United States in 1865. But after a "moment in the sun," African Americans living in the former Confederacy were quickly segregated and disenfranchised through "Jim Crow" laws, which criminalized and discriminated against formerly enslaved African-Americans and maintained the racial caste system in the absence of slavery.[20]

The Birth and Mutation of Whiteness

The concept of race has always been fluid, shifting to accommodate the changing demands of capital and the ruling class, while undermining political struggles for equality and liberation. For example, in colonial America, there was little social difference between African slaves and European indentured servants. The colonizing British and Anglo-American population had reduced immigrants and slaves alike into one undifferentiated social group of inferior status. But when they began organizing together against their colonial rulers, the Virginia House of Burgesses introduced the Virginia Slave Codes of 1705. These laws established new property rights for slave owners; allowed for the legal, free trade of slaves; established separate trial courts for whites and blacks; prohibited black people from owning weapons and from striking a white person; prohibited free black people from employing whites; and allowed for the apprehension of suspected runaways.

Throughout the nineteenth and early twentieth centuries, poor, light-skinned Irish-Catholic immigrants living in the United States were initially treated as an inferior race and experienced discrimination as nonwhite. American cartoonists of the time depicted the Irish with the same racist stereotypes they applied to African Americans, illustrating both ethnic groups as subhuman monkeys in an effort to dehumanize them and justify their exploitation.

As the historian Noel Ignatiev observed, the Irish in America had to become white in order to overcome the structural barriers that kept them alongside African Americans on the lowest rung of the economic ladder.[21]

The Irish made the strategic choice to differentiate themselves from African Americans by aggressively aligning themselves with the Democratic Party and labor unions, and by embracing a virulent strain of racism. Trade unions

> defined certain jobs as fit only for whites, and excluded blacks from lowly jobs open to the Irish. Slave owners cultivated Irish American support for slavery by suggesting freedmen would head north to compete for jobs. In essence, the Irish "became" white. In doing so, they helped to create the modern concept of "the white race," by systematically discriminating against blacks. Mediterranean peoples, Eastern Europeans, and light-complexioned Latin Americans underwent similar processes as they immigrated to the United States.

Racial caste has systematically shaped the food system, particularly during periods of labor shortage, as it did during the Second World War, when over 4 million Mexican farmworkers were brought to the United States. Mexican labor was cheap and ruthlessly exploited. This was made socially acceptable through a system of racial norms that classified Mexicans as inferior.[22]

To this day, important sectors of the food system in the United States and Europe continue to be defined by dispossessed and exploited immigrant labor from the Global South. Their systematic mistreatment is justified by the centuries-old racial caste system.

Racism in the Food System

Calls to "fix a broken food system" assume that the capitalist food system used to work well. This assumption ignores the food system's long, racialized history of mistreatment of people of color. The food system is unjust and unsustainable, but it is not broken. It functions precisely as the capitalist food system has always worked, concentrating power in the hands of a privileged minority and passing off the social and environmental "externalities" disproportionately to racially stigmatized groups.

Statistics from the United States confirm the persistence of racial caste in the food system. In 1910 African Americans owned 16 million

Racism Definitions

- **INTERPERSONAL RACISM**: The prejudices and discriminatory behaviors by which one group makes assumptions about the abilities, motives, and intents of other groups based on race. This set of prejudices leads to cruel intentional or unintentional actions toward other groups.
- **INTERNALIZED RACISM**: In a society where one group is politically, socially, and economically dominant, members of stigmatized groups, bombarded with negative messages about their own abilities and intrinsic worth, may internalize those negative messages. It holds people back from achieving their fullest potential and reinforces the negative messages that, in turn, reinforce the oppressive systems.
- **INSTITUTIONAL RACISM**: This is when assumptions about race are structured into the social and economic institutions in our society. Institutional racism occurs when organizations, businesses, or institutions like schools and police departments discriminate, either deliberately or indirectly against certain groups of people to limit their rights. This type of racism reflects the cultural assumptions of the dominant group.
- **STRUCTURAL RACISM**: Although most of the legally based forms of racial discrimination have been outlawed, many of the racial disparities originating in various institutions and practices continue and accumulate as major forces in economic and political structures and cultural traditions. Structural racism refers to the ways in which social structures and institutions, over time, perpetuate and produce cumulative, durable, race-based inequalities. This can occur even in the absence of racist intent on the part of individuals.
- **RACIALIZATION:** The process through which "race" (and its associated meanings) is attributed to something—an individual, community, status, practice, or institution.

Institutions that appear to be neutral can be racialized, shaped by previous racial practices and outcomes so that the institution perpetuates racial disparities, or makes them worse. This is true of the criminal justice system, the education and health systems, and so on.

- **REVERSE RACISM**: Sometimes used to characterize affirmative action programs, though that is inaccurate. Affirmative action programs are attempts to repair the results of institutionalized racism by setting guidelines and establishing procedures for finding qualified applicants from all segments of the population. The term "reverse racism" is also sometimes used to characterize the mistreatment that individual whites may have experienced at the hands of individuals of color. This too is inaccurate. While any form of humans harming other humans is wrong, because no one is entitled to mistreat anyone, we should not confuse the occasional mistreatment experienced by whites at the hands of people of color with the systematic and institutionalized mistreatment experienced by people of color at the hands of whites.
- **RACIAL JUSTICE**: Racial justice refers to a wide range of ways in which groups and individuals struggle to change laws, policies, practices, and ideas that reinforce and perpetuate racial disparities. Proactively, it is first and foremost the struggle for equitable outcomes for people of color.

acres of farmland. But by 1997, after many decades of Jim Crow, several national farm busts, and a generally inattentive (or obstructionist) Department of Agriculture (USDA), fewer than 20,000 black farmers owned just 2 million acres of land.[23] The rate of black land loss has been twice that of white land loss and today less than 1 million acres are farmed.[24] According to the USDA 2012 Census of Agriculture, of the country's 2.1 million farmers, only 8 percent are farmers of color and only half of those are owners of land. Though their farm share is growing, particularly among Latinos, who now number over 67,000 farmers, people of color tend to earn less than $10,000 in annual sales, produce only 3 percent of agricultural value, and farm just 2.8 percent of farm acreage.[25]

While white farmers dominate as operator-owners, farmworkers and food workers—from field to fork—are overwhelmingly people of color.[26] Most are paid poverty wages, have inordinately high levels of food insecurity, and experience nearly twice the levels of wage theft as do white workers. While white food workers have an average annual income of $25,024, workers of color earn only $19,349 a year. White workers hold nearly 75 percent of the managerial positions in the food system. Latinos hold 13 percent and black and Asian workers 6.5 percent.[27]

The resulting poverty from poorly paid jobs is racialized. Of the 47 million people living below the poverty line in the United States, less than 10 percent are white, while 27 percent are African Americans, 26 percent are Native Americans, 25.6 percent are Latinos, and 11.7 percent are Asian Americans.[28]

Poverty results in high levels of food insecurity for people of color. Of the 50 million food-insecure people in the United States, 10.6 percent are white, 26.1 percent are black, 23.7 percent are Latino, and 23 percent are Native American. Even restaurant workers—an occupation dominated by people of color (who should have access to all the food they need)—are twice as food insecure as the national average.[29]

Race, poverty, and food insecurity correlate closely with obesity and diet-related disease; nearly half of African Americans and over 42 percent of Latinos suffer from obesity. While less than 8 percent of non-Hispanic whites suffer from diabetes, 9 percent of Asian Americans, 12.8 percent of Hispanics, 13.2 percent of non-Hispanic African Americans, and 15.9 percent of indigenous people have diabetes. At $245 billion a year, the national expense in medical costs and reduced productivity resulting from diabetes are staggering.[30] The human and economic burdens of diabetes and diet-related disease on the low-income families of color are devastating.

Trauma, Resistance, and Transformation: An Equitable Food System Is Possible

Recognizing racism as foundational in today's capitalist food system helps explain why people of color suffer disproportionately from its social and environmental "externalities": labor abuses, resource inequities, and diet-related diseases. It also helps explain why many of the promising alternatives such as land trusts, farmers' markets, and community-supported agriculture tend to be dominated by people who are privileged by whiteness.[31] Making these alternatives readily accessible to people of color requires a social commitment to racial equity and a fearless commitment to social justice. Ensuring equal access to healthy food, resources, and dignified, living-wage jobs would go a long way toward "fixing" the food system.

The trauma of racism is inescapable. In addition to the pain and indignity of racialized mistreatment, people of color can internalize racial misinformation, reinforcing racial stereotypes. While white privilege benefits white communities, it can also immobilize them with guilt, fear, and hopelessness. Both internalized racism and white guilt are socially and emotionally paralyzing, and make racism difficult to confront and interrupt.

Difficult, but not impossible. Since before the abolition movement and the Underground Railroad of the mid-1800s, people have found ways to build alliances across racial divides. The history of the U.S. food system is replete with examples of resistance and liberation, from the early struggles of the Southern Tenant Farmers Union to the Black Panthers' food programs and the boycotts and strikes by the United Farm Workers. More recently, the Food Chain Workers Alliance has fought for better wages and decent working conditions. The Detroit Food Policy Council is an example of the increase of local food policy councils run by people of color, and the spread of Growing Power's urban farming groups reflect a rise in leadership by those communities with the most at stake in changing a system that some have referred to as "food apartheid." Indigenous peoples and other oppressed communities have developed ways of healing

The Pedagogy of the Oppressed

First published in Portuguese in 1968, Paulo Freire's *Pedagogy of the Oppressed* presented a detailed analysis of the mechanisms of oppression, examining the relationships between those he defined as "the oppressors," or colonizers, and "the oppressed," the colonized. He details how every person, however submerged in the "culture of silence"—the system of dominant social relations that silences and subsumes the oppressed—can gradually come to perceive their social reality through developing a critical consciousness with which they can question and challenge the values, norms, and cultural conditions imposed on them by their oppressors. Liberation, Freire argued, lay in the education of the oppressed, so that they may recognize the oppressive class structures and overcome them:

> [The] great humanistic and historical task of the oppressed [is] to liberate themselves and their oppressors as well. The oppressors, who oppress, exploit, and rape by virtue of their power, cannot find in this power the strength to liberate either the oppressed or themselves. Only power that springs from the weakness of the oppressed will be sufficiently strong to free both. Any attempt to "soften" the power of the oppressor in deference to the weakness of the oppressed almost always manifests itself in the form of false generosity; indeed, the attempt never goes beyond this. In order to have the continued opportunity to express their "generosity," the oppressors must perpetuate injustice as well. An unjust social order is the permanent fount of this "generosity," which is nourished by death, despair, and poverty. That is why the dispensers of false generosity become desperate at the slightest threat to its source.[32]

historical trauma, and there are peer counseling groups with skills for working through the immobilizing feelings of internalized oppression, fear, hopelessness, and guilt. All of these resources and historical lessons can be brought in to the food movement.

Racism still stands in the way of a good-food revolution. If the food movement can begin dismantling racism in the food system and within the food movement itself, it will have opened a path not only for food system transformation, but for ending the system of racial castes.

Class, Food, and Power

Food systems have always had some form of social division, though as we have seen, this didn't always mean that some people had more power over the food supply than others. Power over food began with animal husbandry, the spread of irrigated agriculture, the differentiation of tasks (crafts, rituals, war, and child-rearing), and the struggle to control agriculture's surplus. As hunter-gatherer societies were displaced by agriculture, clans were replaced by kin-based chiefdoms that were in turn replaced with princely states.[33] States divided society into classes of royalty, nobility, commoners, and slaves. Priestly, political, and military castes gained power in the agrarian civilizations of Mesoamerica, Europe and the Mediterranean, Asia, and the Nile River Valley. These elites kept a tight grip on the food produced by slaves, serfs, and peasants.[34] The old social divisions were the substrate upon which capitalism was to construct an entirely different form of social differentiation based not on kinship, caste, or lineage but on capital itself.

Capitalism revolutionized all prior social relationships. The *aristocracy* was overthrown by the *bourgeoisie,* who dispossessed the peasantry to construct an industrial *proletariat* and a massive underemployed *lumpen*-proletariat underclass to ensure a "reserve army of labor." These transformations to the established social order were defined by land, labor, and capital. For example, workers (proletariat) were people who owned their labor-power, which they sold for wages; landowners (gentry) owned land from which they received rent; capitalists (bourgeoisie) owned capital and got an income from profits, either through production or trade. A constellation of small property owners, shopkeepers, merchants, professionals, and civil servants emerged as the *petty* bourgeoisie, who followed the ideology of the more powerful bourgeoisie, but were unable to accumulate as much capital. Then, there was the peasantry, capitalism's eternal "awkward class," which resisted these changes, routinely withheld their surplus and their labor, and were a poor market for capital's products.[35]

The three founders of social science, Karl Marx, Max Weber, and Emile Durkheim, had similar but different ideas about class. Following on the works of economist David Ricardo, Marx (and Engels) centered private property and ownership of the means of production at the core of class conflict. They believed that "the history of all hitherto existing society is the history of class struggles."[36] Weber agreed that property was a driver of class conflict, but he thought that class was one of several aspects of social stratification, which included status and politics. This introduced complexity in that classes could adopt contradictory ideologies and form alliances in unpredictable ways, making Marx's class war likely, but not inevitable. Norms, beliefs, and values undergird Durkheim's theory of "collective consciousness," the objective ideological glue that holds society together at the same time class conflicts pull it apart. (Weber and Durkheim's thinking helps explain why classes "vote against their interests" in elections and support politicians who appeal to social and cultural mores but enact impoverishing economic policies.) All three scholars were trying to explain the cataclysmic changes that capitalist society had wrought upon community life. Their studies of class became foundational for the discipline of sociology. Later, in the revolutionary crucible of the early twentieth century, researcher-activist thinkers and leaders like Rosa Luxemburg[37] and Emma Goldman[38] elaborated on the nature of imperialism, class struggle, and the state itself.

Another important concept is Antonio Gramsci's notion of "hegemony," the multiple ways in which the ruling class exerts its ideological power on the state and civil society in order to obtain the political and social consent of those being ruled.[39] Intellectuals play a fundamental role in extending the worldview of the ruling class over the rest of society, so much so that these views are often taken as natural laws. For example, today under free-market capitalism, the notion that free (liberalized) markets are the natural state of affairs is largely accepted as fact. Not only are liberal markets not really free, the only verifiable fact about them is that they serve the class interests of multinational corporations that seek to move capital across borders, unimpeded by labor or environmental regulations. As Edward Herman and Noam Chomsky point out, the media plays a decisive role in advancing class hegemony because "[among] their other functions, the media serve and propagandize on behalf of the powerful societal interests that control and finance them."[40]

Class relations and theories regarding social stratification have become much more complex since the fathers of sociology published their seminal texts. Ironically, reference to class today is typically limited to income, consumption patterns, and lifestyle choices. Liberal democracies in Western societies don't talk much about class—class interests were supposed to have vanished with the prosperity of capitalism. But as inequality, poverty, and hunger have worsened, the hegemonic ideology of a "classless society" is beginning to crumble. Both class divisions and class alliances are on the rise, especially in the food system.

Food: What Difference Does Class Make?

In the food system, the principal class division is still between workers (field, packing, processing, retail, restaurant) and the owners of the means of production (the food, grain, and chemical monopolies). We don't typically call the former the "food proletariat" and the latter the "food bourgeoisie," but few other modern industries have such a classic division between capital and labor.

Farmers, however, are a more complicated group. Most of the farmers in the world are peasant women who produce food on very small farms both for themselves and for the (usually local) market.

Less than half of the world's food is produced on large, highly capitalized industrial farms for the global market. Many of these producers are large, corporate family farms; others are not so large (and only a couple of crop failures away from bankruptcy). Some of these farmers—like poultry producers—are owners of their means of production in only a tenuous sense. They are more like "food serfs" than the yeoman farmers of Jeffersonian lore. Other farmers may own their land and machinery but are highly leveraged and locked in to growing commodities like genetically modified corn, soybeans, or sugar beets "for the market." There is a small, undercapitalized but highly committed subclass of small-scale family farmers growing for Community Supported Agriculture (CSAs) and farmers' markets in the Global North who live almost as precariously as peasants in the Global South—but without the extended family and village support networks.

Then there is the "food petty bourgeoisie" made up of small restaurateurs, and retailers, producers for high-end niche markets, the technicians and bureaucrats in the agricultural ministries, midsize philanthropic foundations, and "food entrepreneurs" producing everything from liquid meal replacements and boxed meal ingredients to wine aerators and smartphone food apps. Their media presence far outweighs their actual activity in production itself.

The "food intellectuals" also make up a part of this class (and sometimes that of the bourgeoisie). Though it is fashionable to consider the celebrity chefs, individual scientists, technicians, professors, authors, and commentators working in the food system as independent thinkers, they all serve the needs of some class. (Some celebrity chefs are full-blown, multi-million dollar capitalists.) Gramsci believed that every class, except for the peasantry, had their own group of "organic" intellectuals who helped them advance their class interests. "Intellectuals," he wrote, "think of themselves as independent, autonomous, endowed with a character of their own."[41] But for Gramsci, intellectuals were characterized less by the intrinsic nature of their activities and more by the ensemble of social relations in which they carried out their activities. We can see this in our modern food system: some scientists, professors, and internet trolls and food bloggers work in the class interests of the great food monopolies, whereas the work of other intellectuals reflects the interests of small farmers, and farm and food workers, and the efforts of still others reflect the interests of the petty bourgeoisie.

Does this mean that all classes are ultimately doomed to serve the dominant class interests of the bourgeoisie? Not necessarily. The poor want affordable food; capitalists need compound growth rates and a 15 percent return on their food system investments; farmers want parity; workers want at least living wages; and most intellectuals want a comfortable salary and social recognition.

Karl Polanyi wrote, "The fate of classes is much more often determined by the needs of society than the fate of society is determined by the needs of classes."

We can better understand Polanyi's formulation by applying it to our food system. Polanyi did not dismiss class, class interests, class struggle, and class warfare (nor would he likely have dismissed gender or racial equity struggles). On the contrary, in his study of the impact of capitalism on society, he found that *class alliances—more than the independent struggles of classes themselves—were a fundamental aspect of social change*. Success in the struggle against rapacious liberal markets depended on the ability of the most negatively affected classes to ally with other classes. This, in turn, depended on their ability to work for "interests wider than their own." This way of thinking about class is especially important in understanding the transformation of our food systems.

Food embraces the concerns of class, but also those of gender and race. This means that food provides an opportunity to build alliances on the basis of interests "wider than our own." The question is, what kind of alliances, and with whom? What are the transformative interests and social classes of today's food system and which can build an alliance for its transformation?

Given that the food and agriculture sector is the largest employer in the world, it would seem obvious that any transformation of the food system would have to place the interests of the "food proletariat" prominently in any strategy for change. This is not the case. With the exception of the very few farmworker unions and food retail and restaurant workers' coalitions, most of the good-food movement centers on *food access* that, in the words of Slow Food founder Carlo Petrini, is "good, clean and fair." The mainstream media, the internet, and social media all give the impression that the food movement is either about entrepreneurs inventing clever food apps, consumers seeking an authentic food experience, or underserved communities seeking healthy food. Farmers are presented as individuals rather than as a class with material and social demands, and workers are largely ignored.

The prominence of intellectuals, entrepreneurs, and classless consumers in what some analysts call "the dominant food narrative" is an ideological reflection of a food system in which farmers and blue-collar food workers have lost power in relation to multinational corporations.[42] It is also a reflection of a capitalist system unable to resolve chronic crises of overproduction and underemployment. Thus we have a handful of innovative farmers and food entrepreneurs held up as success stories, while tens of thousands of retiring farmers are forced to sell their farms and millions of food workers are underemployed, mistreated, and underpaid. A triumphant "food revolution" is touted on television food channels, on the internet, and in college courses at a time when the relations of production (and the wealth of the food system) are firmly under corporate control. Even initiatives that ostensibly benefit farmers, like Fair Trade, are run by managers and distributors rather than farmers, which helps to explain why the fair trade premium is based on market prices rather than costs of production. Above all, ownership of the most basic factor of production—land—is unquestionably rooted in a capitalist system of private property that economically shuts out new farmers, particularly women and people of color.

The Fetish of Food and the End to Oppression

The popularity of food in the media and talk of food revolutions give the impression that society is transforming the food system by dint of improved technologies, disruptive ideas, and conscious eating. Market-based strategies for farmers, restaurateurs, and incubator kitchens invite us to believe that patriarchy, racism, and class exploitation in the food system can be eliminated if only we help women, people of color, and the poor become better capitalists. The rise of monopoly ownership of the means of production—land, labor-power, and capital—is blithely ignored in favor of a happy narrative of middle-class economic development, precisely at a time when the middle class is disappearing worldwide. This hegemonic food discourse not only reflects the dominant ideology of the corporate food regime, it avoids addressing how the capitalist food system is inextricably based on the oppression and exploitation of women, people of color, and workers. Worse, this dominant food narrative lulls us into the magical belief that somehow we can change the food system without changing the capitalist system in which it is historically embedded. This is the political fetishization of food.

We can't change the food system without transforming capitalism. Yet we can't transform capitalism without changing the food system. And we can't do either of these without ending patriarchy, racism, and classism. So, if we want a better food system, we have to change everything. Admittedly, this is a tall order for any social movement. The question for the food movement, however, is not "how do we change everything," but "how is the food system strategically positioned to influence systemic change?"

Clearly, a true food revolution would upend the social relations of patriarchy, racism, and classism in the food system and in society as a whole. A food revolution would also smash the monopoly ownership of the means of production by disabling the mechanisms of monopoly power: corporate personhood and intellectual property rights, corporate amnesty (from paying the health and environmental costs of the industrial model of food production), corporate financialization of land, food speculation, and the ability to buy elections and determine food, labor, and environmental policy.

These instruments of power must be addressed if patriarchy, racism, and classism are to be eliminated in the food system; they are precisely what hold these oppressions in place. The food movement's strategic advantage in the struggle for food system transformation is that the main oppressions within it are the primary oppressions of capitalism itself. If hunger, food insecurity, poverty, and social disenfranchisement are addressed not as "problems" to be "fixed" within the existing food system, but rather as part of a historically constructed capitalism based on gender, race, and class oppression, the road to transformational change within and beyond the food system becomes increasingly clear.

The next question is, of course, who will lead this transformation? History indicates that those with the most at stake in system change are the most effective leaders. Peasants have led movements for agrarian reforms; workers have led struggles for wage and workplace improvement; women have led the struggles for equality and suffrage; and African Americans have led the movements for civil rights in the United States. Two things were essential to the successes of all of these movements: cross-class alliances and legitimate "organic" leadership.

The movements for good food, food justice, food democracy, and food sovereignty that have gained traction around the globe are often led by women, people of color, workers, and peasants. However, the gatekeepers of the dominant food movement discourse are professionals, academics, intellectuals, and bureaucrats who are mostly white males. This disjuncture ultimately depoliticizes the food movement, taking its attention away from capitalism and impeding effective alliances, which are difficult under the best of circumstances. Supporting the radical leadership of women, people of color, peasants, farmers, and food workers—and centering food system change within capitalist transformation—will go a long way to overcoming these obstacles.

— 6 —

Food, Capitalism, Crises, and Solutions

The industrial agrifood complex tells us that only big, industrial agriculture with more and more technologies (including those that are needed to fix the problems caused by current technologies) are the only way to feed a global population predicted to reach 10 billion people by 2050. This "Golden Fact" is actually a "Big Lie." We produce one and a half times more than enough food for everyone on the planet—already enough to feed 10 billion people. But more than one billion people are still going hungry because they are too poor to buy the food being produced. Just producing more commodities won't help them. No matter, corporate salesmen tell farmers to increase production with GMOs and chemicals. My co-op even tries to demonstrate how farmers' yield will increase by throwing everything in the spray tank except the kitchen sink. Why not the kitchen sink? Because Monsanto doesn't sell kitchen sinks.[1]

—GEORGE NAYLOR, IOWA FARMER

In 2015 the United Nations announced that the Millennium Development Goals were going to be met and that we were on track to end hunger and poverty.[2] After all, the world was actually producing 1½ times more than enough food for everyone. At the same time, the FAO insisted that we had to double our food supply over the next thirty years in order to feed 10 billion people.

What can we make of this? Nearly a billion people are going hungry even though there is too much food. If we are already overproducing food, how will producing more food end hunger? When it comes to the call to produce more food, hunger gets stretched. When it comes to the effectiveness of the capitalist food system, astonishingly, hunger shrinks. As Alice in Wonderland remarked as she shrank and grew, things get "curiouser and curiouser."[3]

The market-led, neoliberal approach to meeting this curious food demand bases its policies on an assumption of food scarcity and an unshakable belief in the power of enterprise, technology, and free trade. In this view, to solve hunger we must rely on the best and the newest that capitalism and free markets have to offer, namely big agriculture and big data, precision agriculture and nanotechnology, synthetic biology, genetic engineering, glyphosate, Agent Orange, CAFOs, growth hormones, antibiotics, and liberalized trade.

Neoliberal approaches tend to underplay health and environmental concerns, claiming that there is no evidence of any harm from industrial technologies or that newer, more efficient technologies will replace the old ones soon enough. The answer to market failure (as in 2008 when a billion people could not afford to buy food), is to produce more, further liberalize trade, accept corporate monopoly concentration to attain better market efficiencies, automate supermarkets, and add nutrients to staple crops and cheap, processed food. Too poor to buy food? Don't worry, be entrepreneurial.

Reformist approaches to hunger are a little more nuanced and a bit more empathetic to the plight of the poor. While they work from the same neoliberal premise of scarcity, reformers tend to recognize some socioeconomic and environmental failures in the food system. For example, they agree with the neoliberal technological and market proposals, but believe food aid and development programs should help the poor by making sure they have enough calories and can access new technologies and global markets. They sometimes argue that the problem of hunger is so big and so urgent that "all solutions," including organic farming, should be employed in the battle against hunger and environmental degradation (a bit like George Naylor's "kitchen sink" approach). This perspective doesn't attribute the problems in the food system to capitalism per se, but to badly implemented capitalism. Typical reform initiatives, like USAID's Feed the Future (a government-sponsored, overseas agricultural development program), claim to spread the benefits of the capitalist food system to the poor. Other reformist proposals, like reducing and repurposing food waste to end hunger, never ask *why* people are poor or *why* the food system produces so much waste to begin with. Reformist policies do not challenge capitalist structures, like concentrated land ownership, the financialization of food and land, corporate concentration, or market fundamentalism. Nor do they consider whether it is socially just that a basic human need like food is considered a commodity, the same as any other, as part of an economic system that does not guarantee people good-paying jobs, or even any job for that matter.

The True Extent of Hunger: What the FAO Isn't Telling You[3]

In 1996, 840 million people were hungry worldwide. Leaders from 185 countries met at the World Food Summit in Italy and drafted the *Rome Declaration*, promising to reduce the total number of poor and hungry people by half to 420 million people by 2015.

Four years later, in 2000, the *Millennium Declaration* diluted the commitment laid out by the Rome Declaration. Leaders at the Millennium Summit utilized a numbers game that ultimately made the hunger reduction commitment weaker and easier to reach. Instead of sticking to a commitment to reduce hunger by a certain number of people (420 million), they changed the goal to decrease the percentage of hungry people. Because of population growth, this adjustment meant ending hunger for only 296 million people. This sleight of hand allowed leaders to claim quick progress on paper, when in reality the fight to end hunger was proceeding slower than anyone wanted to admit.

Official hunger reduction goals were again eased when the base year was backdated from 2000 to 1990. This allowed the inclusion of China's accomplishments in the 1990s in which millions were pulled from poverty and hunger, even though China was not a part of the Millennium Declaration. It also extended the period of population growth, and as a result, the proportion of people saved from hunger. This modified time frame actually increased the "acceptable" number of hungry from 420 million to 591 million.

As if shifting the goal posts was not misleading enough, the United Nations Food and Agriculture Organization (FAO) misrepresented the true extent of world hunger by using an inaccurate definition of hunger itself. The FAO only counts people as hungry when caloric intake is inadequate to cover minimum needs for a sedentary lifestyle for over one year. But we know most hungry people are peasant farmers engaged in demanding physical labor and need much more than the FAO's "sedentary" minimum caloric threshold. Incredibly, people who go hungry for 11 months out of the year are not classified as hungry by the FAO.

If we measure hunger at the level of calories required for intense activity, the number of hungry people today is closer to 2.5 billion, and this does not count those suffering from serious vitamin and nutrient deficiencies, or those hungry seasonally or for months at a time (but less than a full year). This estimate is two times higher than the FAO's numbers would have us believe.

Through the Millennium Development Goals, the FAO misrepresented the true extent of hunger. In reality, between 1.5 and 2.5 billion people lack access to adequate food. And the numbers are rising, not falling.

Figure 6.1: Rome Declaration

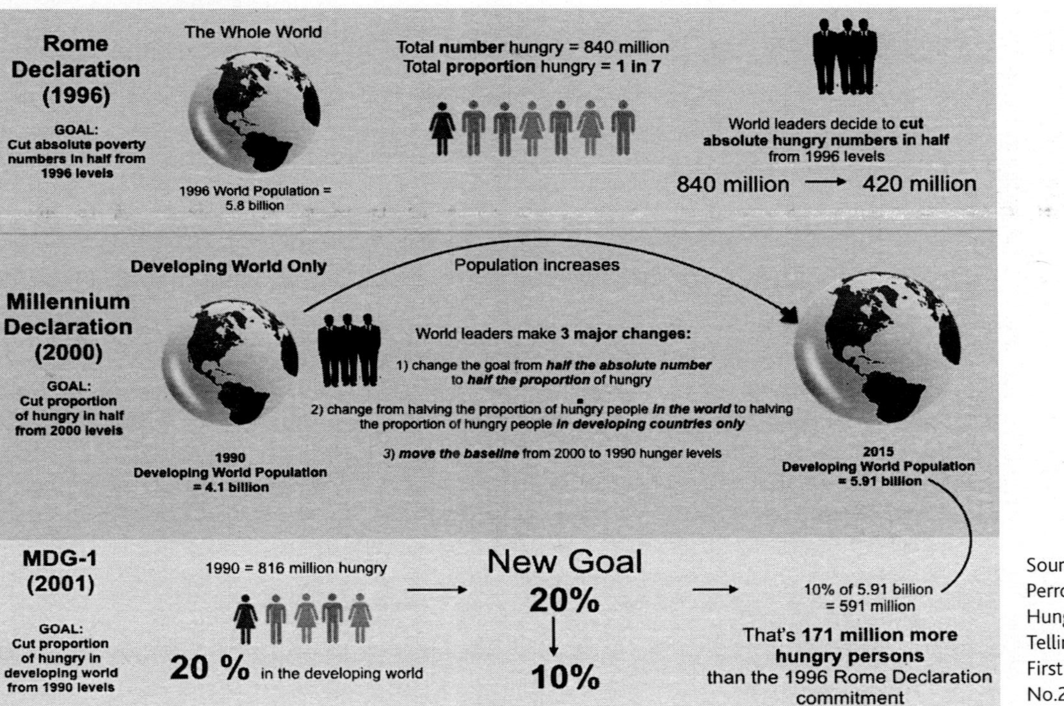

Source: Infographic by ©Eva Perroni in "The True Extent of Hunger: What the FAO Isn't Telling You." Food First. Food First Backgrounder. Vol. 22, No.2A. Summer 2016.

Let's look at a few of the neoliberal and reformist proposals coming from the corporate food regime.

Sustainable Intensification: Less Is More, or Less . . .

Development experts have advanced "sustainable intensification" as a solution for producing more food in a way that does not damage the environment. Sustainable intensification "is based on the principle that in a complex world with a growing population, the more effective use of inputs and the reduction of undesirable outputs in order to achieve greater yields—intensification—is fundamentally required in order to achieve sustainability."[4] Specifically, "sustainable intensification [is] a form of production wherein 'yields are increased without adverse environmental impacts and without the cultivation of more land.'"[5]

These principles ostensibly work for all farms, large and small, from the Global North and the Global South, poor or rich, and for women or men. Sustainable intensification is a big-basket approach that encompasses all technologies, including nanotechnology, big data, precision agriculture, pesticides, genetic engineering, commercial fertilizers, organic farming, agroecology, and permaculture, as long as it produces more food on less land without increasing its negative environmental impact. Sustainable intensification generally assumes a particular form of production as given and then attempts to improve upon it. It avoids making comparisons or addressing the conflicts between one form of agriculture and another.

At its core, sustainable intensification seeks to feed more people while at the same time "sparing land" (mostly forests and wetlands) from further agricultural encroachment. A number of economic and environmental assumptions are built in to the land-sparing argument that fly in the face of how capitalist agriculture, and agroecosystems, actually work. As our farmer friend George Naylor points out:

> The Golden Fact/Big Lie also claims that by increasing yields on existing farmland, we can avoid the need to convert virgin

land—like the rainforest, marshland, or the savanna—to commodity production. The opposite is actually true; any time you increase yields, you cut the cost of production, making cultivation on marginal land even more likely.[6]

Land Sparing

Land sparing is the notion that if production on agricultural land is intensified, the pressure to expand farmland to forests, wetlands, and other natural areas will decrease, thus sparing these areas from agricultural development and thus conserving their biodiversity.

The land-sparing environmental argument is loosely based on the theory of "island biogeography" developed by E. O. Wilson and Robert MacArthur.[7] Island biogeography modeled the rates of species colonization and extinction on islands in the ocean. The bigger and closer the islands were to the mainland, the greater the biodiversity—the numbers and kinds of birds and plants. Conservation biologists applied the theory to forest biodiversity. They treated the forest as a species-rich "mainland" and the neighboring agricultural fields as an inert "ocean" they called a matrix. The bigger and closer forest fragments in the agricultural matrix were to the forest "mainland," the richer they would be in biodiversity. The agricultural matrix was also assumed to be devoid of species and biodiversity. This is fairly true for large-scale, industrial agriculture that only permits the growth of one species: the commodity crop.

However, though this theory may hold for industrial agriculture, it does not hold for extensive patchworks of small, diversified, agroecological farms. In *Nature's Matrix* researchers Vandermeer, Perfecto, and Wright quantitatively demonstrated that agroecological farms are rich in biodiversity and actually serve to replenish and enrich biodiversity in the surrounding forests.[8]

Under current free market conditions, if farmers find ways to increase yields, they may well expand rather than reduce the area under cultivation in order to make more money. Suppliers of chemicals, seeds, big data, and farm machinery will be happy to sell them more inputs. Banks and financial investors will also be glad to lend more money or financialize larger and larger areas of profitable agricultural land. And if agricultural commodity prices decline because of more production by many farmers, these farmers will try to increase production to have sufficient income to pay for their fixed costs.

Sustainable intensification ranges from a narrow calculus of a simple yield per hectare increase accompanied by a reduction in chemical inputs to broader considerations that take into account water, biodiversity, greenhouse gas emissions, animal welfare, nutrition, market demand, and governance. In the end, however, sustainable intensification, much like English high farming and the Green Revolution before it, avoids challenging existing political and regulatory issues, just as it avoids addressing the driving force behind the spread of industrial agriculture in the first place: capitalism. The social *conditions* of production negotiated by people, governments, and the private sector are left to the status quo. As is the commodity nature of the end product, food.

In essence, sustainable intensification does not address the *mode* of production (capitalism), the inequitable distribution of the *means* of production (land, labor capital), or the unequal distribution of income and wealth that leaves a people unable to purchase sufficient amounts of healthy food. Rather, it calls for technological changes to the *forms* or *techniques* of production within the existing politics and structures of the corporate food regime. The underlying premise is that new agricultural technologies or changes in the way we apply existing technologies are sufficient to solve the problem of hunger and environmental degradation, will eventually drive new innovations, or are the best we can hope to accomplish within capitalist agriculture at this time.

By putting capitalism safely outside of its purview, sustainable intensification not only affirms and normalizes capitalist agriculture, it avoids addressing how capital favors some forms of production over others and ignores how some forms can exploit others. For example, large-scale agriculture for feed and fuel crops crowds out food-growing smallholders without providing jobs to compensate for the loss of livelihoods. Contract farming traps farmers in a serf-like form of debt bondage, no matter how sustainable the intensification. Large-scale monocultures and CAFOs, with all their inherent ecological and economic risk, fit nicely within the sustainable intensification framework. All they have to do is reduce the footprint of their manure ponds and be more efficient with the tremendous quantities of chemicals, hormones, antibiotics, water, and energy they consume. The quality of the food and the diets of consumers are of no concern, nor is the steadily concentrating power and wealth of the monopolies that supply seeds, fertilizers, pesticides, and services to industrial agriculture and are financially invested in continuing this form of production.

But wouldn't it be better if all farms produced more food on less land and were more sustainable? Well, perhaps. But do we *want* to sustain CAFOs, contract farming, and monocultures on huge farms? Shouldn't we be looking at the small-scale agroecological farms that are already producing high yields using practices that work in concert with the environment and redistribute wealth within the food system? Sustainable intensification steers us away from these questions.

Climate Change, Agriculture, and Two Primary Contradictions of Capitalism

The capitalist food system may not be sowing the seeds of its own destruction, but it may well be sowing the seeds of ours. Capitalism is not only a crisis-ridden system, it is crisis prone. Two primary contradictions inherent to capitalism lead to cyclical crises.

The first contradiction is between capital and labor. Capital keeps wages low in order to extract surplus value and make ever-increasing profits. In a competitive environment, capitalists intensify productivity by paying workers less or using fewer workers to produce the same amount of goods (exploitation). But low-wage workers can't buy very much. This leads to a crisis of accumulation, or "realization," when goods pile up unsold or need to be unloaded at a loss. Capitalism often resolves this crisis by expanding into new markets to find consumers who can afford their products. This fix works until the new markets are saturated. Other mechanisms can then be implemented. Capital can find new areas of even lower wage labor to make products for the workers with higher wages. Advertising is used to stimulate more sales. In the area of processed foods (especially junk food), a lot of laboratory effort is devoted to find just the right combination of artificial flavors, salt, sugar, and fat to make products more appealing and addictive. Corporations can provide backing for governments to go to war to protect sources of raw materials or markets, with side effects such as provision of government-funded jobs and creation of more disposable income. Capitalist wars are very efficient at producing profits. The products of the war industry—arms, ammunition, ships, vehicles, chemicals—are destroyed in the course of war, and so don't pile up, thus resolving the crisis of overproduction. Lowering prices of goods through automation may help sell cheaper products, but if workers are thrown out of work by machines and end up unemployed or in lower-wage work, they aren't going to be able to buy as much as they did previously. Credit is a great invention to increase purchasing power of consumers, but sooner or later, the bills come due. All of these fixes are temporary and can end up exacerbating the inevitable crisis in the long run.

Another problem for capital is that global population growth is leveling off and in some countries even declining. This reduces the growth potential of markets and profits. It forces companies to rely more on export markets for future growth and raises the issue of a redistribution of wealth downward in order to maintain consumer demand. Though capitalist institutions continuously warn us of the threat of overpopulation in order to justify the industrialization of the food supply, the truth is that far-sighted capitalists are terrified by the projected *end* of population growth in 2050.

When economies are growing, companies can always find profitable investment opportunities, either expanding production or opening up new endeavors. However, problems arise when economic growth slows, as it has over the last decades. Monopoly (or oligopoly) power may enable companies to maintain profits. But then the problem becomes how to use the accumulated wealth. Companies may accumulate more capital than they literally know what to do with. Outside the finance sector, U.S. corporations have over $1.5 trillion in cash and cash equivalents. During cyclical crises of accumulation, capitalists typically restructure industries and business sectors through mergers, buying other companies, pushing for devaluation and deregulation, and so on, ridding their businesses of excess capital at society's expense. But capital also restructures the *relations of production* as well, by restructuring the division of labor from labor-intensive manufacture to automation, or replacing national with foreign labor by offshoring, or by substituting "free" (unorganized) labor for unionized labor, for example; restructuring family and civic relations (as when education and prisons are privatized); and by altering and destroying nature.

This brings us to a second contradiction of capitalism, between the desires of the wealthy and corporations and the finite qualities and quantities of soil, forests, water tables, oceans, biodiversity, and even the biology of people and communities. In other words, there is a systemic contradiction between capitalism, which is impelled to continually grow and acknowledges no limits to the supply of natural resources nor of the availability of "sinks" to absorb and dilute pollution associated with production, and the environmental and social conditions that people need to live and reproduce as a society.[9]

Some of the contradictions of capital—getting rid of the vast quantity of goods produced, finding new profitable investment opportunities, and finding new sources of natural resources needed for industry—have historically been resolved by expansion into new territories. After the Second World War, most former colonies became independent and blatant colonialism fell out of favor. "Development" stepped in to serve the colonizing function for capitalism, opening markets, appropriating existing forms of production, and pulling new labor, land, and resources into the circuits of Northern capitalism. The problem in today's world is that capital is running out of easy territories to colonize, leading it to revisit areas that have proven difficult to capitalist development, like the Arctic Sea and sub-Saharan Africa.

One of the greatest contradictions of capitalism is dramatic and far-reaching, namely global climate change. Along with other negative environmental and social side-effects in the way the system operates, climate change is referred to as an "externality." These are "externalities" only in the sense that they are external to business balance sheets. But this leaves humanity and the biosphere to bear the system's environmental and social costs. It is significant that the food system is a large contributor to greenhouse gases (GHG). Industrial agriculture, particularly livestock, is a significant contributor to GHG emissions. The plastic packaging and 2,500 average food miles that characterize the global food system also play a role in GHG emissions. Rising global temperatures and erratic weather patterns are already disrupting agriculture around the world, particularly in the Global South. This has created terrible hardships, but, ironically, new opportunities for corporate profit.

Climate-Smart Agribusiness

Solutions to global warming range from embracing CO_2 emissions (plants love it!) to carbon offsets, carbon markets, carbon taxes, and irreversible global experiments in geoengineering. Within the food system, one high-profile approach is "climate-smart agriculture" (CSA). According to the FAO, climate-smart agriculture is "agriculture that sustainably increases productivity, resilience (adaptation), reduces/removes GHGs (mitigation), and enhances achievement of national food security and development goals."[10]

What's the difference between sustainable intensification and climate-smart agriculture? Since both are fairly vague in their application, not much. However, while sustainable intensification is primarily a strategy to justify the continuation of large industrial farms, CSA is generally reserved for poor smallholders:

> The majority of the world's poor live in rural areas and agriculture is their most important income source. Developing the potential to increase the productivity and incomes from smallholder crop, livestock, fish and forest production systems will be the key to achieving global food security over the next twenty years. Climate change is expected to hit developing countries the hardest. Its effects include higher temperatures, changes in precipitation patterns, rising sea levels and more frequent extreme weather events. All of these pose risks for agriculture, food and water supplies. Resilience is therefore a predominant concern. Agriculture is a major source of greenhouse gas emissions. Mitigation can often be a significant co-benefit of actions to strengthen adaptation and enhance food security, and thus mitigation action compatible with national development priorities for agriculture is an important aspect of CSA.[11]

Climate-Smart Seeds

Although climate-smart agriculture has been heartily embraced by industry (particularly the fertilizer and chemical monopolies), there has been considerable pushback from farmers' organizations and civil society against the concept.[12] Most of this opposition concerns the regulatory work in favor of genetic engineering and proprietary seed technology. The African continent is a clear example. African governments working with the Alliance for a New Green Revolution for Africa (AGRA), USAID's Feed the Future program, the industry-led Global Alliance for Climate-Smart Agriculture, and the African Agricultural Technology Foundation (AATF) are developing a suite of climate-smart seeds, including drought-resistant maize. The Water-Efficient Maize for Africa project (WEMA) is a public/private partnership, led by the Kenyan-based AATF and funded by the Bill and Melinda Gates Foundation, the Howard G. Buffett Foundation, and USAID.

The AATF champions WEMA's use of conventional breeding, marker-assisted breeding, and biotechnology, and plans to make these varieties available to sub-Saharan smallholders in Kenya, Mozambique, South Africa, Tanzania, and Uganda. Though not yet commercially available, WEMA seed is going to be offered royalty-free. This doesn't mean the seed is free. It means that Monsanto is not going to charge a premium for the seed's drought-resistant trait. However, WEMA seeds will be "stacked" with the *Bacillus thuringiensis* (Bt) gene for pest control, and a gene for resistance to glyphosate and other Monsanto weed killers. Though it is unclear whether farmers will have to pay royalties for the other traits, the glyphosate and fertilizer required by these seeds will definitely not be free. The unstated objective behind climate-smart seeds is finding ways for seed, chemical, and fertilizer companies to break into the African markets. WEMA seeds with a free, drought-tolerant gene are not only an excellent package for the sale of Monsanto's other products, they usher in the required regulatory frameworks for the commodification of *all* African seed. Whether or not these seeds actually help small farmers in the long run is irrelevant to capital. Once Africa's seeds are commodified, companies can sell them to the large farmers that will end up displacing the continent's smallholders. In line with the classical agrarian transition, the model for agricultural development pursued by industries like Syngenta and endorsed by the World Bank and the Bill and Melinda Gates Foundation plans on helping smallholders by pushing most of them out of agriculture (see Figure 6.2).[13]

The convergence of different forms of capital from philanthropy, finance, industry, and government is not new, but the "private-public partnerships" and the scales in which these sectors operate—from nano-particles to entire continents—are unprecedented. The diminished power of government to set research agendas through public universities and the increased power of industry and speculative capital to produce product-oriented research is a characteristic of neoliberal development.

By investing in and regulating the private capture of genetic material and new genetically engineered products, capitalism creates "biocapital," a form of value based on the commodification of the building blocks of life itself.[14] Biocapital in the form of seeds not only

Figure 6.2: Syngenta's Version of Agricultural Development

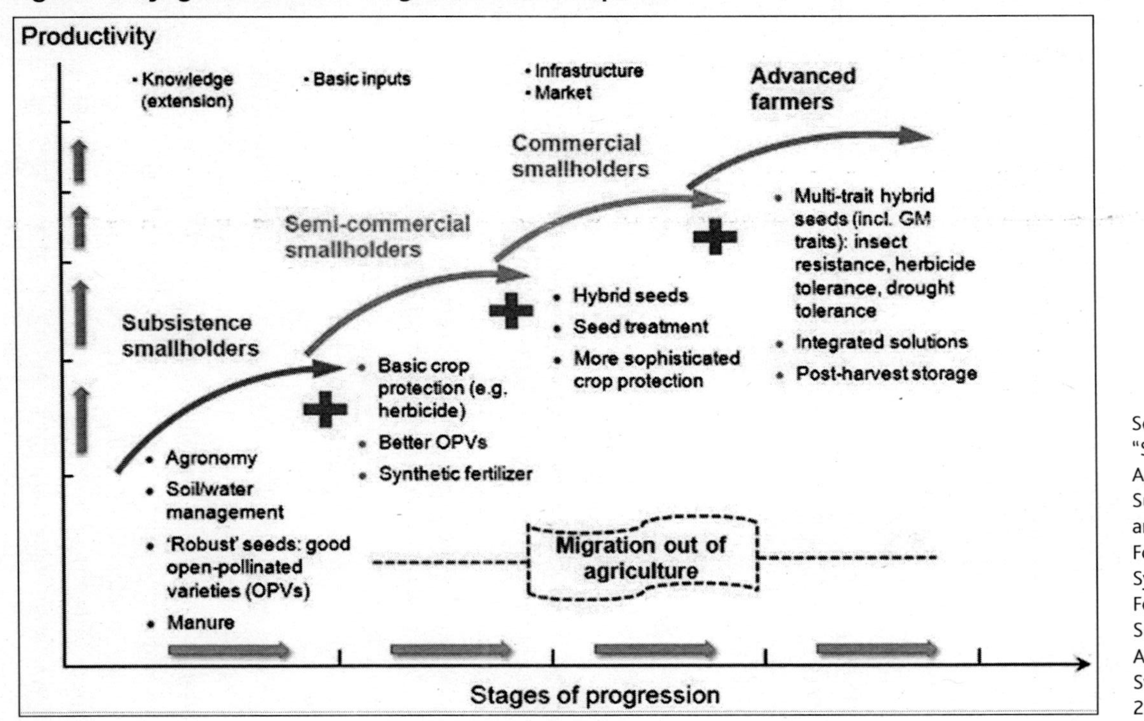

Source: Yuan Zhou, "Smallholder Agriculture, Sustainability and the Syngenta Foundation," Syngenta Foundation for Sustainable Agriculture, Basel, Switzerland, April 2010, 4.

unleashes the power of speculative capital investment in agribusiness, it recruits and creates a vast socioeconomic and political network of scientists, technicians, extensionists, investment firms, foundations, development agencies, and public relations firms invested in a genetically modified future.

Whether any of this has anything to do with actually ending hunger is questionable, especially since hunger could be wiped out rapidly by distributing wealth and income more evenly. If the World Bank, CGIAR, the Bill and Melinda Gates Foundation, USAID, Monsanto, Bayer, and Syngenta were really interested in ending hunger they would have launched a new Green Revolution in Asia, not Africa. After all, that is where most of the world's hungry people actually reside. Why insist on Africa? Because Asia already *had* a Green Revolution and is still going hungry. Hunger is beside the point. Asia's markets for Green Revolution products are already saturated. Africa is the great frontier.

But don't Africa's farmers need new, drought-resistant seeds to be able to adapt to climate change? Because climate change is increasing drought and heat waves in sub-Saharan Africa, no doubt Africa's farmers would welcome more drought resistance. But that doesn't mean that a gene-centered or commodity-centered approach is necessarily the right fit for farmers who don't have enough money for the required inputs and machinery, and who generally fare poorly in global commodity markets.

An agroecological approach to climate resilience, in which the entire agroecosystem (soil fertility and conservation, crop diversity, agroforestry, biomass management, water harvesting, and biological pest management) would better fit the livelihood needs and farming styles of Africa's smallholders. Agroecology's whole farm approach to resilience has much more to offer smallholders in terms of adaptation and mitigation than the gene-by-gene approach of climate-smart agriculture. The problem with agroecology is that it doesn't fit the model for capitalist development because agroecological farmers use fewer rather than more commercial inputs. This explains agroecology's subordinate status in most large-scale development programs, despite its endorsement from farmers' movements and its proven ability to increase yields.

Hidden Hunger and the Trojan Horse of Fortified Commodities

In 2016, Maria Andrade, Robert Mwanga, Jan Low, and Howarth Bouis were crowned the 2016 World Food Prize Laureates during a ceremony at the U.S. State Department.[15] Celebrated as "biofortification pioneers," their combined efforts have been heralded as potentially impacting over 10 million rural poor across Africa, Asia, and Latin America through *biofortification*, the process of scientifically breeding vitamins and nutrients into staple crops.[16] Researchers Andrade and Mwanga developed a carotene-rich, orange-fleshed sweet potato (OFSP) bred for Vitamin A, while Jan Low promoted the product, convincing 2 million people in Africa to adopt it. Howarth Boisas spent twenty-five years promoting iron- and zinc-fortified beans, rice, wheat, and pearl millet, along with Vitamin A-enriched cassava, maize, and OFSP. The biofortification of crops is carried out by scientists at the international centers for agricultural research and funded largely by public monies and big philanthrocapitalists. Proponents claim they are improving the diets of people in over forty countries.

Upstream in the food regime, scientists are breeding and genetically engineering crops to address the hidden hunger that affects 2 billion people worldwide. Hidden hunger is not limited to poor countries in the Global South. Vitamin and mineral deficiencies occur in the high-density, low-nutrient diets of the Global North as well, where obesity can often mask nutrient deficiency. The ravages of hidden hunger can affect all aspects of social and economic life. According to the Global Hunger Index:

> Effects of hidden hunger include child and maternal death, physical disabilities, weakened immune systems, and compromised intellects. Where hidden hunger has taken root, it not only prevents people from surviving and thriving as productive members of society, it also holds countries back in a cycle of poor nutrition,

> poor health, lost productivity, persistent poverty, and reduced economic growth. This demonstrates why not only the right to food, but also access to the right type of food at the right time, is important for both individual well-being and countries as a whole.[17]

The biofortification network grew out of the mandate to shift micronutrient interventions from nutritionally fortified foods (eaten by urban dwellers) to "hard to reach" rural populations that grew their own food. Along with rice and maize, so-called poor man's crops such as sweet potato, millet, beans, sorghum, cassava, and banana became the targets of biofortification programs.[18] Biofortified crop varieties have been heralded as the new miracle seeds, able to address the problem of micronutrient malnutrition through the introduction of "nutrient-rich" crop varieties, even in remote rural areas.[19]

The project emerges out of a twenty-year collaboration between public research institutions, philanthropic organizations, and transnational seed corporations. Decades of advanced research and development in raising the beta-carotene levels in the genetically engineered "Golden Rice," for example, has been primarily funded and supported by the Rockefeller Foundation and agribusiness giant Syngenta. DuPont collaborates with the nonprofit Africa Harvest Biotech Foundation International (Africa Harvest), and Monsanto donates to the BioCassava Plus (BC+) program of the Donald Danforth Center. The Bill and Melinda Gates Foundation is the biggest philanthropic donor of biofortification programs, having committed more than $160 million, worldwide.[20]

Promoters frame biofortification as a nutritional silver bullet: technical, generic, and scalable, putting nutrients into crops much like putting fluoride in water systems.[21] This promotion of biofortification fits into a broader discourse of "benevolent biotechnology" upheld and supported by transnational ag-biotech corporations, international regulatory bodies, and governments with "modern scientific knowledge and practice within market-oriented, poverty-reduction strategies with the aim of integrating rural agricultural communities into the global agricultural system." Promotion of biofortified crops is a promising way for companies to expand into the staple crop seed market that is still presently supplied by farmer-to-farmer seed systems. In this context, biofortification is a vehicle (some say a Trojan horse) for the corporate consolidation and control of food systems still operating outside of their control.[22]

Nowhere in the biofortification discourse does anyone ask why farmers are nutrient-poor. Poor nutrition is assumed to be some sort of natural state, to be remedied by injecting nutrients into staple crops. How and why smallholder farms lost their capacity to produce a balanced diet based on a diversified cropping system is not of concern.

Fortification and Nutritionism

Downstream, industrial food companies are not only reducing salts, sugars, and preservatives in their food products, they are "fortifying" them to contain the nutrients lost in a standard processed foods diet. Fortification is as old as iodized salt and baby formula. In the 1960s, as the diets of the poor were being decimated by the spread of export agriculture, government food supplement programs in developing countries added micronutrients to staple products such as flour, oil, sugar, and margarine. Today, the task of fortifying food has fallen to food industry giants like Nestlé, Unilever, PepsiCo, Kellogg, Danone, and General Mills, who use the market to channel nutrients to the undernourished. To support the trend, in 2005 the World Bank started the Business Alliance for Food Fortification (BAFF). Chaired by Coca-Cola, the partnership includes the major players in the global food industry, like Nestlé, Heinz, Ajinomoto, Danone, and Unilever.[23]

But fortified foods often fail to reach the poorest of the poor, those who live on the margins of the market economy. Due to their low purchasing power and underdeveloped distribution channels, processed fortified food items have limited reach and impact for subsistence farmers and rural people who consume locally produced food. Nevertheless, there is tremendous support for fortification in capitalist food systems. Science plays an important role in this.

The scientific framework used to buttress the claims of the

nutritional superiority of foods specifically engineered for enhanced nutrient content over whole foods is called "nutritionism." Nutritionism is specifically tailored to support the consumption of newly fashioned, ultra-fortified commodities. Just as the Green Revolution produced a "science of scarcity" to justify the overproduction of agricultural commodities (which needed inputs like fertilizers and pesticides), nutritionism has produced the "science of insufficiency" to justify cramming nutrients into staple foods eaten by farmers, and into food products sold to the poor by global monopolies. Nutritionism is a reductionist form of science that avoids addressing the *causes* of malnutrition and simplifies and exaggerates the role of nutrients in dietary health.[24] Ideologically, nutritionism reduces world hunger to a problem of insufficient nutrients—without asking why nutrients are lacking—and carves out a space for nutrient-enriched products offered by the market.

When hidden hunger is reduced to a problem of micronutrient deficiencies, addressing hunger serves a political and economic function. First, it gives power and profit to whichever corporation provides the micronutrients. Second, it masks the ways the global food system has destroyed traditional sources of nutrients and impoverished people's diets. In its extreme version, champions of fortification even claim that human beings cannot obtain their necessary nutrients by eating a healthy diet made up of diverse, whole, and fresh foods, but need personally targeted nutrients, to be administered by the food industry.

Arguing for Nestlé's vision of a "scientifically engineered Garden of Eden" based on fortified food products, outgoing chairman Peter Brabeck-Letmathe claims, "Nature is not good to human beings. Nature would kill human beings. The reason why *Homo sapiens* have become what we are is because we learned to overcome nature."[25] The political economy behind fortification tells another story. Like many monopolies, Nestlé's corporate growth has dropped by 50 percent over the last five years, leading it to seek profits by morphing its mass food products into the more lucrative pharmaceutical sector.

This focus on the inability of humans to feed themselves and the baffling "scarcity" of nutrients enables food industries and biotechnology corporations to sell more products and obtain better profit margins, thus satisfying their shareholders. It also allows governments and industry to depoliticize the causes of world hunger and nutrient deficiency by recasting them as technical problems to be solved by technical solutions rather than structural measures like land reform, promotion of agroecological approaches to farming, market reforms, and living wages. Biofortification pioneers and tech-savvy food companies invite us to believe that ending hunger is simply about getting the science right. This suggests that hunger is caused by no one and nothing, it just happens. And lucky for us, science and industry can end it.

People are hungry because they cannot afford to buy food, not because science hasn't figured out what to feed them. Farmers are nutrient-deficient because they don't have enough land to grow a balanced diet. These are political, not technical problems.

The Problem with Food Waste

Forty percent of food grown in the United States and around the world is "wasted," generating global concern about the social and environmental costs of food waste. The difference in how waste is viewed is the difference between need and demand, and between sustenance and commodities. In the first instance, waste is food that is "lost" to the eater. In the second, food waste is a factor of production that has simply been used up.

The term *waste* is based on the Latin *vastus,* meaning "unoccupied" or "uncultivated." When we think of wasting food—our sustenance—we invoke the term as a verb, "to use or expend carelessly, extravagantly, or to no purpose . . . to fail to make full or good use of." But capitalism tends to treat food waste as an adjective, as "A material, substance or by-product eliminated or discarded as no longer useful or required after the completion of a process."[26]

The US Food Waste Challenge is a private-public initiative between the USDA and the agrifoods industry to reduce food waste by 50 percent by 2030.[27] The industry is eliminating "shrinkage" in packing, shipping, and processing. Supermarkets are giving expired products to food banks or selling old produce for animal feed. Walmart and other stores are selling "ugly fruit." These efforts follow international trends. France recently passed legislation prohibiting grocery stores from throwing away expired food.

Because food provisioning uses 10 percent of the total U.S. energy budget, 50 percent of national land, and 80 percent of all freshwater consumed, it means that Americans are throwing away the equivalent of $165 billion in resources each year.[28] Theoretically, reducing food losses by just 15 percent could save enough to feed over 25 million Americans yearly. This calculus has prompted the USDA and major philanthropic foundations to fund projects to reduce and repurpose food waste and at the same time reduce environmental pollution, create jobs, and improve food security. The geography of food waste is influenced by gender and age, location in the supply chain, and whether a society is industrialized or agricultural. Even socioeconomic status differentiates the kinds of food waste. This has led to diverse responses: everything from composting and energy generation to food banks and processing is being thrown at the problem.

Most of these measures could help reduce some of the externalities related to food waste (landfills, GHG emissions, overuse of natural resources), and that's a good thing. What is curious about the proposals to deal with food waste, however, is the focus on the *effects* and a complete avoidance of one of the major *causes* of food waste: overproduction.

The defining characteristic of capitalism is its tendency to overproduce. The food system is no exception. Our cheap grain policy drives farmers to overproduce. Farmers tend to increase production when prices are high (as is the norm in capitalism), but they also increase production in response to low prices. Although it seems contrary to what they should do, farms have so many fixed costs that even when there are low or even no profits, more output means that they can at least cover these costs. This leads to constant gluts unless there are weather-related reductions in yields. The glut of grain is bought at discounted prices by grain, agrifood, and energy companies, which turn it into cheap food products, feed for CAFOs, and ethanol. The

Food Waste at a Glance

An estimated 30 to 50 percent of the world's food goes uneaten. In the United States 40 percent of food is wasted.[29]

Food waste is not uniform across the globe: 28 percent of global food loss and waste occurred in industrialized Asia with 23 percent in South and Southeast Asia, 14 percent in North America and Oceania, 14 percent in Europe, 9 percent in sub-Saharan Africa, 7 percent in North Africa and West and Central Africa, and 6 percent in Latin America. While more food is lost in production and storage in developing countries, food waste occurs on a higher scale in the consumption stage in developed countries.[30]

As household incomes grow, particularly in transition economies (Brazil, Russia, India, and China), the consumption of starchy food staples declines and diets diversify with fresh fruits and vegetables, dairy, meat, and fish. This shift toward shorter shelf-life food items is associated with greater food waste and a greater use of resources.[31]

Adults waste more food than children, and larger households waste less per person than smaller households. There is less food loss in low-income households than in high-income households, and young people tend to waste more than older people. Hispanic households in the United States waste approximately 25 percent less food than non-Hispanics. "For the average U.S. household of four, food waste translates into an estimated $1,350 to $2,275 in annual losses."[32]

In farming, production losses are greatest for fresh produce. Produce may not be harvested because of damage caused by pests, disease, weather, or low market prices. It is difficult for farmers to grow the exact amount that will match demand, and so they may grow too much food. Approximately 7 percent of planted fields in the United States are not harvested each year, costing an estimated $140 million in crop losses.[33]

Loss can occur due to storage, inadequate packaging, and frequent handling by food processors, brokers, and wholesalers. According to some studies, a typical food product is handled an average of 33 times before it is touched by a consumer. Of the estimated 5.4 billion pounds of food discarded at the retail level in 1995, nearly half of the losses came from dairy products and fresh fruits and vegetables.[34]

Twenty percent of consumer waste occurs because of date label confusion.[35] In most cases, people throw away food once the date passes because they mistakenly think the date indicates that it is no longer safe to eat when in fact the date indicates how long the manufacturers think the food will be at its peak quality. Factor in that food labels range in phrasing from "sell by" to "best before" to "use by," and it is no wonder that retailers and consumers alike are confused.

objective is to sell as much as possible. Similar trends occur in fruits and vegetables, for which low prices, standardization, and the big lots demanded by the agrifoods industry drive farmers to produce more, flooding the market. Even the much-touted farmers' markets that connect local producers and consumers can drive local farmers to overproduce. Because these markets are largely saturated with farmers competing with one another to sell the same products, farmers select only the most cosmetically attractive produce for display and sale. The rest tends to get thrown or given away (or composted). These farmers work on thin margins and tend to pay high rent or mortgages for farmland that is close to urban markets.[36] Producing food waste is a collateral effect of their market strategy for economic survival.

Waste is endemic to capitalist overproduction. Turning food waste into a commodity or donating it to food banks does nothing to address the cause of waste, though it might create new economic activities that depend on food waste for their existence. The key to ending food waste is to end overproduction.

Meet the New Agrifoods Transition

From seed to fork, the food system is being primed for further intensification. Today's techniques in genetic engineering have surpassed the crude technologies of earlier genetically modified seeds by light years, allowing direct manipulation of DNA without having to resort to inaccurate and expensive genetic transfer.[37] Anyone can download a "genetic map" from the internet and use it to directly manipulate DNA, changing a metabolic pathway to express any phenotypic characteristic, not only to produce seeds but also *to make any kind of lifeform*. What we could only dream of doing with DNA can now be realized.[38] New technologies collapse and shorten the innovation time between conception and commercialization. And they are accessible to any molecular biologist.

Corporations are investing in "digital agriculture," in which massive amounts of information about the environment, climate, soil, and cultivars are carefully recorded by satellite, then analyzed and sold to farmers, allowing them to apply inputs with great precision. All major corporations in the food chain, from Monsanto, John Deere, and Cargill to Nestlé, Walmart, and Amazon are using these big data information systems.

The integrated control of genetic and environmental information increases the tendency of land and corporate consolidation: among the six monopolies that control 51 percent of seed and 72 percent of the pesticides in the international market there is strong pressure to merge. Syngenta, ChemChina, Monsanto, Bayer, Dow, and DuPont are all negotiating mergers. When two merge, the others have no choice but to merge as well. Vertical consolidation is also underway. Amazon's 2017 purchase of the high-end organic foods supermarket Whole Foods is another example of corporate consolidation. In open war with the Walmart model, Amazon is planning to sell food through huge supply centers to be delivered by food taxis and drones. Amazon's new Amazon Go stores will be fully automated, allowing consumers to walk through the store selecting items, and walk out without going through checkout. A smartphone application will register their purchase and charge their credit card.[39]

And what will you find in the store? Food products made from commodified ingredients with slightly lower transfats, sodium, and sugar levels than before, but now fortified with micronutrients and disease-preventing, plant-derived compounds called *phytonutrients*. Nestlé, the 150-year-old fortification pioneer—and the world's largest packaged foods monopoly—will sell you a "health chip" to implant under your skin. These will measure your nutrient levels and communicate by satellite with your physician and your smartphone, individually tailoring your shopping experience by indicating which fortified (Nestlé) products you should buy—perhaps an anti-Alzheimer's frozen pizza or some cancer-fighting Hot Pockets.

All the financial and structural pressure of the multitrillion-dollar agrifoods industry leads to even larger scales of production. Seeds, inputs, machinery, financing, insurance, nanotechnology, and mass information will deliver larger and larger batches of uniform products to the supermarket shelves. And the monopolies of the food regime will be even bigger and more concentrated than ever before.

The agrifoods transition will exacerbate both the first and second contradictions of capitalism: inequality, with workers having insufficient purchasing power to absorb all that is produced, and ecological havoc resulting from the system's inability to relate to the environment in ways that maintain a healthy and thriving biosphere. In the first case, it will steadily eliminate labor, not only through automation in the Global North and the emerging economies, but by driving a large portion of the 2.5 billion rural poor, a third of humanity, off the land through land grabs and the industrialization of agriculture in the Global South. The intensification of overproduction will lead to more, rather than less, GHG's, greater losses of agrobiodiversity, and further contamination of the earth's water, soil, and genetic diversity, thus accelerating the second—ecological—contradiction of capital. Where will a third of humanity find work? How many will be able to afford the fortified, food-like substances to ensure their health?

George Naylor: An Iowa Farm Leader Calls for Food Sovereignty[40]

I believe we need to transform our food system. To do this, we need everybody to be a piece in the same puzzle—a puzzle for democratic, egalitarian social change that respects our ecological limits, not a puzzle that supports the status quo and creates more problems for our democracy, our health, our society, and our environment.

The typical farmer in the Midwest owns probably only 10 percent of the land they farm; the rest is cash rented. Landlords often take the highest rent bid from the biggest, most industrialized farmer. Through the years, farmers have invested in bigger and bigger livestock facilities, only to lose money, watch their facilities become "obsolete," and abandon their beneficial crop rotations. Today, almost all the pigs, chickens and even market cattle in the United States are owned by corporations and fed in giant feedlots and confined animal feeding operations (CAFOs). The millions of gallons of CAFO manure, along with the remaining farmers' fencerow-to-fencerow corn and soybeans rotation, pollute our lakes and waterways. Getting bigger is clearly not the answer to our problems.

When a big farmer is going broke, I often hear, "Well, do you really feel sorry for them? They brought it on themselves." My answer to that is, "We should all feel sorry for ourselves for losing one of our most precious institutions, the family farm." Farm depressions do not reverse farm consolidation; the land will continue to be farmed, but by some other farmer who pursues the inevitable call to "get big or get out." In some cases, corporations are already doing the farming. We are headed to a time of "farming without farmers," where the bottom line drives every decision.

Fortunately, some farmers who defy the odds by farming agroecologically or organically are preserving inherited wisdom and developing new methods and techniques. We will all need these practices when our society recognizes that we *can* provide healthy food and leave a beautiful planet for future generations. And likewise, simply voting with our fork won't do the trick. We need to recognize how market forces affect farmers, the land, and consumer behavior, and demand policy solutions to achieve a sustainable future.

We need to de-commoditize food and land. Unless we recognize that industrialized agriculture depends on the production, consumption, and sale of commodities (often speculatively), and that our most basic assumptions and economic behavior actually reinforce the industrial status quo, we can't begin to address the problems of land concentration, unhealthy food, and the degradation of rural environments.

The biggest market for chemical and biotech products is the production of storable commodities: feed grains, mostly corn; food grains, mostly wheat and rice; and oilseeds, mostly soybeans. There are approximately 250 million acres of these storable commodities, versus only about 12 million acres of fruits and vegetables in the US. The feed grains and oilseeds comprise most of the feed for producing industrial milk, meat, and eggs—not food that hungry people can afford when shipped from thousands of miles away. Much of the corn and soybeans are used to produce biofuels and biochemicals—again nothing that will relieve anyone's hunger.

Farmers are going broke growing these commodities and spending big bucks on inputs. Why do they do this? Another big lie is that farmers produce commodities because they are subsidized. Almost everyone in the food movement, people that I love and respect, repeats this lie *ad infinitum*.

The truth is, commodities like grains and oilseeds are storable—not perishable—and can be converted to cash throughout the year. Raised on the vast motherlode of arable soils we have in the US, much of it far from city populations, these commodities were traditionally stored and fed to livestock. If just 10 percent of these commodity acres were converted to fruits and vegetables, the production of these foods would triple, and you'd see those farmers going broke as perishable food rotted in the fields. We can use a lot more produce raised locally, but to think that a corn and soybean farmer could convert their land to fruits and vegetables is unrealistic. Midwestern farmers plant corn and soybeans fencerow-to-fencerow because there are really no alternatives in the capitalist commodity system.

The subsidies paid to commodity farmers from the US Department of the Treasury only partially make up for low grain prices. It is important to understand that these subsidy programs weren't designed to make farmers rich or create the economic framework for diversified family farms; on the contrary, these payments are only intended to keep the commodity system itself from self-destructing.

In addition, cheap grain policy makes it very easy for industrial livestock companies to order all the feed they need over the phone. They don't need to grow the feed or take any responsibility for the environmental and social damage involved in producing mountains of corn and soybeans using chemicals and genetically modified crops. It's simply not true that most of the subsidies go to big farmers, and even mid-sized family farms need subsidies to stay afloat. Diversified farms that raise their own feed with sustainable crop rotations—including hay and pasture along with responsible use of manure—can't compete with this bifurcated system. The subsidy system is an agribusiness scheme to have our citizens pay for the destruction of the very kind of sustainable farm we all want.

Under the current laissez-faire policy of planting fencerow-to-fencerow, a farmer is always going to try to produce more bushels to sell—either out of greed or fear of going broke. If a chemical input can seemingly increase income over the cost, they'll use it. But when all farmers follow suit, overproduction results in low prices and our land and water are degraded.

What if each farm had a quota based on their history of production and an assessment of how a good crop rotation along with conservation plantings could regenerate the soil and biodiversity? What if farmers were compensated with a price that stabilized his or her income? Their thinking and practices would be the opposite of the laissez-faire, free market straightjacket. If a farm has a quota of 10,000 bushels of corn, that farmer would think, "How can I produce 10,000 bushels of corn with the *least* amount of chemicals and fertilizer and the most amount of conservation? Maybe I could use some of the other land for soil-saving hay and pasture to feed a new herd for grass-fed beef or dairy." That farmer would be well on the way to becoming organic.

We citizens of the United States, with a heritage of democratic ideals, and today's food movement that values farmers, well-paid farm workers, properly labeled healthy food, and ecological food production, have a great responsibility to make "Parity" our national policy. With "Parity" we can achieve the kind of nutrition, farm communities, and conservation within the agrarian traditions we desire. What we all need for a well-nourished, democratic, and peaceful world is food sovereignty. This will go a long way to establishing a rational food system and to providing land access to those who truly want to live a good life farming sustainably.

Agroecology: Lessons from the Awkward Science

A third of the world's people depend on smallholder agriculture that produces three-quarters of the world's food on a quarter of the arable land. Nearly 15 percent of the world's food is produced in small urban farms and gardens. Contrary to conventional thought, and a lot of corporate rhetoric, most poor people in the world are farmers or are fed by poor farmers.

These simple facts are strong indications that the agrarian transition to capitalist agriculture is far from complete. For three hundred years capitalism has colonized food up and down the value chain in an attempt to turn every aspect of production and consumption into a profit-generating commodity. In this massive historical transition, the research, practice, and politics of food have all been steadily influenced and disciplined by the logic of capitalism. But twenty-first-century capitalism has been stymied by decades of stagnant global economic growth. Smallholder agriculture appears to capital both as a sector for potential market expansion and as an opportunity for the accumulation by dispossession of land, labor, and resources.[41]

Though global economic growth may be slow, the purchasing power of the nearly 4 billion people at the economic "base of the pyramid" is growing steadily at 8 percent a year.[42] This growth represents a huge potential market for capital. But what can you sell people who are too poor to buy smartphones, flat-screen televisions, and electric cars? *Processed food.* What can you sell the 2.5 billion farmers who already feed the poor? *Seeds. Fertilizer. Pesticides.* The base of the pyramid is not just attractive to global capital, it is essential to its survival. The unstated irony behind the push for a new, genetically engineered Green Revolution is that it responds to the needs of the rich, not the poor.

But the food systems of the poor do not conform easily to the logic of capital. Around the world, rural communities resist, contest, and avoid the capitalist food regime while constructing new forms of production and consumption. These communities sit precariously on the blurry divide between the market economy and the moral economy, employing different forms of production and consumption in ways that provide them with a degree of autonomy from capital. Forms of ownership may be individual, cooperative, communal, or collective; consumption may be local, extended, or mixed; labor may be performed by family, paid, reciprocal, permanent, or temporary; production may be rural, urban, organic, or not. The mix of farming and consumption styles depends on the context of each local food system.

Capitalism assumes these communities are backward and in need of development. Ignored is the fact that many are trying to recover from the environmental destruction of the Green Revolution and the devastation visited upon their livelihoods by global markets. That they might choose to organize their food system differently, or would want to pick and choose what aspects of capitalism to adopt or reject, is irrelevant to capital expansion. Nobel Laureate Milton Friedman's famous thesis that unfettered capitalism leaves people "free to choose" does not allow for a choice *against* free-market capitalism. Nor does it allow much choice for the poor, who have real unmet needs but lack the money to exert "effective demand" in a capitalist system.

Agroecology has emerged as part of the agrarian contestation against capitalism. Its principles are drawn from careful ecological observations of millennia-old peasant farming systems and reapplied, together with new knowledge based on scientific experimentation, and farming innovations developed by today's smallholders.[43] Agroecology relies on farmer-led, ecosystem management that aims to develop productive, healthy and resilient fields, farms, and regions. The aim is to avoid agronomic and agroecological problems rather than apply chemical inputs to solve farm system malfunction. Agroecology is knowledge intensive rather than capital intensive, and tends toward small, highly diversified farms. The practice of agroecology is largely passed farmer-to-farmer with the help of farmers' organizations and NGOs rather than through government extension services or corporate outreach.[44] Because it was originally developed in collaboration with farmers who are fighting for land, water, and resource rights, agroecology is both part of the resistance to capitalist agriculture and the agricultural basis for the construction of a new food system.

Taken together, the planet's smallholders and the practice of agroecology constitute *a means and a barrier* to the expansion of capitalist agriculture. Smallholders subsidize capitalist agriculture with cheap labor and offer a vast, low-end market for seeds and chemical inputs. At the same time, family labor, small farm size, diversified farming, and knowledge systems, and smallholders' diversified livelihood strategies preserve smallholder farming systems (including growing food for their families), presenting barriers to entry and competition for capitalist agriculture.[46] This is one reason why, despite being

A Brief Political Economy of Agroecology

If we apply the basic questions of political economy—Who owns what? Who does what? Who gets what? What do they do with it?—we can get an idea of why agroecology is so widespread, despite the lack of resources dedicated to its expansion.

Imagine the soil as a fertility "endowment" in which wealth is made up of all the mineral and biotic components of fertility—humus, biota, minerals, nutrients, water, clay, silt, sand, pH, and so on. This makes up the "principal" of the fertility endowment. Now imagine that the nutrients and water used by plants represent debits to the endowment. As long as plants rely on the interest rather than the principal, they can be grown and harvested forever, especially if the nutrients they use are returned to the soil through decomposition or the manure of grazing animals. While this happens in natural systems, in agriculture these nutrients are taken out to feed people. Because of the metabolic rift, (see chapter four), they are not always returned. Over time, agriculture can consume both the interest and the principal of the fertility endowment.

Conventional agriculture replenishes part of the "interest" of the fertility endowment with synthetic fertilizer. Over time, however, cultivation steadily draws from the "principal" by depleting micronutrients, killing off the biota, burning up the humus, and drying out the soil. On fragile, thin, or mineral soils, this can happen in just a few years. The farmer must purchase these inputs as commodities and will become dependent on them as the principal of the soil steadily evaporates.

Rather than paying fertilizer companies for "interest," agroecology concentrates on building the principal, through compost, green manures, biomass production and management, and biological nitrogen fixation, so that it continually replenishes the original interest. In Central America, farmers in the Campesino a Campesino movement grow the velvet bean (*Muncna pruriens*) in association with maize. The velvet bean fixes nitrogen and produces a thick mat of biomass that smothers weeds, thus reducing labor costs. When the plant dies, the leaves decompose, adding to the humus (principal) of the soil.

Agroecologists have discovered that the traditional practice of polycultures (companion planting) increases agriculture's net primary productivity. Three hectares planted to a mixture of maize, beans, and squash yields much more than a hectare of maize, a hectare of beans, and a hectare of squash. This "over-yielding" can be calculated with the Land-Equivalent Ratio or "LER." In this case, the agroecological labor process yields a surplus beyond conventional methods.[45]

The process of accumulation of agroecological wealth—fertility, agrobiodiversity, soil and water conservation—occurs largely outside the circulation of commodities and is controlled by the farmer rather than capital. The precondition for this is the long-term usufruct of the land. Sharecroppers, renters, and squatters are unlikely to make the labor investment in agroecological methods because there is no guarantee they will reap the benefits of these farm improvements.

marginalized to some of the planet's worst agricultural lands, smallholders persist in agriculture today.[47]

When smallholder farms began crashing under Green Revolution methods in the 1970s, many farmers turned to agroecology in an effort to restore soil organic matter, conserve water, restore agro-biodiversity, and manage pests.[48] Agroecology does not preclude small-scale mechanization to eliminate drudgery, but it does require the constant attention, skill, and inventiveness of the farmer. In the first stage of development, agroecology reduces the needs for external chemical inputs (commercial fertilizers and pesticides); in the second stage it replaces these chemicals for organic and local inputs; and in the third stage the ecological redesign of the farm organizes production on the basis of internal ecological management.

Since the early 1980s, hundreds of nongovernmental organizations (NGOs) in Africa, Latin America, and Asia have promoted thousands of agroecology projects that incorporate elements of traditional knowledge and modern agroecological science.[49] With the food, livelihoods, and climate crises on the rise, the importance of the social and environmental services provided by agroecological agriculture are becoming widely recognized.[50]

Corporate agriculture's champions have criticized agroecology's alleged low productivity. These criticisms are based on low output per farmworker, because much of the land farmed agroecologically is not mechanized. But they ignore the evidence demonstrating the high productivity per unit of land and the strong resilience of agroecologically managed peasant agriculture,[51] and forget that the first Green Revolution required the massive structural mobilization of state and private-sector resources.[52] While agroecology has spread widely through the efforts of NGOs, farmers' movements, and university projects, it remains marginal to official agricultural development plans and is dwarfed by the resources provided to genetic engineering and Green Revolution technologies. In contrast, the remarkable spread of agroecology in Cuba stems, in large part, from the government's strong structural support.[53] Asking "Why don't all farmers practice agroecology?" begs the question "What is holding agroecology back?" The simple answer is: capitalism.

A capitalist agrarian transition could conceivably concentrate food production worldwide on some 50,000 industrial farms.[54] Given the best land, subsidized inputs, and favorable market access, these farms could potentially produce the world's food (although not very sustainably) using relatively little labor. But how would 2.5 billion displaced smallholders buy this food? A full global transition to capitalist agriculture would condemn a third of humanity to unprecedented unemployment, disruption, and suffering.

The challenge for our planet is not how to (over)produce food, but how to keep smallholders on the land while sustainably producing

Figure 6.3: Vision of the International Assessment of Agricultural Knowledge, Science and Technology for Development (IAASTD)

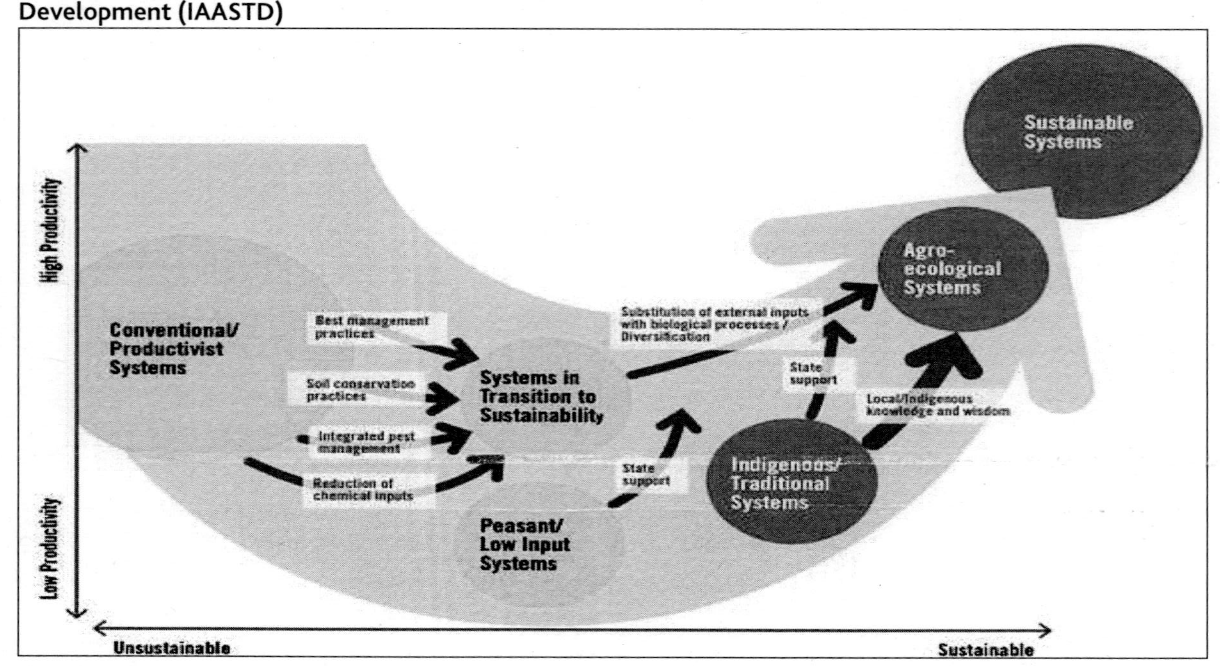

Source: IAASTD, "Toward Multifunctional Agriculture for Environmental, Social and Economic Sustainability."[55]

healthy food. The challenge is not to attempt to engineer "climate-smart" commodities or nutritionally fortified crops, but to build overall nutrition and resilience into the whole agroecosystem. This will take more—not fewer—highly skilled farmers. For this to happen, farmers need support from universities, schools, and government in order to develop agroecology in the face of rapidly changing climatic conditions. Markets need to be organized around the principles of parity. The countryside itself needs to be a good place to live with electricity, clean drinking water, sanitation facilities, roads, schools, cultural activities, clinics, and social services. Above all, the world's farmers need enough land and resources to be able to live well, what indigenous people in Latin America call *El Buen Vivir*. This requires a social investment in agriculture that capitalism is unwilling to make.

CONCLUSION

Changing Everything: Food, Capitalism, and the Challenges of Our Time

> Philosophers have hitherto only interpreted the world in various ways; the point is to change it.
>
> —KARL MARX[1]

Food, energy, the environment, and livelihoods are the urgent—and inescapable—challenges of our time. Our food systems should and *could* feed everyone equitably and sustainably while providing dignified livelihoods and ensuring a good quality of life. To build a good, clean, and fair food system, we need to build an alternative to capitalism, a system designed to concentrate massive amounts of wealth and power in fewer and fewer hands, no matter the cost to people or the planet.

How we produce and consume determines how our society is organized, but how we organize socially and politically can also determine how we produce and consume. The implications of this are profound: our food systems are vessels of unmatched social and economic power and pivotal sites for systemic transformation.

When we assess the potential for different approaches to end poverty, hunger, and malnutrition, or to reverse global warming and environmental destruction, we must also ask how these strategies will affect the relations of power in our food system. Do they challenge the status quo or accommodate it? Are they regressive or redistributive? Will they concentrate power within the halls of unaccountable corporate control, or work to decentralize and democratize our food system in favor of the poor? Will they strengthen or weaken social movements? Do these approaches mitigate the externalities of the corporate food regime, or help us transcend the regime itself?

What kind of changes to the food system are desirable or will actually make a difference in the long run? Are we content to "tinker around the edges" or can we introduce structural transformations? Do we need incremental or drastic change? Should we simply try to improve conditions within our own communities, hoping for the eventual evolution of a better food system? Or should we, as the Black Panthers proposed in the 1970s, pursue "survival pending revolution"?

It's easier to pose these questions than it is to answer them. But that doesn't let us off the hook. In our current system, if you don't set the menu, you're on the menu. Just as we need an understanding of capitalism to know *what* to change in the food system, we need an understanding of power to figure out *how* to bring about regime change. As this book demonstrates, the power of social movements is key to both resisting the ravages of capitalism and forcing reforms upon the changing regimes. Can the food movement build enough power to transform the food regime? Can the movement unite with other groups seeking progressive social and economic change in order to create the critical mass to make it happen? Perhaps. The task is daunting, but history may be on our side.

Liberalization and Reform: Two Sides of the Capitalist Coin

As we saw in chapter 1, the corporate food regime, like the capitalist economic system, goes through periods of *liberalization* characterized by unregulated markets and massive capital concentration, followed

Capitalism and Democracy

Capitalism and democracy evolved together. The particular form of democracy associated with capitalism is "liberal democracy," which is based on the rights of property and the rights of the individual (or corporations, which are treated as if they were individuals). While the combination of capitalism and liberal democracy is frequently understood unproblematically as "freedom," it harbors a core contradiction because the inherent tendency of capital to concentrate wealth is antithetical to the distribution of power integral to democracy. In the early days of capitalism this tension was managed by restricting suffrage to the privileged economic classes and white, male property owners. But as political democracy began to spread to broader spheres of society, the tension between what the majority of people wanted and what the captains of capitalism wanted became harder to manage. The forms of control became more sophisticated, but so did the social forms of exercising democracy. What is important to remember is that economic liberalism and political liberalism are different but related aspects of capitalism.

This is reflected in the ways political parties link economic issues with social issues. For example, in the United States, starting with the Clinton administration, the Democratic Party has linked a neoliberal economic agenda to a progressive social agenda in a form of ***progressive neoliberalism***. According to Nancy Fraser:

"In its U.S. form, progressive neoliberalism is an alliance of mainstream currents of new social movements (feminism, anti-racism, multiculturalism, and LGBTQ rights), on the one side, and high-end 'symbolic' and service-based business sectors (Wall Street, Silicon Valley, and Hollywood), on the other. In this alliance, progressive forces are effectively joined with the forces of cognitive capitalism, especially financialization. However unwittingly, the former lend their charisma to the latter. Ideals like diversity and empowerment, which could in principle serve different ends, now gloss policies that have devastated manufacturing and what were once middle-class lives."[2]

The Republican Party linked the same neoliberal economic agenda to a reactionary social agenda in a form of ***conservative neoliberalism***. Billionaire candidate Donald Trump's clever trick was to mobilize social discontent against the political establishment by condemning both economic neoliberalism and social progressivism in a virulent form of *reactionary neoliberalism.*

by devastating financial busts and social upheaval. These are followed by *reformist* periods in which markets are regulated in an effort to re-stabilize the regime. Although these phases appear politically distinct, they are actually two sides of the same capitalist coin. If unregulated capitalist markets ran rampant indefinitely, they would eventually destroy the social and natural resource base of capitalism itself.

However, necessary reforms do not result from the good intentions of reformists. As liberal markets undermine society and environment, social conditions deteriorate, giving rise to social *counter-movements* that force governments to reform their markets and institutions. The politics of these counter-movements—and the balance of power within the regime—influences the nature of the reforms.

During a capitalist crisis, liberals, conservatives, populists, social democrats, socialists, libertarians, and fascists will champion some combination of social and economic issues based on their own political calculus. They'll align with particular political parties, like Democrats, Republicans, Conservatives, Labor, Nationalists, and Greens. There are many possible combinations, confounded by the fact that party names are rarely consistent with their politics. In the United States, on social issues Republicans tend to align with social conservatives and Democrats with social progressives; but both align with the economic neoliberalism of the corporate food regime.

Today's counter-movement to neoliberalism has been growing around the world as people struggle to defend their livelihoods, their communities, and their environment from uncontrolled capitalist markets. Women, ethnic minorities, people of color, family farmers, peasants, workers, immigrants, indigenous peoples, and environmentalists have steadily been organizing and advancing practical and political alternatives to neoliberalism. There are other reactions against neoliberalism as well, and some can be quite contradictory or reactionary. Co-optation of anti-liberalization movements is to be expected. For example, in the United States, the *progressive neoliberalism* of Democrats co-opts social progressives into accepting economic neoliberalism.[3] The *reactionary populism* of the Tea Party co-opts social conservatives into the neoliberal economic platform. The irony of politics under capitalism is that forces that oppose *economic* liberalization can often be persuaded to fight each other (rather than capitalism) on the basis of opposing *social* agendas.

One of the prominent currents within the global counter-movement to neoliberalism is the food movement. The food movement is very broad, and there are plenty of people and proposals that align with neoliberal, reformist, progressive, and radical economic trends. However, by definition, the part of the food movement that can be considered as part of the counter-movement falls within progressive and radical trends.

There are neoliberal and reformist economic trends within the corporate food regime. Both share a power base rooted in G-8 governments (United Kingdom, United States, France, Italy, Germany, Japan, Canada, and Russia), multilateral institutions, monopoly corporations, and big philanthropy. The neoliberal trend is hegemonic, grounded in economic liberalism, driven by corporate agrifood monopolies, and managed by institutions such as the U.S. Department of Agriculture, the Common Agricultural Policy, the World Trade Organization, the private-sector financing arm of the World Bank (International Finance Corporation), and the International Monetary Fund. Big philanthropy, like the Bill and Melinda Gates Foundation and the Rockefeller Fund, believe in the power of technology and

POLITICS, PRODUCTION MODELS,		
	Corporate Food Regime	
POLITICS	NEOLIBERAL	REFORMIST
Reactionary Neoliberalism	Conservative Neoliberalism	Progressive
Discourse	Food Enterprise	Food Security
Main Institutions	International Finance Corporation (World Bank); IMF; WTO; USDA; Global Food Security Bill; Green Revolution; Millennium Challenge; Heritage Foundation; Chicago Global Council; Bill and Melinda Gates Foundation	International Bank for Reconstruction and Development (World Bank); FAO; UN Commission on Sustainable Development; International Federation of Agricultural Producers; mainstream Fair Trade; Slow Food; some Food Policy Councils; most food banks and food aid programs
Orientation	Corporate	Development
Model	Overproduction; corporate concentration; unregulated markets and monopolies; monocultures (including organic); GMOs; agrofuels; mass global consumption of industrial food; phasing out of peasant and family agriculture and local retail	Mainstreaming/ certification of niche markets (for example, organic, fair, local, sustainable); maintaining Northern agricultural subsidies; "sustainable" roundtables for agrofuels, soy, forest products, etc.; market-led land reform
Approach to the food and environmental crises	Increased industrial production; unregulated corporate monopolies; land grabs; expansion of GMOs; public-private partnerships; sustainable intensification and climate-smart agriculture; l iberal markets; internationally sourced food aid	Same as Neoliberal but w/increased middle peasant production and some locally sourced food aid; more agricultural aid, but tied to GMOs and "bio-fortified/climate-resistant" crops
Guiding document	WB 2009 Development Report	WB 2009 Development Report

AND APPROACHES

Food Movements	
PROGRESSIVE	RADICAL
Neoliberalism	Diverse, Re-Politicized Counter-Movement
Food Justice Alternative Fair Trade and Slow Foods chapters; many organizations in the Community Food Security Movement; CSAs; many Food Policy Councils and Youth-led food and justice movements; many farmworker and labor organizations Empowerment	Food Sovereignty Via Campesina; International Planning Committee on Food Sovereignty; Global March for Women; many Food Justice and rights-based movements Entitlement
Agroecologically produced local food; investment in underserved communities; new business models and community benefit packages for production, processing and retail; better wages for ag. workers; solidarity economies; land access; regulated markets and supply	Democratization of food system; dismantle corporate agri-foods monopoly power; parity; redistributive land reform; community rights to water and seed; regionally based food systems; sustainable livelihoods; ; protection from dumping/ overproduction; revival of agroecologically managed peasant agriculture to distribute wealth and cool the planet
Institutionalizing the Right to Food; better safety nets; sustainably produced, locally sourced food; agroecologically based agricultural development International Assessment of Agricultural Knowledge, Science and Technology for Development (IAASTD)	Human right to food sovereignty; locally sourced, sustainably produced, culturally appropriate, democratically controlled focus on UN/FAO negotiations

Table adapted from Eric Holt-Giménez and A. Shattuck, "Food Crises, Food Regimes, and Food Movements: Rumblings of Reform or Tides of Transformation?" *Journal of Peasant Studies* 38, no. 1 (January 2011): 109–44.

entrepreneurship. They promote the Green Revolution, capital-intensive agriculture, and global markets as an answer to poverty and hunger.

The reformist trend is much weaker than the neoliberal trend and is sometimes backed by subordinate branches of the same institutions, such as the United Nations, the public-sector financing arm of the World Bank (International Bank for Reconstruction and Development), and many large development NGOs. Though the mission of reform is to mitigate the excesses of the market, its "job" is identical to that of the neoliberal trend of maintaining and reproducing the corporate food regime. Reformists call for mild reforms like food aid, social safety nets, fair trade, organic niche markets, industrial-scale organic farms, Green Revolution technologies for small farmers, and technology-focused renderings of agroecology. They also appeal to (or fund) progressive organizations within the counter-movement on the basis of social rather than economic arguments.

Global food movements are characterized by two major trends: progressive and radical. Many actors within the progressive trend advance practical alternatives to industrial agrifoods, such as sustainable, agroecological, and organic agriculture, Community Supported Agriculture, farmers' markets, farm-to-school programs, urban gardens, and food hubs. Food justice movements calling for racially equitable food access are found in this trend. The radical trend also calls for practical alternatives like agroecology, but focuses more on structural issues like agrarian reform, an end to free trade agreements, and smashing the corporate power of food monopolies. Radical proposals (as in "go to the root") address structural issues and include food sovereignty, agrarian reform, and the democratization of food systems in favor of the poor.

All of these general trends are blurry around the edges. People, communities, and organizations can straddle different trends, oscillate between them, and build different kinds of tactical and strategic alliances across trends. However, if history is any guide, effective counter-movements come about through powerful, broad-based alliances. The progressive trend is pivotal in this regard. If progressives ally with reformists (progressive neoliberalism), as they have for the last twenty years, then the food movement is split, and there is little chance of pushing through substantive reforms. But what if progressives ally with the radicals? Would the food movement not be made stronger?

Because we happen to be in a thirty-year period of privatization and deregulation, neoliberalism is much more powerful worldwide than the reformist, progressive, or radical trends. Neoliberal policies are currently supported by all mainstream political parties around the world, regardless of their social agendas or political persuasions. In the United States, both Republicans and Democrats champion neoliberalism. There has been notable nativist, or neo-"populist," opposition to some parts of the neoliberal agenda, especially regarding immigration and the international agreements like the European Union, the Transatlantic Trade and Investment Partnership (TTIP), and the Trans-Pacific Partnership (TPP). The Brexit vote in Great Britain and Donald Trump's presidential election in the United States are both a reflection of backlash against neoliberalism. Indeed, among Trump's first executive actions was to remove the United States from the TPP and announce a shift toward bilateral, rather than multilateral, trade agreements. These events, as important as they may be, do not threaten corporate power over the long term.

How will this affect the food system? In the first instance, through labor. Though operationally unworkable, Trump's calls to deport 11 million undocumented immigrants and build an impenetrable wall between Mexico and the United States reflect a move to both lower the value of labor and secure a stable—foreign—workforce. Despite xenophobic claims that "immigrants are taking our jobs," the fact is undocumented immigration into the United States is at a historical low. In part, this is because of improvements in the Mexican and Central American economies. In part, it is because increased border enforcement has prevented workers from going back and forth across the border—immigrants simply stay in the United States rather than risk a border crossing. The longer they are in the United States, the more likely they are to move out of low-end agricultural work and into better-paid sectors, like construction. Both Republicans and

Democrats propose guest-worker programs that tightly control the flow of workers and the wages paid to labor. These programs also control dissent. If participating workers try to organize or otherwise stand up for their rights, their contracts are cancelled and they are shipped home.

In summary, neoliberalism will continue managing the food system as an unregulated corporate enterprise; right-wing nationalists seek to limit immigration; reformism will include some safety nets; progressive approaches seek incremental changes to the system; and radical demands seek structural change. In this scenario, the progressive trend is pivotal for the construction of a powerful counter-movement to transform the food system. If progressives align with reformist and neoliberal projects, the counter-movement (of progressives and radicals) will split, weakening the transformative impact of the food movement. If they align with radicals, the counter-movement can be strengthened to force substantive reforms from the corporate food regime.[4]

The Challenges Facing the Counter-Movement

Historically, liberalization proceeds by privatizing and deregulating capital, by concentrating massive amounts of wealth in fewer and fewer hands, and continually building capacity to produce as if there were no limits to consumption. A crisis of accumulation then results, bringing a financial crash and a depression or recession, as in 1929 and 2008. Reforms that restrict speculation and capital accumulation, control overproduction, and protect producers, workers, and national industries are introduced for economic recovery. However, both the nature and the success of reform depends on the strength of the counter-movement and its ability to create political will among politicians. Although the 1929 stock market crash and the Great Depression ushered in the many important reforms of the New Deal in the United States, the 2008 financial crash ended up bailing out the banks rather than homeowners, and ultimately reinforced neoliberal economic politics. Why weren't reforms introduced?

The simple answer is that the counter-movement was simply not strong enough to create the political will for reforms. Remember, during the Great Depression, the streets were full of millions of unemployed workers demanding food and jobs. The Communist Party and the Congress of Industrial Organizations (CIO) brought together thousands of loggers, farmworkers, miners, shipbuilders, autoworkers, steelworkers, and others, in every sector of the economy, who engaged in massive strikes and direct action.[5] Unions and progressive political parties were able to channel dissent into powerful political platforms—platforms that were a serious threat to the government and to capitalism itself. Given the very real possibility of political collapse—and the strong appeal of communism and socialism to working men and women—reforms were introduced that lasted for nearly half a century. (That wasn't the case in 2008, though ironically many of the reforms introduced in the 1930s, like Social Security and unemployment insurance, were instrumental in mitigating the degree of livelihood disruption and political dissent in 2008.)

But after the Second World War, New Deal reforms were followed by an attack on the very social movements that had demanded these reforms. In 1947, the U.S. Congress passed the Taft-Hartley Act, restricting the right to strike and boycott, and purging union leadership of communists.[6] This set off a "Red Scare" that continued into the 1950s.[7] Championed by Wisconsin senator Joseph McCarthy, politicians took aim at alleged communists in government and the armed forces. The House Un-American Activities Committee (HUAC) turned on the film industry, "blacklisting" writers, actors, and entertainers, sending them to jail when they refused to testify. Many left the country or went underground when they could no longer find work. The Red Scare ruined the careers and lives of many prominent American citizens—like Charlie Chaplin, Dalton Trumbo, and Paul Robeson. It also helped catapult right-wing politicians—like Richard Nixon and Ronald Reagan—into political power.[8]

Capital's ability to use the raw power of the state to destroy its opposition, even in a liberal democracy, and its sustained attacks on labor and progressive politics, not only steadily undermined the gains to farmers and labor under the New Deal,[9] it purged criticism of capitalism from mainstream U.S. society, creating the illusion of class harmony. Today, even talking about class, injustice, or the staggering inequalities of capitalism is denounced by right-wing pundits as fomenting "class warfare." One of the richest men in the world, Berkshire Hathaway's CEO Warren Buffet, agreed, sort of, when he said, "There's class warfare, all right . . . but it's my class, the rich class, that's making war, and we're winning."[10]

The pushback by capitalists against the power of labor and against regulations that inhibit their ability to function as they wish; the force used to destroy the left and trade unions; the attacks on civil rights, human rights, liberation movements, and even environmentalists have all served to intimidate and erode political opposition to capital. The results have been the decline of unions and the left, and the spectacular growth of inequality of income and wealth. According to a 2017 Oxfam report, eight people—you could fit them in a van—control more wealth than the bottom half of the global population, some 3.6 billion people.[11] The weak political opposition to neoliberalism follows on a half-century of systematic attacks against any and all organizations that questioned capitalism. The hegemony of neoliberal ideology, even within some sectors of the food movement, has been secured by well-funded right-wing think tanks, which have been able to shift the national dialogue in favor of the privatization of everything. Things once unthinkable, like doing away with public schools, are now a real possibility.

The counter-movement and the threats to capitalism are very different today than they were in the 1930s. Rather than being defined and led by labor and left political parties, the counter-movement is made up of a diverse range of interests representing indigenous communities, environmentalists, feminists, peasants and family farmers, food workers, farmworkers, people of color, immigrants, and young people. Although food worker and farmworker organizations fight for the majority of people working in the food system, the strategic voice of labor is relatively quiet within the food movement. Political parties are absent, or weakly involved. The biggest threat to capitalism is no longer communism but climate change. Globally, the possibility of widespread un-governability resulting from a deadly combination of poverty, hunger, climate disasters, and mass migrations is growing daily. Our capitalist food system doesn't just need to be reformed, it must be transformed. And it is not only the food system, but the entire way that production is carried out. We need a new system in which the people doing the producing make the critical decisions in ways that environmental and social considerations can be put at the top of the agenda. The purpose of production must change from growing commodities to sell in markets to using ecologically sound regenerative practices to produce healthy food to feed people.

Philanthropy, Depoliticization, and Fragmentation

All the ingredients are present to build a strong counter-movement capable of advancing reforms—economic crisis, social discontent, systemic threats—yet few substantive reforms are forthcoming. On the contrary, extreme, right-wing "populism" (read: neo-fascism) is challenging neoliberalism. What needs to happen to catalyze the counter-movement? What is holding it back?

The highly diverse agendas of today's social movements make it challenging to unify forces, particularly when progressive neoliberalism has ideologically coopted many organizations into political agendas that work against their economic interests. This has been possible because of the *depoliticization* of social movements following the decline of radical unions and political parties. This does not necessarily mean that today's social movements do not vote or lobby for their respective causes. Depoliticization is the cultural process by which structural issues—like capitalism—are taken off the social change agenda. There is no discussion of who should make economic decisions, what should be the purpose of production, or how we should meet human needs. With progressive neoliberalism, social movements are seduced into accepting the status quo of capitalism in exchange for the advancement of their respective social issues.

As neoliberalism privatizes public institutions and social services, as it deregulates and prioritizes the interests of capital, it steadily reduces the public sphere, the social arena where, ideally, people can debate issues, take political action, and hold their governments accountable to public opinion. Under neoliberalism, all important decisions are turned over to the "magic of the marketplace." While this sounds like a free and unbiased way of allocating resources and making decisions, what it means in practice is that whoever has the most market power (transnational corporations, the wealthy elite, and their political allies) gets to decide how society will address the issues of food, energy, housing, employment, education, and the environment. The use of force is always lurking in the background, ready to be deployed should anyone refuse to go along with the market's "magic." As public institutions and public goods have either disappeared or been privatized, the public sphere itself has crumbled.

While wealth has steadily concentrated at the top, the role of government in providing for the social welfare has diminished and the political influence of big philanthropy has grown enormously. Starting with the Carnegie, Ford, and Rockefeller Foundations in the early 1900s, philanthropy has grown to over 200,000 foundations, worldwide, with 86,000 registered in the United States.[12] Once occupied with building libraries, supporting the fine arts, and providing emergency assistance, big philanthropy (organizations with $4 billion to $40 billion in assets) now figures prominently in global development financing. Its sheer size is instrumental in determining the social agenda of development, which is the promotion of liberal markets.

Smaller family foundations are active in the arena of social services and social justice, where over the last twenty years they have created thousands of community-based organizations (CBOs) and transnational non-governmental organizations (NGOs). Even though there is more foundation money than ever before, philanthropic foundations have created so many community organizations that they can only afford to dole out limited tranches of short-term project money, rather than multi-year core funding. This makes it very difficult for community organizations committed to social justice to actually work for social change. Instead they work to provide services, build self-esteem, or assert "rights" within the existing political structures of capitalism. All of these are necessary activities and important to all who are exploited, oppressed, and marginalized. However, these organizations rarely have the resources to address the structural *causes* of the lack of services or injustice, and often place the responsibility for solving social problems on individuals rather than the structures of oppression.

Most CBOs and NGOs tend to rely on only one or two major sources of grant funding. The loss of a major funder can mean the end of the organization. Because they decide which kinds of projects and organizations get funded, the charitable sector also ends up setting the overall political agenda of the nonprofit sector. Despite an emphasis on "justice," "empowerment," "partnerships," and "stakeholders," these arrangements pit local organizations against one another as they compete for the scraps of capitalism's enormous wealth, offered charitably (though not without conditions) by the foundations.

The net effect is to divide social movements into the "grassroots"—the communities needing services—and the "grass shoots," the NGOs who provide them. The economic survival of NGOs depends on anticipating the latest trends in charitable project funding and convincing funders they can implement these projects efficiently. This makes NGOs institutionally accountable to funders. Politically and socially, of course, NGOs are accountable to the communities they serve. These two forms of accountability are politically very different and require NGOs to develop distinct agreements, strategies, and competencies to serve both funders and constituents. This difficult balance of accountability provides funders with tremendous political influence over the relationships between CBOs/NGOs and their constituent communities. Many small and midsized foundations are genuinely progressive and make a strong effort to maintain dialogue with the organizations they fund. However, other than refusing to take their money, there is no way for NGOs or communities to hold funders accountable for what, who, or how they choose to fund. The reproduction of capitalist structural relations within civil society—along with the ideological confusion introduced by progressive neoliberalism—makes it difficult to build real grassroots political power, despite everyone's good intentions. This would not be such a big problem if organizations in the counter-movement were not so dependent on the charitable sector for their institutional existence. Stronger unions and stronger political parties, and stronger social movements (like Black Lives Matter) could provide a larger framework for social and institutional accountability, and help to create a better balance of power among the different actors in the counter-movement.

Just like the rest of the world's social movements, the food movement is subject to ideological confusion. The historical divisions of racism, classism, and sexism have been exacerbated with the neoliberal shrinking of the state and the erosion of the public sphere. Not only have the social functions of government been gutted; the social networks within communities have been weakened, increasing the violence, intensifying racial tensions, and deepening cultural divides. People are challenged to confront the problems of hunger, violence, poverty, and climate change in an environment in which society has been restructured to serve global markets rather than local communities.[13]

To break this political impasse, the challenge for the food movement is how to repoliticize its organizations while finding ways to converge in all of its diversity. But how? The critical reconstruction of the public sphere may be a good place to start. Since reactionary and socially conservative neoliberalism has long celebrated the state's withdrawal from health, education, and welfare, right-wing funders see no need to provide safety nets to the poor, to women, immigrants, or minorities whose lives are devastated by privatization and liberal markets. They have channeled their funding directly to reactionary social movements and to the right-wing think tanks, which have been very successful in ideologically empowering conservative and reactionary pressure groups. Unfortunately, most progressive foundations exhaust their budgets funding community organizations to provide social services, so there is very little money left over to fund progressive think tanks. This has the effect of pulling politics and ideologies strongly to the right, and of depoliticizing the language of progressive social change. However, perhaps the time is ripe, as the horror of the Trump administration's program begins to sink it, to build an alternative vision of the public sphere.

Building the Critical Public Sphere, Repoliticization, and Convergence in Diversity

The public sphere was first conceived as a "sphere of public authority" in which people came together freely to discuss social issues, develop public opinion, and take political action to pressure national governments.[14] But it was, and still is, much more than that. Nancy Fraser writes:

> The concept of the public sphere was developed not simply to understand communication flows but to contribute a normative political theory of democracy. In that theory, a public sphere is conceived as a space for the communicative generation of public opinion. Insofar as the process is inclusive and fair, publicity is supposed to discredit views that cannot withstand critical scrutiny and to assure the legitimacy of those that do. Thus, it matters who participates and on what terms. In addition, a public sphere is conceived as a vehicle for marshaling public opinion as a political force. Mobilizing the considered sense of civil society, publicity is supposed to hold officials accountable and to assure that the actions of the state express the will of the citizenry. Thus, a public sphere should correlate with a sovereign power. Together, these two ideas—the *normative legitimacy* and *political efficacy* of public opinion—are essential to the concept of the public sphere in democratic theory.[15]

But just what was the "normative legitimacy" and "political efficacy" of this public sphere?

In the early nineteenth century, the public sphere was generally a white, masculine space, dominated by businessmen and property owners who sought to influence national governments to favor their own business interests. People active in the public sphere were citizens of the same country who spoke the same language, read the same newspapers, and utilized their social networks to advance similar class interests. These people determined what political behavior was acceptable in a democratic society. They conferred normative legitimacy on the government. They had the ear of parliaments and congress, and were politically effective at "governing the governors."[16]

The rise of labor unions, populism (in the normal sense of this word, which signifies movements leaning to the left), women's suffrage, abolition movements, and radical political parties gave rise to feminist, proletarian, and agrarian public spheres. Workers met in clubs, eateries, and union halls; farmers met in Grange halls and coffee shops; farmworkers met under trees in the fields. These labor-oriented public spheres not only helped immigrants and people of different national backgrounds influence labor conditions, they influenced social life in general, from community associations and local government to workers' and farmers' cooperatives and national political parties. Their normative legitimacy came from strikes, boycotts, labor solidarity, and their ability to articulate workers' desires for labor justice and farmers' desire for parity. They had a critical analysis of capital and worked to counter elite ideology with working-class norms and rights. By dint of their ability to collectively withhold their labor and their products from capital—essentially shutting down the market—they were also politically effective at "gaining the ear" of industry and government, forcing reformists to institute substantive labor and agrarian reforms.

Today, new technical forms of communication, like television and the internet, have replaced newspapers and meeting halls, removing the direct human contact of the past. Globalization has transnationalized both capital and labor, making national governments less responsive to public demands. Nationalities, languages, customs, and cultures in most countries today are fluid, and highly diverse. In the face of a declining national public sphere, *transnational* public spheres have emerged. Like before, these are dominated by elites on the one hand and rapidly growing popular sectors on the other.

Corporate and philanthropic elites meet yearly in Davos, Switzerland, at the World Economic Forum, the world's most exclusive "public sphere." Here Gates, Rockefeller, Exxon, Walmart, Monsanto, and other philanthropic and corporate entities come together with multilateral institutions like the IMF and the World Bank to discuss the future of capitalism.

But social movements also have their own public spheres that are increasingly crossing borders, languages, cultures, and classes. The World Social Forum (WSF) was started in 2001 in opposition to the World Economic Forum. The WSF has met fifteen times, preceded by dozens of national social forums each year. Hundreds of thousands of people attend from around the world. The international peasant federation, La Vía Campesina and its 200 million members, hold national, regional, and global gatherings to advance the cause of food sovereignty.

Consciously or not, in many ways the U.S. food movement, with its hands-on, participatory projects for a fair, sustainable, healthy food system, is rebuilding our public sphere from the ground up. Even though it is impossible to replace the social functions of the state, the *ways* in which NGOs and CBOs attempt to provide the "services of survival" can and do make a political difference. But do they go far enough? Do the projects for community gardens also result in politically organized community groups that pressure city councils for redistributive forms of regulation? Do farmer-to-farmer workshops train and link community leaders from underserved communities to demand rights to agricultural extension services, water, and land? Do food policy councils also provide social platforms to address labor rights, racism, and sexism in the food system? Does the revival of the Grange among young and aspiring farmers across the United States also address the need for agrarian reform? Are fair food and workers' rights groups linking their work with immigrant rights? While the task of transforming capitalism may seem too daunting to consider, if we first train our sights on building the *critical* public sphere through the institutions and projects that already exist within civil society, we will have taken back essential political territory from which to build political power.

The challenge of building a public sphere for the twenty-first century is not to re-create the past, but to build a new, transnational public sphere that has a critical analysis of capitalism, builds social legitimacy for movements for food justice and food sovereignty, and connects them with the broad environmental and social justice movements. It is not enough to build an apolitical public space in our food system. Creating alternative markets is not the same as shutting down capitalist markets. Both actions are needed for regime transformation. We need a movement that is able to forge a militantly democratic food system in favor of the poor and oppressed globally and locally, and that effectively rolls back the elite, neoliberal food regime. In a critical transnational public sphere we not only need to ask who owns what, does what, gets what, and what do they do with it. We also need to ask, who will transform the food regime, how will it be transformed, and in whose interests, and to what purpose?

But as many organizations have discovered, because of the tremendous diversity of and within our social movements, we can't build a critical public sphere without addressing the issues that divide us. The food movement itself is not immune to the structural injustices that it seeks to overcome. Because of the pervasiveness of white privilege and internalized oppression in our society, racism, classism, and sexism in the food system does resurface within the food movement itself, despite good intentions. It does no good to push the issues aside because this undermines the trust we need to be able to work together. Understanding why, where, and how oppression manifests itself in the food system, recognizing it within our food movement and our organizations (and within ourselves), is not extra work for transforming our food system. It *is* the work.

Changing Everything

Karl Marx wrote that people "make their own history, but they do not make it as they please; they do not make it under self-selected circumstances, but under circumstances existing already, given and transmitted from the past."[17]

A decade prior to the writing of this book, Michael Pollan's *The Omnivore's Dilemma* pushed food to the forefront of the public consciousness, ushering in a generation of "foodies" deliciously obsessed with books, television, documentaries, conferences, and festivals about food. Today more people than ever are fluent on the topics of how food is grown, prepared, consumed, wasted, and how it impacts our health and the environment.

In an era of unprecedented economic inequality, dim millennial futures, and deep political disillusionment, food has also become a surrogate for hope—and freedom. The alienation of people from the products of their labor under capitalism does not stop at the paycheck. Alienation is a part of capitalist culture and all aspects of the value chain from production to consumption, alienating human beings from nature, from community, and from themselves. No wonder so many people try to reconnect to themselves, and with others, through food.

This is understandable and maybe even desirable, but at meal's end, our food isn't allocated by choice, desire, values, or even by need, but through market demand and through active creation of the demand for highly processed junk food. *Capitalism* is the silent ingredient in our food. It means that the 50 million people living in poverty in the richest country on earth—many of whom grow, harvest, process and serve our food—can't afford to be foodies because they're too busy worrying where their next meal is coming from. It means that contrary to the hopeful statistics presented by our governments and the FAO, over a third of the world is going hungry.[18] It is also the food manufacturers' quest for profits that pushes people to consume unhealthy junk foods high in sugar, salt, fat, artificial flavors, and other additives. If we care about people as much as we do about food, and if we really want to change the food system, we'd better become fluent in capitalism.

Political fluency has been the focus of this book. Much like an intensive language course, I have introduced basic political-economic concepts to explain structural and historical aspects of our food system in order for readers to link things like slavery and patriarchy to super-exploitation, the high price of organic food to socially necessary labor time, and land grabs to differential land rent and to investment funds looking for ways to diversify. The point of political fluency is to understand, communicate, engage, and change the world for the better.

For much of the food movement, this doesn't necessarily mean dropping what they are doing, but assuming the politics of what they are doing. The progressive foodies, good food and food justice activists concentrating on the urban gardens, fair trade, farm-to-school, workers' rights, and farmers' markets need to keep working to change the *practices* of our food system. The radical food sovereignty organizations calling for an end to seed, chemical, and food monopolies and agrarian reform need to continue their political work to change the *structures* of our food system. When the work of progressives and radicals comes together, the food movement will be a strong enough counter-movement to force deep transformative reforms upon the food regime. For this convergence, progressives and radicals need to build strong strategic alliances within the food movement and between the food movement and the multitude of groups in the environmental and social justice movements. What do these alliances look like? Where can they be built? And what exactly is a strategic alliance?

Strategic alliances are those in which people and organizations agree to a position or actions that share a basic political platform. For example, La Vía Campesina (LVC) and the World March of Women (WMW) established a strategic alliance when WMW assumed food sovereignty as a plank in the platform for women's liberation, and LVC committed to an end to all violence against women as a necessary condition for food sovereignty. The convergence of two of the most powerful social movements in the world has far-reaching political ramifications, particularly for women, who grow most of the world's food.

Tactical alliances are also important, but they converge around actions rather than positions, for example, a shared project or campaign. People and organizations can work together, but don't necessarily change their political position by doing so. This caveat is needed because many organizations in the food movement depend on grants from philanthropic foundations. This may begin as a tactical alliance in which the organization implements food security projects to better engage with the community and build community power to address the causes of food insecurity. Over time, however, the need for constant grant funding can draw the organization away from the radical work of deep social change toward a more reformist, service-oriented position. The tactical has defined the strategic.

Both strategic and tactical alliances are needed to build a strong social movement. The trick is to understand the difference and to make sure strong strategic alliances are not compromised by tactical demands. This also does not mean that food justice and food sovereignty organizations cannot build strategic alliances with funders. They can and do. There are many progressive family foundations and even consortia of progressive funders who support fairly radical organizations on the ground. The danger is when the strength of an organization comes from its funders rather than its constituency or its membership. Without a strong constituency, it is impossible to effectively advance a political position.

The greater political challenge for the food movement is how to build strategic and tactical alliances *outside* the food movement, with labor, women, movements led by indigenous peoples, people of color, environmentalists, progressive and radical political parties, anti-growth movements, and popular social movements for radical democracy, alternative economics, and others within the progressive-radical trends of the world's growing counter-movements. The need for cross-sector alliance responds to the centrality of food to society and to capitalism. We won't be able to change the food system without transforming our economic system. This means that to change the food system, we have to change everything. That's a big order. But if we build strategic alliances, we'll have plenty of help.

Never Waste a Crisis

Antonio Gramsci wrote: "The old world is dying and the new world struggles to be born: now is the time of monsters."[19] Today, neoliberalism, capitalism, and liberal democracy are in crisis. In the absence of strong radical unions and progressive political parties, and when most social organizations are funded *not* to be political, neoliberal capitalism proceeds unchecked, wreaking havoc on society, the economy, the environment, and the culture of politics itself. Around the world, right-wing, neo-fascist demagogues like U.S. president Donald Trump are leaping into the vacuum of political leadership, channeling the widespread frustration with mainstream politicians into a toxic ideology that ostensibly denounces business as usual, but targets and scapegoats Muslims, immigrants, people of color, feminists, and "liberal elites." Although U.S. presidential cabinets have typically been a revolving door between business and government, with a net worth larger than a third of all Americans combined, the present Trump cabinet indicates that far from abandoning neoliberalism, Donald Trump is *privatizing* the presidency by putting the country under direct billionaire management.

The United States was founded by colonial elites who, at first, ran the new republic themselves. With time, they turned management over to professional politicians. True, most of the U.S. presidents have been multimillionaires, or became rich after leaving office. But a crony cabinet of billionaires with little to no understanding of, or respect for, the mechanisms of liberal democracy reflects a breakdown in the model that has managed capitalism for the past two hundred years. The billionaire capture of the White House is less a reflection of elite power than of a crisis *within* elite power. Trump represents a break in the political ranks of the rich, not their consolidation. We can expect him and his cabinet to maintain the general mantle of neoliberalism while seeking competitive advantages for themselves. What will be much more difficult for the Trump administration is to manage the tension between democracy and keeping the masses quiet while corporate elites plunder the economy. We can also expect a lot of anger, nativism, bigotry, and scapegoating as "crony neoliberalism" pushes our health, housing, labor, energy, environment—and our food system—over the edge.

But by calling for an end to free trade agreements, aren't the new so-called "populists" against neoliberalism? What is important to understand about neoliberalism is that it is not just a collection of activities for privatization, deregulation, regressive taxation, and financialization on a global scale. Neoliberalism is a *class* project, designed to undermine the power of labor and to consolidate the power of elites.[20] As free trade agreements cease to be useful to this project, they will be happily abandoned, as will other agreements and proposals.

Much like the 1930s, liberal democracy is finding it difficult to resolve the contradiction between the voracious corporate appetites of the 1 percent and the erosion of the social and environmental conditions for the functioning of capitalism. At that time, the United States ushered in the New Deal; Germany and Italy ushered in fascism. The world is facing similar choices today.

The food movement cannot escape the political crisis of capitalism. Nor should it try. A political crisis is a moment of tremendous social convergence and deep politicization of society. A crisis is precisely what the food movement needs in order to mobilize the tremendous power of the food system. At the time of this writing, hundreds of thousands of people across the United States and around the world have taken to the streets to protest the monstrous moves on the part of the Trump administration to scapegoat Muslims and people of color, dismantle due process, and consolidate power in the hands of a small cabal of family members, "alt-right" zealots, and billionaire cronies.

Can the food movement reverse capitalism's ugly turn? Yes, but not alone. The food movement is well positioned, however, to help build the broad-based political alliance we will need to resist the fascist trends gaining power within capitalism. The construction of alternative food systems already begun at the local level brings together a wide array of farmers, communities, churches, social workers, educators, small entrepreneurs, restauranteurs, food and farm workers, and local politicians. These relationships are part of a new public sphere that is now challenged to change the system in which we produce and consume our food. The food movement must continue to do the practical, everyday work to build a new food system. But for these alternatives to have a chance, we must also build a different food regime by changing the rules and the institutions that govern our food. This means we also need to invest in our political education: studying, analyzing, and discussing the political-economic challenges and contradictions of our food systems within the larger context of capitalism and its devastating crises.

We cannot choose the circumstances for advancing social change, only adapt our work to present conditions. For the food movement, this means using the moment of crisis to build a powerful movement for transformation, one that is capable of mobilizing resistance and inspiring change. This in turn means constructing fierce alliances with and supporting the leadership of women, people of color, immigrants, and others who are not only central to our food system, but who have suffered the most under neoliberalism and are now bearing the brunt of the attack on civil liberties.

We don't know what the outcome will be of such a struggle, but do know the outcome if we don't struggle. It's time to organize and take action to transform the food system. There never was a better time.

Postscript: The Secret Ingredient to Change the World

When I was a young agronomist working with peasant farmers in the Campesino a Campesino (farmer to farmer) movement in Mesoamerica, I got to know a lot of fine, hardworking men and women who lived in grinding poverty and farmed on steep, eroded hillsides. They were systematically subjected to oppression, economic exploitation, and social derision by landowners, traders, agricultural technicians, and government officials. These people had advised me that the peasants were fatalistic, superstitious, and permanently numbed by a life of tradition and drudgery. I quickly discovered these impressions were an excuse to justify the status quo. Peasants lived a very hard life that nonetheless had wonderful moments of simple and spontaneous joy. Campesino a Campesino was a peasant-led movement for sustainable agriculture. They used small-scale experimentation to develop agroecological farming methods that conserved soil and water, restored fertility, reforested their hillsides, and improved their livelihoods. They shared their innovations with others during farm visits and hands-on workshops. They had triumphs (and plenty of failures), but always seemed convinced that their movement was making their world a better place.

As a rural development worker, I accompanied the movement for years, but knew that their vision of peasant-led sustainable agriculture, and local economies stitched together by mutual aid, would never be accepted by the ministries of agriculture, powerful agribusiness corporations, the large landowners, and the agricultural development agencies that were committed to eradicating the peasantry. I loved the movement, but was not optimistic about its future.

One day in a farmer-to-farmer workshop, the farmer teaching the session on soil and water conservation bent on one knee to clean out a smooth surface on the hard red earth. Then, using the point of his machete, he drew a stick figure. "This is our movement," he said, pointing to the ground. "It walks on two legs: solidarity and innovation. It works with two hands: production and protection." He drew a head on the shoulders, and a mouth, then added two small stones for eyes. "We have eyes to see a future—with us in it—in which our soil is fertile, our land is productive, our rivers clean and our children healthy. We have a mouth. We can speak for peasant justice and for an agriculture that sustains us as it does nature." Then, using his long, slender index finger, he carefully drew a heart in the figure's chest. "*Compañeros*," he said, "farming is hard! To change the way we farm is even harder. To convince others is harder still. But if you want to be in this movement you must work harder than you have ever worked in your life!"

I sighed inwardly. These subsistence farmers already worked harder than anyone I had ever known. Telling them they had to work harder didn't seem like a good recruiting strategy for the Campesino a Campesino movement.

But then the farmer pointed to the heart drawn in the earth. "You can't do this work if you don't love," he said. "You must love the land, love agriculture, love your family, love your village, and love peasant people. You must love your God! If you don't love, you will never last, it's just too hard. We must *love* to change the world!"

The group nodded in agreement and a lively discussion ensued about love, hope, and peasant agriculture. I sat silently, a little overcome as I listened to a group of poor, illiterate farmers on a desolate hillside deep within the Mesoamerican countryside chat enthusiastically about changing the world.

Nearly thirty years later, I still ponder the meaning of that moment. It led to the most strategic decision of my life—one that has helped me overcome the pessimism that too much analyzing can bring. I allied myself with those for whom giving up hope was not an option.

There are two lessons in this book that I hope stick with you. One is that to change our food system we need to understand capitalism. I've spilled a lot of ink trying to convince you of that. The other, which you'll have to take on faith, is that love alone won't transform our food system, but without it we'll never change the world.

Glossary

Agrarian: Relating to the cultivation of land, land tenure, and the division and distribution of land, labor, capital, and resources in the countryside.

Agrarianism: A philosophy promoting agrarian reform and rural life as the foundation of society.

Agrarian reform: Policies and government intervention that promote land and resource redistribution to increase land ownership by peasant farmers and small-scale producers. A common example is Brazil's Land Statute of 1988, which states that if land is not being used for its "social function" then it can be redistributed to others who will fulfill this duty. The Landless Rural Workers Movement (MST) takes advantage of this statute to take back land for rural peasants and unemployed urban dwellers.

Agrarian transition: The transitioning from peasant/subsistence agriculture to capitalist/industrial agriculture through market pressures, government interventions, and/or violent displacement. This process began in the seventeenth century and continues.

Agrarian question: Addresses how to bring the peasantry's agricultural and labor surplus out of the peasant sector and into the industrial sector (including industrial agriculture) in a way that eventually moves the peasantry out of agriculture; also addresses the issue of how to mobilize the peasantry in a class war against the aristocracy and/or bourgeoisie.

Agroecology: The science, practice, and social movement for sustainable agricultural systems; the application of ecological concepts and principles to the design, development, and management of farming systems, landscapes, and food systems.

Appropriationism: The process by which capital appropriates the labor process on the upstream (production) side of agriculture by replacing agroecological management practices (for example, the use of green manures, cover crops, animal-based fertilization, biological and biodiverse forms of pest control, and farm-grown seed stock) with synthetic fertilizers, pesticides, and genetically engineered seeds.

Arbitrage: The purchase of a good or asset (land, commodities, financial instruments, etc.) for sale at a higher price without adding any other value to the good.

Biofortification: The addition of nutrients to crops by inserting genes into the crop genome to improve nutritional content. Golden Rice is an example of biofortification. This orange-colored rice contains beta-carotene that can be transformed into vitamin A when consumed. The beta-carotene content of Golden Rice is achieved by inserting genes from a soil bacteria and maize into the rice genome.

Biofuels: Fuels derived from plant material. Crops that can be processed for fuel (rather than food or feed) include maize and sugarcane that can be turned into ethanol.

Biological speed-up: The selective breeding, genetic engineering, and use of antibiotics and growth hormones to speed up the growing period of animals, increase their size, and increase their productivity of meat and milk. Breeding and genetic engineering can also be used to the same purpose with plants.

Bracero Program: Also known as the Mexican Farm Labor Program Agreement of 1942, this U.S. government program brought millions of Mexican guest workers to the United States to work as agricultural laborers during the Second World War's labor shortage. Though workers were provided rights and safeguards in their contracts, these were often violated and *braceros* were often overworked, underpaid, and abused. Guest worker programs being proposed today are modeled on the Bracero Program.

British Poor Laws: Also known as English Poor Laws, these originated in the mid-1300s in England and Wales during a prolonged labor shortage following the Black Death. Decrees were issued to keep food and labor prices down and force serfs and vassals to work. Poor Laws in the 1400s and 1500s legitimized whipping of the able-bodied unemployed and placing them in stocks as punishment. Vagabonds were forced to return to their place of birth to work. The disabled were cared for by their parish, and parishioners were bound by law to contribute to their food, clothing, and shelter. Later, workhouses and indentured servitude became the fate of the poor and unemployed.

Capital accumulation: The process of acquiring assets that can be used to acquire more wealth.

Capital logic: The economic and political logic that obeys the tendency of capital to invest, expand, expropriate, and accumulate wealth. The tendency of the rate of profit to fall and the tendency toward monopoly follow a capitalist logic.

Capitalist differentiation: In agriculture, differentiation leads to the formation of stratified classes of farmers and agricultural workers. As capitalist investment in agriculture takes place, it tends to favor larger farmers who already have some wealth. These farmers have an advantage in acquiring credit, new technologies, and access to markets, and become wealthier and bigger over time. Poorer farmers are not able to invest in this way and tend to fall behind economically. This tendency results in smaller farmers being driven to become farm laborers on larger farms and poor farmers becoming landless workers. A poor working class, a middle worker-owner class, and a rich owning class develop as capital penetrates further and further into agriculture.

Carbon markets: Develop when permits are traded that allow a certain amount of carbon emissions, hence the term "emissions trading." Permit trading is combined with an obligatory cap on the amount of allowable emissions. When a company exceeds the cap, it can continue to pollute by purchasing emission permits from another entity that has not exceeded the cap on carbon emissions.

Climate-smart agriculture (CSA): A set of guiding principles and management practices that mitigate the effects of climate change and increase agriculture's resilience to climate-related hazards, such as drought or flooding. The three main objectives of climate-smart agriculture are to reduce carbon emissions, increase agricultural productivity, and strengthen agricultural resilience.

Commodity: A good that can be specifically produced to be bought and sold on the market for profit. During the agrarian transition, agricultural goods shifted from being produced for subsistence or barter to being produced for the main purpose of selling on the market. In the late nineteenth century, there was a drastic global increase in commodity production as European empires expanded.

Commons: A resource that is exclusively owned and managed by a specified community in which all members share equal power over the resource. Non-community members can be denied access to a commons. Traditional commons are frequently pastures, forests, and fishing grounds. Things like air, outer space, and the open ocean are not commons but open-access resources.

Common property rights: A form of property ownership in which a plot of land is collectively owned and managed. Before the Enclosures (see below), which initiated the transition from feudalism to capitalism, most peasant land was managed collectively through communal food cultivation and grazing.

Confined Animal Feedlot Operation (CAFO): Large, enclosed areas where hundreds of thousands of animals (cattle, pigs, poultry) are raised on concentrated animal feed. Intensive use of hormones and antibiotics is required to intensify production and manage ever-present diseases. Manure is often channeled into large, open-air lagoons.

Cooperative model: A form of enterprise ownership based on the principle of one person, one vote. Cooperatives can be formed for production, consumption, or delivery of services and ideally follow seven principles: voluntary and open membership; democratic member control; economic participation by members; autonomy and independence; education, training, and information; cooperation among cooperatives; and concern for community.

Conservation easement: A legal agreement between a private landowner and private organization or public entity that limits certain types of uses or prevents further development of the land. An easement does not affect the ownership of the land, only its use. The owner either donates or sells the rights to sell, subdivide, or develop the land. Easements are often used to conserve wetlands, forests, and other landscapes for environmental conservation.

Conservative neoliberalism: A form of economic neoliberalism (support for free markets and the privatization of public goods and services) that usually adheres to conservative social values, for example, anti-abortion, anti-same-sex marriage, etc.

Consultative Group on International Agricultural Research (CGIAR): Founded in 1971, CGIAR, also known as Consortium of International Agricultural Research Centers, is a member organization that directs fifteen centers of international agricultural research around the world. Funded by governments and big philanthropies, it has been the primary institution advancing the Green Revolution.

Contract farming: A modern version of sharecropping and tenant farming, here farmers give exclusive rights to a firm to buy their product using a fixed-term agreement. In a *market-specification contract,* the firm guarantees the producer a buyer, based on agreements regarding price and quality. With a *resource-providing contract* the firm also provides production inputs (such as fertilizer, hatchlings, or technical assistance). If the firm provides all the inputs and buys all of the product, it essentially controls the production process, while the farmer basically provides land and labor.

Corn Laws: English laws instituted in 1815 that placed steep tariffs on imported grain thereby keeping the price of food—something most rural people had previously been able to grow rather than buy—relatively high. The tariffs favored large landholders, and thus were opposed by emerging industrialists who wanted cheap food for workers so that they could keep wages low.

Cost-price squeeze: A situation in which the costs of production increase while the price of the produced goods go down, a chronic condition for most of the world's farmers.

Counter-movement: In Karl Polanyi's analysis, the broad alliance of classes opposing economic liberalization. The food counter-movement is a reaction against the severe deterioration in the social and economic conditions of society as the result of privatization, liberalization of markets, and extreme concentration of wealth.

Cover crop: Planted to enrich and conserve the soil and return nutrients to it that were removed by prior crops. Common cover crops include annual cereals (rye, wheat, barley, oats) and legumes (beans, peas, peanuts, clover).

Cost of reproduction of labor: The human cost of raising a child to productive working age and of maintaining a functioning labor force. This includes all household costs, including the physical and emotional care largely provided by women. It also includes the public and private costs of health, education, and welfare. When a worker migrates, the costs of raising them to working age were already assumed by their country of origin and so are free to the country receiving their labor (and lost to the home country).

Dead zone: Areas in oceans and lakes with extremely low oxygen concentration (hypoxia) due to algal blooms caused by high nitrogen fertilizer runoff. When algae die, they sink and decompose, a process that uses up all the oxygen, suffocating animal life. Dead zones grow and shrink with agricultural seasons. Dead zones are found in the Gulf of Mexico, the Great Lakes, and on the eastern seaboard.

Depoliticization: The process by which social movements, institutions, and individuals fail to address the underlying capitalist structures of violence and injustice.

Desertification: The process in which a landscape loses its plant life and organic matter (trees, bushes, grasses, humus, etc.), rendering it a desert. This process is often induced by unsustainable changes in grazing regimes, water use, and deforestation. Desertification frequently takes place on the edges of existing deserts or in fragile, semi-dry savannas.

***Ejido* system**: In Mexico, commonly held land governed by a democratic assembly and farmed cooperatively or individually is known as an *ejido*. *Ejidos* were formed when estates (*haciendas*) belonging to large landowners were expropriated and distributed to the peasantry after the Mexican Revolution.

Enclosures: In seventeenth-century England, powerful lords began fencing off common lands and claiming private property rights. This began the displacement of peasants, who used the commons for many livelihood needs. The Enclosures marked the beginning of a transition from a feudal to a capitalist mode of production.

***Encomienda* system**: Large land grants from the Spanish Crown, called *encomiendas*, were given to generals and lords in the New World. The recipients gained the right to extract labor and resources from the indigenous inhabitants and in return were expected to send a portion of their wealth to the Spanish Crown.

Entrepreneurial farm: Midsized family farms that primarily produce commodities, and generally rely on family labor.

Environmental resiliency: The capacity of an environment to "bounce back," recover, or return to its original state after a major shock or disturbance.

Fair trade: A form of trade in which a price premium is paid to a producer that has been certified by a fair trade organization. Fair trade is based on the willingness of consumers to pay a higher price for the product (for example, coffee) in order to improve farmer income.

Financialization: Refers to the growing power and influence of the finance sector over the economy, politics, and society. The term reflects a tendency for profits to derive more from extremely complex financial markets than from productive activities. Increasingly, the financial value of something, such as farmland, grows many times higher as a financial asset than as a source of actual production.

Food regime: All of the institutions, treaties, and regulations shaping and governing food on a global scale. Food regimes developed in tandem with capitalism.

Colonial Food Regime: Established in the nineteenth century, this was the first regime to dominate the entire global food system. The flow of food and raw materials was from the colonies of the South to the empires of the North. The regime was instrumental in the transfer of wealth from South to North, which allowed the North to industrialize.

Second Global Food Regime: A neocolonial regime established after the Second World War in which resources continued to flow from South to North, but increasingly, surplus grain from the North flowed to the South, destroying local markets and making Southern urban populations more dependent on food from the North. At the same time, the model of industrial food production was exported from the Global North to the Global South, largely as part of an anti-communist, Cold War development strategy.

Corporate Food Regime: After the fall of communism and the end of the Cold War, economic development programs were largely abandoned in favor of free markets. Structural Adjustment Programs opened the South to Northern capital, globalizing Southern food systems and making Southern populations dependent on global markets for their food. Also known as the Neoliberal Food Regime.

Food sovereignty: The democratization of the food system in favor of the poor, known as food sovereignty, was introduced by La Via Campesina in the 1990s to counter the notion of food security. Whereas food security addresses access to enough food to live a productive life—without addressing *how*, *where*, or *by whom* it is produced—food sovereignty asserts the rights of farmers and peoples to produce their own food and control their own systems of production and consumption.

Functional dualism: A theory proposed by academic researcher Alain de Janvry asserting that as part of a transition to capitalist agriculture (specifically in Latin America), a relationship emerged in which peasant farmers, pushed to ever smaller plots, were forced to work as wage laborers on industrial farms. Because they continued to grow food to feed themselves—and sold extra food cheaply in the market—they were able to work for very low wages and keep the general price of food low. This provided a food and labor "subsidy" to industrial agriculture.

Genome property: If a biological or genetic material is patented by an individual, organization, or corporation it becomes a genome property. This has led to the privatization and commodification of life itself.

GMO (Genetically Modified Organism): An organism in which the DNA has been altered using genetic engineering technology. In agriculture, the most common GMOs are herbicide-resistant maize and soy produced by chemical companies that sell herbicides. New technologies using RNA and DNA "markers" that manipulate the genome without the introduction of foreign DNA are making transgenic GMOs—organisms that receive DNA from unrelated life forms—obsolete.

Great Migrations of 1910–1930 and 1940–1970: The periods when over six million African Americans migrated out of the southern United States to industrial cities in the North to escape racial discrimination and the violent racial oppression of the Jim Crow South in search of economic opportunity. The first wave consisted primarily of farming people from rural areas, and the second wave included many urban migrants.

Green grabbing: Another form of land grabbing, it occurs when so-called environmental agendas legitimize the appropriation of land. The green-grabbing term also encompasses the many ways in which ecosystems are commodified, underlying the idea that economic growth is compatible with environmental sustainability. The appropriation of land for biofuels or for nature reserves are examples.

Green Revolution: An agricultural development campaign initiated by the Ford and Rockefeller Foundations in the 1960s to spread industrial agriculture from the United States to the Global South. The Green Revolution was implemented by the U.S. government, the United Nations, the FAO, and the publicly funded Consultative Group on International Agricultural Research (CGIAR) which established International Centers for Agricultural Research (IARCs) around the world. The IARCs developed high-yielding varieties of cereals that required irrigation, chemical fertilizers, and pesticides. Beginning in Mexico, massive government support spread the Green Revolution successfully to India and Asia where conditions were optimal. It was not successful in Africa where conditions were much more difficult. The Green Revolution became part of a Cold War strategy as a way to build agrarian support against communism.

Greenhouse Gas Emissions (GHG): Gases that absorb solar radiation and trap heat in the atmosphere, causing the greenhouse effect. The major GHGs include carbon dioxide (CO_2), methane (CH_4), nitrous oxide (N_2O), and fluorinated gases (hydrofluorocarbons, perfluorocarbons, sulfur hexafluoride, and nitrogen trifluoride). The three sectors responsible for the most GHG emissions are electricity and heat production, agriculture, and transportation.

Guest worker programs: Supplying agricultural and other industries with cheap, temporary labor from abroad, these programs (like the current H-2A program) make it possible for both the state and corporations to better control migrant laborers. The immigration status of guest workers is often tied to their jobs, meaning they are legally prevented from changing jobs if their wages are too low or the conditions too terrible. In certain industries such programs deliberately drive down wages and working conditions while undermining unions for workers. See **Bracero Program**.

Hedging: A financial investment tactic in which an investor seeks to offset risk by investing in a particular asset. After the financial meltdown in 2007–2008, many investors sought what were perceived to be more stable investment opportunities, such as oil, primary commodities, and land. Land assets are seen as investments that, unlike purely financial assets, will continually appreciate and not devalue with inflation.

Hegemony: Associated with the Italian theorist Antonio Gramsci, the term hegemony describes when certain classes in a society dominate the values, politics, and economic and military structures of that society, leading to control and subordination of all other classes. Hegemony can be exercised by any privileged group to control others; for example, patriarchal hegemony, colonial hegemony, or white hegemony.

Heirloom crop varieties: Heirloom food crops are open-pollinated or standard varieties that, unlike hybrids (a cross between two varieties), "breed true." This means that seeds can be collected and replanted year after year and the plant will continue to express the same characteristics, unlike hybrids that frequently express regressive traits from a parent variety. Heirlooms were originally bred by farmers and gardeners over many generations for their taste, storage, or agronomic properties. In general, heirloom crops were developed by traditional breeding methods before the 1950s.

High farming: A set of intensive farming techniques practiced by larger, wealthier farms in nineteenth-century England that relied on imported guano for fertilization.

Hybrid seeds: A seed produced by cross-pollinating two different varieties and then backcrossing the new plant with one of the parent varieties. Hybrid seeds are generally unstable and will lose "hybrid vigor" after the first year of planting. This leads to purchasing new seeds each year, making farmers dependent on seed companies for their seeds.

Inputs: In agriculture, inputs refers to the seeds, fertilizers, pesticides, herbicides, and irrigation invested in crop production. Inputs can be either synthetic (chemical) or organic; called "external inputs" if produced off-farm (like chemical fertilizers and pesticides), and "on-farm inputs" if produced by the farmer (like seeds or compost).

Input substitution: The substitution of organic inputs (usually fertilizers and pesticides) for chemical inputs. Common on large, industrial, organic farms. This can be an intermediary step toward redesigning the farm agroecologically.

Intercropping: The practice of planting different crops that complement each other in the same bed or row, for example, plants with shallow roots beside plants with a deep tap root. This is done in order to increase yields, mimic natural symbiotic relationships, and return nutrients to the soil.

Jim Crow laws: Laws enacted in previously Confederate states after the Civil War (1880s) that mandated racial segregation in all public spaces including schools, buses, and libraries. Under the guise of states' rights, these laws led to many more discriminatory and cruel practices such as political disenfranchisement and arbitrary incarceration and labor exploitation of African Americans. The last of the Jim Crow laws were struck down by the Supreme Court in the 1960s through the efforts of the civil rights movement.

Land grabs: Viewed as a quick fix to the crisis of capitalist over-accumulation, land grabs are large-scale acquisitions that bring land into global markets. Although finance is seen as the major driving force behind recent land grabs, many different actors, from extractive industries and the real estate sector, to life insurance companies and wealthy individuals, have engaged in this process.

Land reform: The act of changing the pattern of land ownership, usually through distribution of land titles (private or collective) to the landless. Land reform may or may not include the breakup and redistribution of large landholdings, and it may or may not be linked to more sweeping agrarian reforms affecting markets and services.

Land justice: A term for equitable access to land in both urban and rural contexts.

Land sovereignty: The right of working people to occupy and have effective access to, use of, and control over land and its benefits.

Latifundio: A component of the land tenure structure common in Latin America, a *latifundio* is a large agricultural estate (over 500 hectares) farmed for commercial purposes.

Marker-assisted breeding: Also known as marker-assisted selection (MAS), this genetic engineering technique entails selecting for specific genetic traits based on morphological, biochemical, or DNA markers that are linked to the desired plant trait. MAS is much faster than conventional crop breeding.

Market economy: An economic system, also known as a "self-regulating economy," in which goods and services are allocated based on supply and demand, without government intervention.

Mass food: Highly processed, corporate-owned, GMO-laden foods that fill grocery store shelves today are known as mass foods. They are associated with many environmental and social costs, such as diet-related diseases and greenhouse gas emissions.

Means of production: Excluding labor, all the inputs that generate use value (in pre-capitalist and socialist societies) or both use and exchange value (in capitalist societies), such as machines, factories, resources, goods, and services for society. In an agrarian society, the land and the tools used to work the land are the means of production. In an industrial or contemporary society, the means of production are the machines, factories, transportation, offices, stores, etc. The means of production create wealth and provide the material foundation for society, and under capitalism are privately owned.

Mercantilism: A colonial phase in capitalist development that subsidized exports, kept wages low, and prohibited the colonies from industrializing, forcing them to buy the ruling empire's own manufactured products.

Monoculture: The cultivation of one single crop in a field, a common practice of industrial agriculture and characteristic of the Green Revolution. Monocultures require increased use of fertilizers, pesticides, and herbicides to maintain soil fertility and control weeds and pests.

Neoliberalism: An ideology and set of policies implemented over the last thirty years characterized by a transfer of power and assets from the public sector to the private sector. This involves increasing privatization of government-provided goods and services, fiscal austerity, deregulation, free trade, and the reduction of top marginal tax rates. Consequences of neoliberalism include high levels of global inequality and the disappearance of the public sphere from political life.

Non-profit industrial complex (NPIC): A system of relationships among the state/government, capitalist elites, foundations (for example, the Bill and Melinda Gates Foundation), and non-governmental organizations (NGOs). Because these NGOs are dependent on funding from foundations, corporations, or the government, their missions and actions are influenced by those funding them.

Normative legitimacy: The legitimacy conferred on a regime, government, or social movement that allows it to rule (or contest existing rule) based on a set of shared beliefs regarding what is socially desirable, acceptable, or unacceptable.

Nutritionism: An approach and ideology dominating food science that reduces the understanding of healthy food to key nutrients alone, rather than on the food system and well-balanced diets.

Open-access frontier: An area in which resources (land, water, minerals, etc.) do not have clear ownership and/or are in dispute; for example, the air, the oceans, and parts of the Amazon rainforest.

Over-accumulation: A cyclical economic crisis (recession) in which goods and services pile up, unsold because the general population is suffering from underemployment and unemployment.

Parity: The agrarian concept that farmers should be paid a fair price for their product, a price that allows them to have a decent and dignified livelihood. Parity prices paid to farmers rise commensurately with the rising costs of production.

Peasant farms: Small-scale, subsistence-oriented farms that are less entrenched in commodity relations and use on-farm inputs such as green manures, animal traction, and family labor.

Peasantry: A term commonly used to refer to the world's approximately 1.5 billion poor and landless farmers. During the transition from feudalism to capitalism, much of this population was displaced and dispossessed of the land they farmed and became the cheap labor fueling the Industrial Revolution in urban areas. This displacement and dispossession of the peasantry continues today.

Primitive accumulation: Also known as original accumulation or accumulation by dispossession, this refers to the expropriation of land and resources for privatization under a new regime. Imperial conquests of other territories for raw materials and fertile lands are an example.

Progressive neoliberalism: A form of economic neoliberalism (support for free markets and the privatization of public goods and services) that also supports liberal social values such as racial equality, LGBTQ rights, and being pro-choice, or pro-immigrant.

Proletariat: The class of workers in a capitalist society who, lacking ownership of the means of production, must sell their labor in return for wages.

Purchase of Agricultural Conservation Easements (PACE) Program: Also known as the Purchase of Development Rights Program, this program protects agricultural land from development when landowners sell portions of land to public entities (for example, land trusts) that then hold the easement, preventing development. The landowner still holds other ownership rights such as the right to farm the land, transfer, or bequeath it.

Rational agriculture: A form of agriculture that does not overexploit people or the planet. It is the opposite of capitalist "irrational agriculture."

Reactionary populism: A virulent form of right-wing populism that relies on nationalism, xenophobia, scapegoating, and white supremacist discourse to appeal to working and middle classes, a form of neo-fascism.

Reformist: The tendency or positions within governance regimes that promote social projects and reforms but do not challenge the basic political-economic structures of the regime.

Relay cropping: Planting crops in the same field in a staggered sequence so that one is in seedling stage while another is maturing. The objective is to make optimal use of time and space. Many relay crop combinations are also advantageous for pest control and/or fertility management.

Rent-seeking behavior: The practice of profiting without producing wealth, through speculation, arbitrage, or accessing undeserved tax breaks or subsidies. Also known as neo-rentism.

Resources:

Common pool resources, Common property resources (CPR): Held and managed in common, these are different from public goods, because with CPR, access and benefits are exclusive to the specific group rather than the general public.

Open-access resources: These do not fall under a governance regime or private property laws.

Slash-and-burn agriculture: A method used widely for thousands of years in the tropics in which trees are cut down and remaining vegetation is burned, forming a layer of nutrient-rich ash over a formerly forested area. This area is then planted with crops for several years until weeds prevent cultivation. Farmers then shift to a new wooded area and repeat the process, eventually returning to the same areas they had previously farmed after new growth has been established.

Socially necessary labor time: The average amount of labor required to accomplish a task by a worker of average skill, using generally available tools and technologies.

Subsistence crop: A crop grown to be eaten by the farmer and their family and/or community rather than sold on the market for a profit.

Substitutionism: A process whereby farm products are broken down to their basic ingredients (protein, carbohydrates, fats, and oils) and reconstituted into industrial products like soft drinks, processed foods, biodiesel, and cosmetics.

Superexploitation: The non-wage, subsistence-producing labor of women and others such as slaves, colonized subjects, contract workers, and peasants, which make possible wage-labor exploitation.

Surplus mobilization: The transfer of wealth from one sector to another through unequal terms of trade and exchange. For example, in 1914 in the United States, a bushel of corn bought five gallons of gasoline. In 1921 it took two bushels of corn just to buy one gallon of gasoline. The change in the terms of trade mobilized agriculture's wealth out of the countryside and into industry.

Sustainable intensification: A broad term that describes increasing agricultural productivity while lowering the amount of chemical and energy inputs used for production. Sustainable intensification does not contemplate structural changes to agriculture but seeks to fine-tune existing industrial systems.

Tenant farmers: Those who farm and live on rented land and, in turn, have limited rights and temporary access to the land. In some cases, part of the production must be turned over to the landowner.

Territorial restructuring: The restructuring of laws, regulations and infrastructure at a territorial scale in order to access resources and extract wealth.

Trade-Related Aspects of Intellectual Property (TRIPs): An international agreement between all member nations of the World Trade Organization (WTO) that created regulations for national governments to protect various forms of intellectual property (such as genetic information in GMO seeds). It was the first time intellectual property was introduced into the international trade system.

Value:

Exchange value: The value a commodity holds when it is compared to another object on the market, with money being the "universal equivalent" dictating value.

Labor theory of value: A concept explored by Marx, Ricardo, and Smith (in differing ways) that the economic value of a product or service is determined by the amount of labor required to produce it.

Use value: The usefulness of a commodity, meaning the direct value that it serves, such as providing sustenance or shelter, or performing work.

Surplus value: The new value embodied in a commodity that results after the cost of the workers' labor (labor-power) is taken into account. In a commodity market, this surplus value is the profit the capitalist attains after a product or service is sold.

Absolute surplus value: The increase in value that accrues to the capitalist when the amount of labor is increased in the production of a commodity (an increase in hours or number of laborers).

Relative surplus value: The increase in value that accrues to a product when wages paid to workers are reduced for the same amount of work, or when productivity is increased (intensified) without increasing wages.

Notes

Introduction

1. Nancy Fraser, "The End of Progressive Neoliberalism," *Dissent*, January 2, 2017,
2. Henry Bernstein, *Class Dynamics of Agrarian Change* (Halifax: Fernwood, 2010), 22.

1. How Our Capitalist Food System Came to Be

1. Fukuyama, Francis (1989). "The National Interest" (16): 3–18. ISSN 0884-9382. JSTOR 24027184.
2. Adam Smith, *An Inquiry into the Nature and Causes of the Wealth of Nations* (London: W. Strahan; and T. Cadell, 1776).
3. Thomas Malthus, *An Essay on the Principles of Population* (London: Fox J. Johnson, 1798).
4. David Ricardo, *The Principles of Political Economy and Taxation* (London: John Murray, Albemarle Street, 1817).
5. Karl Marx, *Capital: A Critique of Political Economy*, vol. 1, 3 vols. (New York: International Publishers, 1967).
6. Ibid., 1:718.
7. Frederick Engels, *The Condition of the Working Class in England* (Oxford: Oxford University Press, 1993). Engels had initially introduced the reserve army perspective, though in less developed form, in his "Outlines of a Critique of Political Economy" in 1843 (Karl Marx and Frederick Engels, *Collected Works*, vol. 6 [New York: International Publishers, 1975], 438, 443).
8. P. J. Perry, "High Farming in Victorian Britain: Prospect and Retrospect," *Agricultural History* 55 (April 1981): 156–66.

9. Robert L. Heilbroner, *The Worldly Philosophers: The Lives, Times, and Ideas of the Great Economic Thinkers*, 7th ed. (New York: Touchstone, 1999), 38, http://starbooksfeaa.weebly.com/uploads/5/4/8/6/54869709/the_wordly_philosophers.pdf.
10. Ellen Meiksins Wood, "Capitalism's Gravediggers," *Jacobin*, December 5, 2014, https://www.jacobinmag.com/2014/12/capitalisms-gravediggers/.
11. David Harvey, *The New Imperialism* (New York: Oxford University Press, 2003) and in "The 'New' Imperialism: Accumulation by Dispossession," *The Socialist Register*. Vol 40: 64.
12. Sidney Mintz, *Tasting Food, Tasting Freedom: Excursions into Eating, Culture, and the Past* (Boston: Beacon Press, 1996).
13. John Bellamy Foster, "Marx as a Food Theorist," *Monthly Review* 68/7 (December 2016), http://monthlyreview.org/2016/12/01/marx-as-a-food-theorist/.
14. Charles Mann, *1493: Uncovering the New World Columbus Created* (New York: Vintage, 2012).
15. Cecil Woodham-Smith, *The Great Hunger: Ireland 1845–1849* (London: Penguin Books, 1962).
16. Derek Byerlee and Carl Eiker K., *Africa's Emerging Maize Revolution* (Boulder, CO: Lynne Rienner Publishers, 1997).
17. Europeans who tried subsisting only on maize, as they did with barley, potatoes, and wheat, contracted pellagra, a nutrient-deficiency disease. Indigenous communities of the Americas didn't suffer from pellagra because they combined maize with beans and other cultivars and prepared their maize using the process of nixtamalization that uses lime and greatly improves the nutrient content. Arturo Warman, *Corn and Capitalism: How a Botanical Bastard Grew to Global Dominance* (Chapel Hill: University of North Carolina Press, 2003).
18. Ibid.
19. Judith Ann Carney, "From Hands to Tutors: African Expertise in South Carolina Rice Economy," *Agricultural History* 67/3 (1993): 1–30; Judith Ann Carney, *Black Rice: The African Origins of Rice Cultivation in the Americas* (Cambridge and London: Harvard University Press, 2001).
20. Charles Mann, *1493: Uncovering the New World Columbus Created* (New York: Vintage, 2012).
21. Edward E. Baptist, *The Half Has Never Been Told: Slavery and the Making of American Capitalism* (New York: Basic Books 2014).
22. Sven Beckert, "Slavery and Capitalism," *The Chronicle of Higher Education*, December 12, 2014, http://chronicle.com/article/SlaveryCapitalism/150787.
23. Judith Ann Carney, "'With Grains in Her Hair': Rice in Colonial Brazil," *Slavery and Abolition* 25/1 (2004): 1–27.
24. Judith Ann Carney, *Black Rice: The African Origins of Rice Cultivation in the Americas* (Cambridge and London: University of Harvard Press, 2001),76
25. Ibid.
26. Gail Meyers and Owusu Bandele "Roots" in *Land Justice: Re-imagining*

Land, Food and the Commons in the United States, 2016 (Oakland: Food First Books 2016), 25

27. Judith Ann Carney, *Black Rice: The African Origins of Rice Cultivation in the Americas* (Cambridge and London: Harvard University Press, 2001).
28. Meyers and Bandele, 2016.
29. Philip McMichael, "A Food Regime Genealogy," *Journal of Peasant Studies* 36/1 (2009).
30. Karl Kautsky, *The Agrarian Question*, vol. 1 (London: Zwan Publishers, 1988).
31. Alexander Chayanov, *The Theory of Peasant Economy* (Manchester, UK: Manchester University Press, 1966).
32. E. Wolf, *Peasant Wars of the Twentieth Century* (New York: Harper & Row, 1969).
33. T. Shanin, "Peasantry as a Political Factor," *Sociological Review* 14/1 (1966): 5–27.
34. GRAIN, "Hungry for Land: Small Farmers Feed the World with Less than a Quarter of All Farmland" (Barcelona: GRAIN, May 2014), http://www.grain.org/article/entries/4929-hungry-for-land-small-farmers-feed-the-world-with-less-than-a-quarter-of-all-farmland.
35. Janet Poppendiek, *Breadlines Knee-Deep in Wheat: Food Assistance in the Great Depression* (New Brunswick, NJ: Rutgers University Press, 1986).
36. Daniel Cryan, Sharron Shatil, and Piero, *Capitalism: A Graphic Guide* (London: Icon Books, 2009).
37. Poppendiek, *Breadlines Knee-Deep in Wheat.*
38. George Naylor, "Agricultural Parity for Land De-Commodification," in *Land Justice: Re-Imagining Land, Food and the Commons in the United States* (Oakland, CA: Food First Books, in press).
39. David W. Galenson, "The Rise and Fall of Indentured Servitude in the Americas: An Economic Analysis," *Journal of Economic History* 44/1 (1984): 1–26.
40. James Ciment and John Radzilowski, *American Immigration: An Encyclopedia of Political, Social, and Cultural Change* (London: Routledge, 2015).
41. Philip Martin and Elizabeth Midgley, "Immigration to the United States," *Population Bulletin*. Report, Vol 54, No 2 (June 1999).
42. Mae Ngai, *Impossible Subjects: Illegal Aliens and the Making of Modern America* (Princeton: Princeton University Press, 2004), 37.
43. Marcel Paret, "Legality and Exploitation: Immigration Enforcement and the US Migrant Labor System," *Latino Studies* 12/4 (2014): 503–26.
44. Center for History and News Media, "Bracero History Archive," 2014, http://braceroarchive.org/.
45. The co-evolution of agricultural chemicals and chemicals for warfare dates from the turn of the twentieth century. For an in-depth account see Edmund Russell, *War and Nature: Fighting Humans and Insects with Chemicals from World War I to Silent Spring* (New York: Cambridge University Press, 2001).

46. U. Lele and A. A. Goldsmith, "The Development of National Agricultural Research Capacity: India's Experience with the Rockefeller Foundation and Its Significance for Africa," *Economic Development and Cultural Change* 37/2 (1989): 305–43; Peter Wallersteen, "Scarce Goods as Political Weapons: The Case of Food," *Journal of Peace Research* 13 (1976): 277–98.
47. Eric Holt-Giménez, Raj Patel, and Annie Shattuck, *Food Rebellions: Crisis and the Hunger for Justice* (Oakland, CA, and London: Food First Books/ Pambazooka Press, 2009).
48. Ibid.
49. Frances Lappé, Joseph Collins, and Peter Rosset, *World Hunger: Twelve Myths*, 2nd ed. (New York: Grove Press, Food First Books, 1986).
50. Cynthia Hewitt de Alcántara, *Modernizing Mexican Agriculture* (Geneva: United Nations Research Institute for Social Development, 1976); Andrew Pearse, *Seeds of Plenty, Seeds of Want: Social and Economic Implications of the Green Revolution*, ed. UN Research Institute for Social Development (Oxford: Clarendon Press, 1980).
51. Mike Davis, "Planet of Slums: Urban Involution and the Informal Proletariat," *New Left Review* 26 (2004).
52. Alain de Janvry, *The Agrarian Question and Reformism in Latin America* (Baltimore and London: Johns Hopkins University Press, 1981).
53. With the help of the farmers' movement called *Campesino a Campesino* (Farmer to Farmer), Gabriel and his family managed to restore fertility and reestablish production on the farm by painstakingly rebuilding the organic matter in the soil, implementing soil and water conservation practices, and replacing the hybrid maize and fertilizers with a traditional corn-bean-squash polyculture. He introduced agroforestry and added a complex mix of leguminous and perennial plants and beehives to his farm. Gabriel's experience of increasing investment and diminishing returns in capitalist agriculture is a common one for peasants and small-scale farmers in Latin America. His recovery—by using agroecological practices—is less common, but growing. E. Holt-Giménez, *The Campesino a Campesino Movement: Farmer-Led Sustainable Agriculture in Central America and Mexico* (Oakland: Food First Books, 1996).
54. Luigi Russi, *Hungry Capital: The Financialization of Food* (Winchester, UK, and Washington, DC: Zero Books, 2013).
55. Heinz Sonntag, "Modernism, Development and Modernization," *Pensamiento Propio* 11 (January-June 2000): 3–30.
56. Charles Gore, "The Rise and Fall of the Washington Consensus as a Paradigm for Developing Countries," *World Development* 28/5 (2000): 789–804; J. N. Pieterse, "My Paradigm or Yours? Alternative Development, Post-Development, Reflexive Development," *Development and Change* 29 (1998): 343–73.
57. Holt-Giménez, Patel, and Shattuck, *Food Rebellions: Crisis and the Hunger for Justice.*
58. Jennifer Clapp, *Food* (Cambridge: Polity Press, 2012).

59. Naomi Klein, *This Changes Everything: Capitalism vs. The Climate* (New York: Simon & Schuster, 2014).

2. Food, A Special Commodity

1. Karl Marx, *Capital: A Critique of Political Economy*, vol. 1, 3 vols. (New York: International Publishers, 1967). Marx's first volume of *Das Kapital*, published in 1861 in Hamburg, Germany, was not translated into English until after Marx's death in 1883—at the height of a continental depression following an expansive free-market boom. Frederick Engels, Marx's collaborator, editor, and benefactor, called *Capital* "The Bible of the Working Class." Before Marx, political economists simply accepted the existence of profit without asking how it was appropriated from the value of the product. Marx's fundamental contribution to political economy of the nineteenth century was to explore the nature of surplus value.
2. See, for example, David Harvey, *A Companion to Marx's Capital*, vol. 1, 2 vols. (London and Brooklyn: Verso, 2010).
3. Peter Rosset, *Food Is Different: Why We Must Get the WTO out of Agriculture* (London: Zed Books, 2006).
4. "Organic" refers to crops that are grown and animals that are raised without the application of synthetic chemicals or the ingestion of hormones or chemically treated crops. In the United States, the United States Department of Agriculture inspects and certifies organic products. Though a large percentage of the world's farmers grow food without synthetic chemical inputs they sell their products in conventional markets without organic certification.
5. Tanya Kerssen, "Quinoa: To Buy or Not to Buy . . . Is This the Right Question?," Food First.org blog, February 15, 2013, http://foodfirst.org/quinoa-to-buy-or-not-to-buy-is-this-the-right-question/.
6. Tim Weis, *The Global Food Economy: The Battle for the Future of Farming* (London: Zed Books, 2007).
7. Much of capitalism's petroleum comes from the Middle East. Publicly funded, trillion-dollar wars have (and are) being waged to ensure oil access. These costs do not show up on the corporate balance sheet, nor at the pump.
8. Peter Rosset, "The Multiple Functions and Benefits of Small Farm Agriculture in the Conext of Global Trade Negotiations," *Food First Policy Brief* (Oakland, CA: Food First/Institute for Food and Development Policy, 1999).
9. Harvey, *A Companion to Marx's Capital.*
10. William Kandel, "Profile of Hired Farmworkers, a 2008 Update," Economic Research Service (Washington D.C.: U.S. Department of Agriculture, 2008), https://www.ers.usda.gov/webdocs/publications/err60/12055_err60_reportsummary_1_.pdf.
11. Karin Astrid Siegmann, "Reflections on the Fair Food Agreement between the Coalition of Immokalee Workers and Retail Multinational," *Global*

Labor Column, August 1, 2015, http://column.global-labour-university.org/2015/08/reflections-on-fair-food-agreement.html.

12. CIW, "The Fair Food Program," 2017, http://www.fairfoodprogram.org/.
13. CIW "The Anti-Slavery Program" 2017, http://www.ciw-online.org/slavery/.
14. Lorin Kusmin, "Rural America at a Glance, 2013 Edition" (Washington, D.C.: U.S. Department of Agriculture Economic Research Service, 2013), http://www.ers.usda.gov/publications/eb-economic-brief/eb24.aspx#.U072hfldWN2.
15. According to the USDA 2012 Census of Agriculture, of the country's 2.1 million farmers only 8 percent are farmers of color (Native American, Asian, Latino, or African American), though their share is growing, particularly among Latinos, who now number over 67,000 farmers. The percentage of women farmers is 14 percent. Three-quarters of them earn less than $10,000 in annual sales. Seventy-five percent of farms in the United States have sales of under $50,000, but the number of high-income mega farms is increasing. The percentage of farmers under 35 years old has declined 8 percent since the last census, while the number of older farmers has increased. The average age for a farmer in the United States is now 58. Although these statistics paint the picture of a stereotypically white, male, aging farmer, they belie a growing movement of young, predominantly female and non-white beginning farmers. Eric Holt-Giménez, "This Land Is Whose Land? Dispossession, Resistance and Reform in the United States," *Backgrounder* (Oakland, CA: Food First/Institute for Food and Development Policy, Spring 2014), http://foodfirst.org/publication/this-land-is-whose-land/.
16. J. D. van der Ploeg, "The Peasantries of the Twenty-First Century: The Commodification Debate Revisited," *Journal of Peasant Studies* 37 (2010): 1–30.
17. Nicholas Babin, "Agroecology Saves the Farm (Where Fair Trade Failed): Surviving the Coffee Crisis in Costa Rica," *Backgrounder* (Oakland, CA: Food First/Institute for Food and Development Policy, December 10, 2014), http://foodfirst.org/publication/agroecology-saves-the-farm-in-costa-rica/.
18. Raj Patel, *The Value of Nothing: How to Reshape Market Society and Redefine Democracy* (New York: Picador, 2010).
19. Martin Lindstrom, *Buyology: Truth and Lies about Why We Buy*, 2nd ed. (New York: Broadway Books, 2010).
20. Harvey, *A Companion to Marx's Capital*, 1:79.
21. Karl Marx, *Capital: A Critique of Political Economy*, vol. 2: *The Process of Circulation of Capital* (New York: International Publishers, 1967), 27.
22. Stefano Longo, Rebecca Clausen, and Brett Clark, "Capitalism and the Commodification of Salmon: From Wild Fish to a Genetically Modified Species," *Monthly Review* 66/7 (2014): 35–55.
23. Adapted from Fred Magdoff, "A Rational Agriculture Is Incompatible with Capitalism," *Monthly Review* 66/10 (March 2015): 9–11.

3. Land and Property

1. Epigraph: http://www.onthecommons.org/sites/default/files/celebrating-the-commons.pdf.
2. Henry Bernstein, *Class Dynamics of Agrarian Change* (Halifax: Fernwood, 2010)
3. Thomas Piketty, *Capital in the Twenty-First Century* (Cambridge, MA, London, England, Harvard University Press, 2014); Fred Magdoff and John Bellamy Foster, *What Every Environmentalist Needs to Know about Capitalism* (New York: Monthly Review Press, 2011).
4. Eric Holt-Giménez, Raj Patel, and Annie Shattuck, *Food Rebellions!: Crisis and the Hunger for Justice* (Oakland, CA: Food First Books, 2009).
5. Jeremy Waldron, "Property and Ownership," *The Stanford Encyclopedia of Philosophy* (Palo Alto, CA: Stanford University Press, 2012), http://plato.stanford.edu/archives/spr2012/entries/property/.
6. Environmental Commons, "History of the Commons," 2015, http://www.environmentalcommons.org/commons.html.
7. The Commons has not disappeared under capitalism, and millions of hectares of common-pool resources (agricultural land, grazing land, forests, rivers lakes) can be found around the world in developed and developing countries including sub-Saharan African (500 million people), Fiji, Mexico, Taiwan, India, Nepal, Jamaica, the United States (lobster fisheries), Scandinavian countries (wild forage mushrooms and berries), Spain (irrigated vegetable gardens), and pasture across Europe, as well as indigenous lands in Mexico, Brazil, Honduras, Venezuela, and Nicaragua. Jose Luis Vivero Pol, "Reframing the Narrative of the Food System," Social Science Research Network, April 23, 2013, http://ssrn.com/abstract=2255447 or http://dx.doi.org/10.2139/ssrn.2255447.
8. Pierre Proudhon, "Property Is Theft!," in *No Gods No Masters: An Anthology of Anarchism*, 2 vols. (Edinburgh: AK Press, 1998), 1:30–40.
9. Elinor Ostrom, *Governing the Commons: The Evolution of Institutions for Collective Action* (New York: Cambridge University Press, 1990).
10. Pierre Proudhon, *What Is Property? An Inquiry into the Principles of Right and Government* (New York: Humboldt Publishing Company, 1840), https://www.marxists.org/reference/subject/economics/proudhon/property/.
11. Elinor Ostrom, "Revisiting the Commons: Local Lessons, Global Challenges," *Science* 284 (April 9, 1999): 278–82.
12. Elinor Ostrom, "A Behavioral Approach to the Rational Choice Theory of Collective Action," *American Political Science Review* 92/1 (1997): 1–22.
13. Ostrom's framework for common pool resources:
    1) Clearly defined boundaries (effective exclusion of external unentitled parties);
    2) Rules regarding the appropriation and provision of common resources that are adapted to local conditions;
    3) Collective-choice arrangements that allow most resource appropriators to participate in the decision-making process;

4) Effective monitoring by monitors who are part of or accountable to the appropriators;
5) A scale of graduated sanctions for resource appropriators who violate community rules;
6) Mechanisms of conflict resolution that are cheap and of easy access;
7) Self-determination of the community recognized by higher-level authorities; and
8) In the case of larger common-pool resources, organization in the form of multiple layers of nested enterprises, with small local common pool resources at the base level.

14. Garrett Hardin, "The Tragedy of the Commons," *Science* 162 (December 1968): 1243–48.
15. FUNDESCA, *El Último Despale . . . La Frontera Agrícola Centroamericana* (San José, Costa Rica: Fundación para el Desarrollo Económico y Social de Centro América, 1994).
16. Stefano Longo, Rebecca Clausen, and Brett Clark, "Capitalism and the Commodification of Salmon: From Wild Fish to a Genetically Modified Species," *Monthly Review* 66/7 (2014): 35–55.
17. Courtney Carrothers, "Tragedy of Commodification: Displacements in Alutiiq Fishing Communities in the Gulf of Alaska," *VB Mast* 9/2 (2010): 95–120.
18. Karl Polanyi, *The Great Transformation: The Political and Economic Origins of Our Time* (Boston: Beacon Press, 1944).
19. In the dreams of economists, a true self-regulating "free market" requires many buyers and sellers, thus allowing no one to dominate the market. Prices reach their "natural" level depending on supply and demand. However, when there are few buyers (as for commercial-scale agricultural production) and/or few sellers (agricultural input industries as well as the food retail sector), there cannot be any such thing as a "free market" in the classical sense.
20. Polanyi, *The Great Transformation*, 73.
21. Ibid.
22. David Bacon, "Unbroken Connection to the Land: An Interview with Farmworker Activist Rosalinda Guillen," in *Land Justice: Re-Imagining Land, Food and the Commons in the United Stated* (Oakland, CA: Food First Books, 2017) 162–163.
23. E Holt-Gimenez, "Biofuels: Myths of the Agro-Fuels Transition," *Backgrounder* (Oakland, CA: Food First Books, 2007), https://foodfirst.org/wp-content/uploads/2013/12/BK13_2-Biofuels2007_English.pdf.
24. World Bank, "World Development Report 2008: Agriculture for Development" (Washington, D.C.: World Bank, 2007).
25. Rosamund Naylor et al., "The Ripple Effect: Biofuels, Food Security, and the Environment," *Environment* 49/9 (2007): 35.
26. Madeleine Fairbairn, "When Farmland Meets Finance: Is Land the Next

Economic Bubble?," Food First Policy Brief, *Land & Sovereignty in the Americas* 5 (May 2014), http://www.mozilla.com/en-US/firefox/central/.

27. S. Varble, S. Secchi, and C. G. Druschke, "An Examination of Growing Trends in Land Tenure and Conservation Practice Adoption: Results from a Farmer Survey in Iowa," *Environmental Management* 57, no. 2 (2016): 318–30.
28. Ibid., 319.
29. Ibid.
30. Michael Carolan, "Barriers to the Adoption of Sustainable Agriculture on Rented Land: An Examination of Contesting Social Fields," R*ural Sociology*, no. 3 (2005): 387–413.
31. Tanya Kerssen and Zoe Brent, "Land & Resource Grabs in the United States: Five Sites of Struggle and Potential Transformation," *Policy Brief* (Oakland, CA: Food First, 2014), https://foodfirst.org/publication/land-resource-grabs-in-the-united-states/.
32. Susan Payne, *Susan Payne Makes a Case for African Farmland* (Des Moines, IO: 2013), http://farmlandgrab.org/post/view/22254-emvest-ceo-susan-payne-makes -case-for-africa-farmland.
33. Camilla Toulmin et al., "Land Tenure and International Investments in Agriculture," High-Level Panel of Experts on Food and Nutrition (Rome: Committee on World Food Security, July 2011).
34. Eric Holt-Giménez, "Territorial Restructuring and the Grounding of Agrarian Reform: Indigenous Communities, Gold Mining and the World Bank," *Working Paper, Land Policy* (Amsterdam: Transnational Institute, 2008).
35. E. Holt-Giménez, "Territorial Restructuring and the Grounding of Agrarian Reform: Indigenous Communities, Gold Mining and the World Bank," in *Land, Poverty, Social Justice and Development*, ed. S. Sauer (Brasilia: 2006); Eric Holt-Giménez, "LAND – GOLD – REFORM: The Territorial Restructuring of Guatemala's Highlands," *Development Report* (Institute for Food and Development Policy, 2007).
36. David Harvey, *The New Imperialism* (New York: Oxford University Press, 2003).
37. L. Solano, *Guatemala: Petróleo Y Minería En Las Entrañas Del Poder* (Guatemala City: Infopress Centroamericana, 2005).
38. Holt- Giménez, "LAND – GOLD – REFORM: The Territorial Restructuring of Guatemala's Highlands."
39. E. Holt- Giménez, "The Campesino a Campesino Movement: Farmer-Led Sustainable Agriculture in Central America and Mexico." *Development Report* No. 10. June 1996. (Oakland, CA: Food First, 1996), 121.
40. Miguel Carter, *Challenging Social Inequality: The Landless Rural Workers Movement and Agrarian Reform in Brazil* (Durham: Duke University Press, 2015).
41. Angus Wright and Wendy Wolford, *To Inherit the Earth: The Landless Movement and the Struggle for a New Brazil* (Food First Books, 2003).

4. Capitalism, Food, and Agriculture

1. Fred Magdoff, "A Rational Agriculture Is Incompatible with Capitalism," *Monthly Review* 66/10 (March 2015): 1–18.
2. M. Edelman, "The Persistence of the Peasantry," *North American Congress on Latin America* 33/5 (2000): 14–19.
3. GRAIN, "Hungry for Land: Small Farmers Feed the World with Less than a Quarter of All Farmland" (Barcelona: GRAIN, May 2014), http://www.grain.org/article/entries/4929-hungry-for-land-small-farmers-feed-the-world-with-less-than-a-quarter-of-all-farmland.
4. Frank Bardacke, *Trampling Out the Vintage: Cesar Chávez and the Two Souls of the United Farm Workers* (New York: Verso, 2011).
5. Karl Marx, *Capital: A Critique of Political Economy*, vol. 2: *The Process of Circulation of Capital* (New York: International Publishers, 1967), 238.
6. S. A. Mann, "Obstacles to the Development of a Capitalist Agriculture," *Journal of Peasant Studies* 5/4 (1978): 473.
7. Peter Rosset, "The Multiple Functions and Benefits of Small Farm Agriculture in the Context of Global Trade Negotiations," *Food First Policy Brief* (Oakland, CA: Food First/Institute for Food and Development Policy, 1999).
8. James MacDonald, "Family Farming in the United States," *Amber Waves*, March 2014.
9. Jan Douwe van der Ploeg, "The Peasantries of the Twenty-First Century: The Commodification Debate Revisited," *Journal of Peasant Studies* 37/1 (2010): 1–30.
10. Richard Levins and William W. Cochran, "The Treadmill Revisited," *Land Economics* 74/4 (1996).
11. John Ikerd, "The New Farm Crisis Calls for New Farm Policy," Missouri Farmers' Union Annual Conference, Jefferson City, MO, 2002, http://web.missouri.edu/ikerdj/papers/FarmUnion.pdf.
12. Richard A. Walker, *The Conquest of Bread: 150 Years of Agribusiness in California* (New York: New Press, 2004).
13. Madeleine Fairbairn, "When Farmland Meets Finance: Is Land the Next Economic Bubble?," Food First Policy Brief, *Land & Sovereignty in the Americas* 5 (May 2014), http://www.mozilla.com/en-US/firefox/central/.
14. "Casino of Hunger: How Wall Street Speculators Fueled the Global Food Crisis" (Washington, D.C.: Food and Water Watch, November 2009), https://www.foodandwaterwatch.org/sites/default/files/casino_hunger_report_dec_2009.pdf.
15. Jennifer Clapp, *Food* (Cambridge: Polity Press, 2012).
16. *Food and Water Watch*, 2009.
17. D. Goodman, B. Sorj, and J. Wilkinson, *From Farming to Biotechnology: A Theory of Agro-Industrial Development* (Oxford: Blackwell, 1987).
18. Walker, *The Conquest of Bread: 150 Years of Agribusiness in California*.
19. S. R. Gliessman, *Agroecology: Ecological Processes in Sustainable Agriculture* (Chelsea MI: Ann Arbor Press, 1998); M. Altieri, "Why Study

Traditional Agriculture?," in *Agroecology*, ed. P. Rosset, Biological Resource Management (New York: McGraw-Hill, 1990), 551–64.

20. Daniel Charles, "The System Supplying America's Chickens Pits Farmer vs. Farmer," *The Salt*, February 20, 2014, http://www.npr.org/sections/thesalt/2014/02/20/279040721/the-system-that-supplies-our-chickens-pits-farmer-against-farmer.
21. From: National Sustainable Agriculture Coalition, "What's All the Flapping About: What Do HBO's John Oliver, Chicken Farmers, and Congress Have in Common?," NSAC blog, May 29, 2016, http://sustainableagriculture.net/blog/whats-all-the-flapping-about/.
22. Martin Prowse, "Contract Farming in Developing Countries: A Review," (Paris: Agence Française de Développement, 2012), 9.
23. World Bank, "World Development Report 2008: Agriculture for Development" (Washington, D.C.: World Bank, 2007).
24. Karl Marx, *Capital: A Critique of Political Economy*, vol. 1 (New York: International Publishers, 1967), 637–38.
25. K. Kautsky, *The Agrarian Question* (London: Zwan, 1988), 214–15.
26. Fred Magdoff and John Bellamy Foster, "Liebig, Marx and the Depletion of Soil Fertility: Relevance for Today's Agriculture," in *Hungry for Profit: The Agribusinss Threat to Farmers, Food and the Environment* (New York: Monthly Review Press, 2000).
27. Magdoff, "A Rational Agriculture Is Incompatible with Capitalism."
28. Working Group III contribution to the IPCC 5th Assessment Report "Climate Change 2014: Mitigation of Climate Change," April 12, 2014,http://report.mitigation2014.org/drafts/final-draft-postplenary/ipcc_wg3_ar5_final-draft_postplenary_chapter11.pdf.
29. Brenda B. Lin et al., "Effects of Industrial Agriculture on Climate Change and the Mitigating Potential of Small-Scale Agro-Ecological Farms," *Animal Science Reviews* 2011 (2012): 69.
30. EPA, "Climate Impacts on Agriculture and Food Supply," September 27, 2014, http://www.epa.gov/climatechange/impacts-adaptation/agriculture.html#impactslivestock.
31. Oakland Institute, "Down on the Farm—Wall Street: America's New Frontier," September 26, 2014, http://www.oaklandinstitute.org/sites/oaklandinstitute.org/files/OI_Report_Down_on_the_Farm.pdf, 4.
32. Magdoff, "A Rational Agriculture Is Incompatible with Capitalism."
33. Altieri, "Why Study Traditional Agriculture?"; S. R. Gliessman, "The Ecological Basis for the Application of Traditional Agricultural Technology in the Management of Tropical Agroecosystems," *Agro-Ecosystems* 50 (1981): 24–31.
34. J. Pretty, *Regenerating Agriculture; Policies and Practice for Sustainability and Self-Reliance* (London: Earthscan Publications, 1995); E. Holt-Giménez, "The Campesino a Campesino Movement: Farmer-Led Sustainable Agriculture in Central America and Mexico" (Oakland, CA: Food First, Development Report No.19, June 1996, https://foodfirst.org/publication/

the-campesino-a-campesino-movement/); R. Bunch, *Two Ears of Corn: A Guide to People-Centered Agricultural Improvement* (Oklahoma City: World Neighbors, 1985).

35. Beverly McIntire et al., "Agriculture at a Crossroads: International Assessment of Agricultural Knowledge, Science and Technology for Development," *Report Synthesis* (Washington, D.C.: Island Press, 2009), http://www.agassessment.org/.
36. Olivier de Schutter, "Agroecology and the Right to Food," *Report of the Special Rapporteur* (Geneva: United Nations, December 2010), http://www.srfood.org/en/report-agroecology-and-the-right-to-food.
37. Eric Holt-Giménez, Raj Patel, and Annie Shattuck, *Food Rebellions: Crisis and the Hunger for Justice* (Oakland, CA, and London: Food First Books, Pambazooka Press, 2009).
38. E. P. Thompson, *Customs in Common: Studies in Traditional Popular Culture* (New York: New Press, 1991), 338.
39. E. Wolf, *Peasant Wars of the Twentieth Century* (New York: Harper & Row, 1969); E. Wolf, *Peasants*, ed. M. Sahlins, vol. 4 (Englewood Cliffs, NJ: Prentice-Hall, 1966); J. Scott, *The Moral Economy of the Peasant* (New Haven and London: Yale University Press, 1976); J. C. Scott, "Everyday Forms of Resistance," in *Everyday Forms of Peasant Resistance*, ed. F. D. Colburn (New York: M.E. Sharpe, 1989), 3–33.
40. Larry Yee and James Cochran, "The Food Commons," *Summary*, 2015, http://www.thefoodcommons.org/summary/; Jose Luis Vivero Pol, "Food as a Commons: Reframing the Narrative of the Food System," Social Science Research Network, April 23, 2015, http://ssrn.com/abstract=2255447 or http://dx.doi.org/10.2139/ssrn.2255447; Jose Luis Vivero Pol, "Reframing the Narrative of the Food System," Social Science Research Network, April 23, 2013, http://ssrn.com/abstract=2255447 or http://dx.doi.org/10.2139/ssrn.2255447.
41. Brian K. Obach and Kathleen Tobin, "Civic Agriculture and Community Engagement," *Agriculture and Human Values* (2014): 307–32, doi:10.1007/s10460-013-9477-z.
42. Jan Douwe van der Ploeg, "Peasant-Driven Agricultural Growth and Food Sovereignty," *Journal of Peasant Studies* (2014), 10, doi:10.1080/03066150.2013.876997.
43. Rosset, "The Multiple Functions and Benefits of Small Farm Agriculture in the Context of Global Trade Negotiations."
44. Van der Ploeg, "Peasant-Driven Agricultural Growth and Food Sovereignty."
45. Ibid.
46. E. Holt-Giménez, "Measuring Farmers' Agroecological Resistance to Hurricane Mitch in Central America" (London: International Institute for Environment and Development, 2001).
47. Eric Holt-Giménez, "Agrarian Questions and the Struggle for Land Justice in the United States," in Justine Williams and Eric Holt-Giménez, editors,

Land Justice: Re-Imagining Land, Food and the Agrarian Question (Oakland, CA: Food First Books, 2017).

5. Power and Privilege in the Food System

1. Margaret Wallhagen and Bill Strawbridge, "When Women Flourish . . . We Can End Hunger," Hunger Report (Washington, D.C.: Bread for the World, 2015).
2. Murray Bookchin, *The Ecology of Freedom* (Palo Alto, CA: Cheshire Books, 1982).
3. Sharon Smith, "Engels and the Origin of Women's Oppression," *International Socialist Review* 2 (1997), http://www.isreview.org/issues/02/engles_family.shtml#top.
4. Friederich Engels, *The Origin of the Family, Private Property and the State* (Hottingen-Zurich: 1884), https://www.marxists.org/archive/marx/works/download/pdf/origin_family.pdf, 30.
5. Cheryl Doss, "If Women Hold Up Half the Sky, How Much of the World's Food Do They Produce?" (New York: UN Food and Agriculture Organization, 2011), http://www.fao.org/3/a-am309e.pdf.
6. Silvia Federici, *Revolution at Point Zero: Housework, Reproduction, and Feminist Struggle* (Oakland, CA: PM Press, 2012).
7. Maria Mies, *Patriarchy and Accumulation on a World Scale: Women in the International Division of Labor* (London: Zed Books, 1986), 46.
8. Ibid., 48.
9. FAO, "Women in Agriculture: Closing the Gender Gap for Development," State of Agriculture yearly report (Rome: Food and Agriculture Organization (FAO), 2012), http://www.fao.org/docrep/013/i2050e/i2050e.pdf.
10. Mary Bauer and Monica Ramirez, "Injustice on Our Plates: Immigrant Women in the U.S. Food Industry" (Montgomery, AL: Southern Poverty Law Center, 2010), https://www.splcenter.org/sites/default/files/d6_legacy_files/downloads/publication/Injustice_on_Our_Plates.pdf.
11. On the new regime of women's impoverishment and exploitation, Silvia Federici writes, "[A] new international division of reproductive work has been organized that has redistributed significant quotas of housework on the shoulders of immigrant women, leading to what is often defined as the globalization of care work. . . . But these developments have not significantly affected the amount of domestic work which the majority of women are still expected to perform, nor have they eliminated the gender-based inequalities built upon it. If we take a global perspective we see that not only do women still do most of the housework in every country, but due to the state's cut of investment in social services and the decentralization of industrial production the amount of domestic work paid and unpaid they perform has actually increased, even when they have had an extra-domestic job." Federici, *Revolution at Point Zero,* 18.
12. This section is taken from an article co-written with A. Breeze Harper, Executive Director of the Sistah Vegan Project, http://www.sistahvegan.com.

13. From David Bacon, "Unbroken Connection to the Land: An Interview with Farmworker Activist Rosalinda Guillen," in *Land Justice: Re-Imagining Land, Food and the Commons in the United Stated* (Oakland, CA: Food First Books, 2017).
14. Alison Hope Alkon, *Black, White and Green: Farmers Markets, Race, and the Green Economy* (Atlanta: University of Georgia Press, 2012).
15. Michelle Alexander, *The New Jim Crow: Mass Incarceration in the Age of Colorblindness*, rev. ed. (New York: New Press, 2011).
16. Roxanne Dunbar-Ortiz, *An Indigenous People's History of the United States* (Boston: Beacon Press, 2014).
17. Edward E. Baptist, *The Half Has Never Been Told: Slavery and the Making of American Capitalism* (New York: Basic Books, 2014).
18. Nell Irvin Painter, *The History of White People:* (New York: W. W. Norton, 2010).
19. Noel Ignatiev, *How the Irish Became White* (New York, London: Routledge, 1995).
20. Alexander, *The New Jim Crow.*
21. Jim Crow laws were state and local laws enforcing racial segregation in the southern United States. Enacted after the Reconstruction period, these laws continued in force until 1965. They mandated *de jure* racial segregation in all public facilities in states of the former Confederate States of America, starting in 1890 with a "separate but equal" status for African Americans. Facilities for African Americans were consistently inferior and underfunded compared to those available to European Americans; sometimes they did not exist at all. This body of law institutionalized a number of economic, educational, and social disadvantages. *De jure* segregation mainly applied to the southern states, whereas Northern segregation was generally *de facto*—patterns of housing segregation enforced by private covenants, bank lending practices, and job discrimination, including discriminatory labor union practices. Jim Crow laws—sometimes, as in Florida, part of the state constitution—mandated the segregation of public schools, public places, and public transportation, and the segregation of restrooms, restaurants, and drinking fountains for whites and blacks. The U.S. military was also segregated, as were federal workplaces, initiated in 1913 under President Woodrow Wilson. By requiring candidates to submit photos, his administration practiced racial discrimination in hiring. These Jim Crow laws followed the 1800–1866 Black Codes, which had previously restricted the civil rights and civil liberties of African Americans. Segregation of public (state-sponsored) schools was declared unconstitutional by the Supreme Court of the United States in 1954 in *Brown v. Board of Education*, although in some cases it took years for this decision to be acted on. Generally, the remaining Jim Crow laws were overruled by the Civil Rights Act of 1964 and the Voting Rights Act of 1965, but years of action and court challenges were needed to unravel numerous means of institutional discrimination.

22. Center for History and News Media, "Bracero History Archive," 2014, http://braceroarchive.org/.
23. Pete Daniel, *Dispossession: Discrimination Against African American Farmers in the Age of Civil Rights* (Chapel Hill: University of North Carolina Press, 2013).
24. Anuradha Mittal and John Powell, "The Last Plantation" (Food First, 2000); John Powell, "Poverty and Race through a Belongingness Lens," *Policy Matters* 1 (April 2012).
25. Eric Holt-Giménez, "This Land Is Whose Land? Dispossession, Resistance and Reform in the United States," *Backgrounder* (Oakland, CA: Food First/Institute for Food and Development Policy, Spring 2014), http://foodfirst.org/publication/this-land-is-whose-land/.
26. Of the total land rented out by operator and non-operator landlords, 97 percent of principal landlords are white. Landlords who are white accounted for 98 percent of rent received, expenses, and the value of land and buildings in 2014. From U.S. Agricultural Census total survey results 2014.
27. Food First, "Food Insecurity of Restaurant Workers," Food Chain Workers Alliance, Restaurant Opportunities Center, 2014, http://foodfirst.org/publication/food-insecurity-of-restaurant-workers/.
28. Carmen DeNavas-Walt, Bernadette Proctor, and Jessica Smith, "Income, Poverty, and Health Insurance Coverage in the United States," in *The U.S. Farm Bill: Corporate Power and Structural Racialization in the United States Food System,* Haas Institute for a Fair and Inclusive Society, UC Berkeley, 2015, http://www.hassinstitute.berkeley.edu.
29. Elsadig Elsheikh and Nadia Barhoum, "Structural Racialization and Food Insecurity in the United States; A Report to the U.N. Human Rights Committee on the International Covenant on Civil and Political Rights," Haas Institute for a Fair and Inclusive Society, UC Berkeley, August 2013.
30. Centers for Disease Control and Prevention, "National Diabetes Statistics Report: Estimates of Diabetes and Its Burden in the United States," U.S. Department of Health and Human Services, 2014, http://www.cdc.gov/diabetes/pubs/statsreport14/national-diabetes-report-web.pdf.
31. Julie Guthman, "If They Only Knew: Color Blindness and Universalism in California Alternative Food Institutions," in *Taking Food Public: Redefining Foodways in a Changing World* (New York, London: Routledge, 2012), 211–23.
32. Paulo Freire, *Pedagogy of the Oppressed* (New York: Herder and Herder, 1970).
33. Tim Flannery, *The Eternal Frontier: An Ecological History of North America and Its Peoples* (London: Penguin Books, 2001).
34. These hierarchies are so well documented that we tend to forget that the food and farming systems of the indigenous societies of North America and the Andes, of Polynesian and Arctic peoples, of aboriginal Australians, and many other societies were highly productive, sustainable and, despite social, political, and cultural divisions, largely egalitarian.

35. T. Shanin, *The Awkward Class: Political Sociology of Peasantry in a Developing Society* (Oxford: Clarendon Press, 1972).
36. Karl Marx and Friederich Engels, "The Communist Manifesto," in *The Marx Engels Reader* (New Yok: Norton,W.W. & Company, Inc., 1978).
37. Hudis Peter and Kevin B. Anderson, *The Rosa Luxemburg Reader* (New York: Monthly Review Press, 2004).
38. Alix Kates Shulman, *Red Emma Speaks: An Emma Goldman Reader*, 3rd ed. (New York: Humanity Books, 1996).
39. Antonio Gramsci, *Selections from the Prison Notebooks*, ed. Q. Hoare (New York: International Publishers, 1971).
40. Edward Herman and Noam Chomsky, *Manufacturing Consent: The Political Economy of the Mass Media* (New York: Pantheon Books, 1988).
41. Gramsci, *Selections from the Prison Notebooks*.
42. Rachel Slocum and Kirsten Valentiine Cadieux, "What Does It Mean to Do Food Justice?," *Journal of Political Ecology* 22 (2015), http://jpe.library.arizona.edu/volume_22/Cadieuxslocum.pdf; Guthman, "If They Only Knew: Color Blindness and Universalism in California Alternative Food Institutions," 211–23.

6. Food, Capitalism, Crises, and Solutions

1. George Naylor, "Agricultural Parity for Land De-Commodification," in *Land Justice: Re-Imagining Land, Food and the Commons in the United States* (Oakland, CA: Food First Books, 2017)
2. Adapted from E. Holt-Gimenez, "The True Extent of Hunger: What the FAO Isn't Telling You," *Backgrounder* (Oakland, CA: Food First/Institute for Food and Development Policy, 2016), https://foodfirst.org/wp-content/uploads/2016/06/Summer2016Backgrounder.pdf.
3. Lewis Carroll, *Alice's Adventures in Wonderland* (London: Cleave Books, 1865), http://www.cleavebooks.co.uk/grol/alice/won02.htm.
4. T. Garnett and J. Godfray, "Sustainable Intensification in Agriculture: Navigating a Course through Competing Food Systems Priorities," Report from Food Climate Research Network and Oxford Martin Programme on the Future of Food workshop, January 2012, 17, http://www.futureoffood.ox.ac.uk/sites/futureoffood.ox.ac.uk/files/SI%20report%20-%20final.pdf.
5. Ibid., 8.
6. Naylor, "Agricultural Parity for Land De-Commodification."
7. E. O. Wilson and Robert MacArthur, *The Theory of Island Biogeography* (Princeton: Princeton University Press, 1967).
8. John Vandermeer, Ivette Perfecto, and Angus Wright, *Nature's Matrix: Linking Agriculture, Conservation and Food Sovereignty* (London: Earthscan, 2009).
9. James O'Connor, *Natural Causes: Essays in Ecological Marxism* (New York, London: Guilford Press, 1998).
10. Leslie Lipper et al., "'Climate-Smart' Agriculture Policies, Practices and Financing for Food Security, Adaptation and Mitigation" (Rome: Food and

Agriculture Organization of the United Nations (FAO), 2010), ii, http://www.fao.org/docrep/013/i1881e/i1881e00.pdf.

11. "Climate-Smart Agriculture" (Food and Agriculture Organization of the United Nations, n.d.), http://www.fao.org/climate-smart-agriculture/overview/en/.
12. See La Vía Campesina https://viacampesina.org/en/.
13. E. Holt-Giménez, Justine Williams, and Caitlyn Hachmyer, "The World Bank Group's 2013–15 Agriculture for Action Plan: A Lesson in Privatization, Lack of Oversight and Tired Development Paradigms," Development Report (Oakland, CA: Food First/Institute for Food and Development Policy, October 2015), https://foodfirst.org/publication/the-world-bank-groups-2013-15-agriculture-for-action-plan-a-lesson-in-privatization-lack-of-oversight-and-tired-development-paradigms/.
14. Rajan Sunder Kashik, *Biocapital: The Constitution of Postgenomic Life* (Durham, N.C.: Duke University Press, 2006).
15. Nicole Barreca, "Biofortification Pioneers Win 2016 World Food Prize to Fight Against Malnutrition," Press release. World Food Prize. Ames, IA. June 28, 2016, https://www.worldfoodprize.org/index.cfm/87428/40322/biofortification_pioneers_win_2016_world_food_prize_for_fight_against_malnutrition.
16. Sally Brooks, *Rice Biofortification: Lessons for Global Science and Development* (London: Earthscan Publications, 2010).
17. Klaus von Grebmer et al., "The Challenge of Hidden Hunger," *Global Hunger Index* (Bonn/Washington D.C./Dublin: International Food Policy Research Institute, October 2014), 3.
18. Elizabeth C. Daño, "Biofortification: Trojan Horse of Corporate Food Control?," *Development* 57/2 (2014): 201–9.
19. Sally Brooks, *Rice Biofortification: Lessons for Global Science and Development.* (London: Earthscan Publications, 2010).
20. Daño, "Biofortification: Trojan Horse of Corporate Food Control?"
21. H. Bouis, "The Dual Global Challenges of Malnutrition and Obesity," World Food Prize International Symposium, Des Moines, Iowa, October 13, 2005, 4, https://www.worldfoodprize.org/documents/filelibrary/images/borlaug_dialogue/2005/Bouis_transcript_31DE91D659E2F.pdf;
22. Daño, "Biofortification: Trojan Horse of Corporate Food Control?"
23. GAIN, "Public-Private Partnership Launched to Improve Nutrition in Developing Countries," Global Alliance for Improved Nutrition, First Annual Forum of the Business Alliance for Food Fortification, 2005, http://www.gainhealth.org/knowledge-centre/first-annual-forum-business-alliance-food-fortification/.
24. George Scrinis, *Nutritionism: The Science and Politics of Dietary Advice* (New York: Columbia University Press, 2013).
25. Chase Purdy, "'Nature Is Not Good to Human Beings': The Chairman of the World's Biggest Food Company Makes the Case for a New Kind of Diet," *Quartz*, December 27, 2016, http://qz.com/856541/

the-worlds-biggest-food-company-makes-the-case-for-its-avant-garde-human-diet/.

26. "Waste," Oxford Living Dictionary, https://en.oxforddictionaries.com/definition/waste.
27. "USDA and EPA Join with Private Sector, Charitable Organizations to Set Nation's First Food Waste Reduction Goals," https://www.usda.gov/oce/foodwaste/.
28. Dana Gunders, "Wasted: How America Is Losing Up to 40 Percent of Its Food from Farm to Fork to Landfill," National Resources Defense Council, August 2012, https://www.nrdc.org/sites/default/files/wasted-food-IP.pdf
29. Dana Gunders, "Wasted: How America Is Losing Up to 40 Percent of Its Food From Farm to Fork to Landfill," National Resources Defense Council, August 2012, https://www.google.com/url?sa=t&rct=j&q=&esrc=s&source=web&cd=1&cad=rja&uact=8&ved=0ahUKEwjmnpXhlaLRAhXhlVQKHTGFC0UQFggcMAA&url=https%3A%2F%2Fwww.nrdc.org%2Fsites%2Fdefault%2Ffiles%2Fwasted-food-IP.pdf&usg=AFQjCNGQByTwl4jY7R-9EryXFloSYw57cg.
30. Brian Lipinski et al., "Reducing Food Loss and Waste," Working Paper, World Resources Institute, May 2013, http://www.wri.org/sites/default/files/reducing_food_loss_and_waste.pdf.
31. Julian Parfitt, Mark Barthel, and Sarah MacNaughton, "Food Waste within Food Supply Chains: Quantification and Potential for Change to 2050," *Philosophical Transactions of the Royal Society* 385 (2010): 3065–81.
32. Gunders, "Wasted: How America Is Losing Up to 40 Percent of Its Food from Farm to Fork to Landfill," 12.
33. Ibid.
34. Linda Scott Kantor et al., "Estimating and Addressing America's Food Losses," *Food Review* 3 (1997), http://gleaningusa.com/PDFs/USDA-Jan97a.pdf.
35. Emily Broad Leib et al., "Consumer Perceptions of Date Labels: National Survey," Consumer Survey, Johns Hopkins Center for a Liveable Future, Harvard Food Law and Policy Clinic, National Consumers League, May 2016, http://www.chlpi.org/wp-content/uploads/2013/12/Consumer-Perceptions-on-Date-Labels_May-2016.pdf.
36. Caitlyn Hachmyer, "Notes from a New Farmer: Rent-Culture, Insecurity, and the Need for Reform," in *Land Justice: Re-Imagining Land, Food and the Commons in the United States* (Oakland, CA: Food First Books, 2017).
37. Michael Specter, "How the DNA Revolution Is Changing Us," *National Geographic*, August 2016, http://www.nationalgeographic.com/magazine/2016/08/dna-crispr-gene-editing-science-ethics/.
38. Pat Mooney, "The Corporate Strategy to Control the Food System," public presentation, World Social Forum. Montreal, Canada. August 13, 2016.
39. Allan Boyle, "The End of Grocery Checkers? Amazon's High-Tech Store Points to the Future of Physical Retail," GeekWire, December 5, 2016, http://www.geekwire.com/2016/the-end-of-grocery-checkers-amazons-high-tech-convenience-store-points-to-future-of-physical-retail/.
40. George Naylor, "Agricultural Parity for Land De-Commodification,"

in Justine M. Williams and Eric Holt-Giménez, editors, *Land Justice: Re-Imagining Land, Food and the Commons in the United States* (Oakland, CA: Food First Books, 2017).

41. David Harvey, *A Brief History of Neoliberalism* (Oxford: Oxford University Press, 2005).

42. Boston Consulting Group, "The Next Billions: Business Strategies to Enhance Food Value Chains and Empower the Poor" (Geneva: World Economic Forum, 2009), http://www3.weforum.org/docs/WEF_FB_FoodValueChainsAndPoor_Report_2009.pdf.

43. Miguel. A. Altieri, *Agroecology: The Scientific Basis of Sustainable Agriculture* (Boulder, CO: Westview Press, 1987); Stephen.R. Gliessman, *Agroecology: The Ecology of Sustainable Food Systems* (New York: Taylor and Francis, 2007).

44. Eric Holt-Giménez, *Campesino a Campesino: Voices from Latin America's Farmer to Farmer Movement* (Oakland, California: Food First, 2006).

45. Gene Wilken, *Good Farmers: Traditional Agricultural Resource Management in Mexico and Central America* (Berkeley: University of California Press, 1988); R. Netting, *Cultural Ecology*, Second Edition (Prospect Heights: Waveland Press, 1986).

46. Sylvia Kantor, "Comparing Yields with Land Equivalent Ration (LER)," Agriculture and Natural Resources Fact Sheet, Washington State University, 2017, https://ay14-15.moodle.wisc.edu/prod/pluginfile.php/59463/mod_resource/content/0/LERfactsheet.pdf.

47. M. Edelman, "The Persistence of the Peasantry," *North American Congress on Latin America* 33/5 (2000): 14–19.

48. Miguel Altieri, "Linking Ecologists and Traditional Farmers in the Search for Sustainable Agriculture," *Frontiers in Ecology and the Environment*, 2004, 35–42.

49. Jules Pretty, *Regenerating Agriculture; Policies and Practice for Sustainability and Self-Reliance* (London: Earthscan Publications, 1995); Norman Uphoff, *Agroecological Innovations: Increasing Food Production with Participatory Development* (London: Earthscan, 2002).

50. Olivier de Schutter, "Agroecology and the Right to Food," Report of the UN Special Rapporteur on the Right to Food (Geneva: United Nations, December 2010), http://www.srfood.org/en/report-agroecology-and-the-right-to-food.

51. C. Badgley et al., "Organic Agriculture and the Global Food Supply," *Renewable Agriculture and Food Systems* 22/2 (2007): 86–108; Jules Pretty and Rachel Hine, "Feeding the World with Sustainable Agriculture: A Summary of New Evidence," Final Report from SAFE-World Research Project (Colchester: University of Essex, 2000); E. Holt-Giménez, "Measuring Farmers' Agroecological Resistance after Hurricane Mitch in Nicaragua: A Case Study in Participatory, Sustainable Land Management Impact Monitoring," *Agriculture, Ecosystems & Environment* 93 (2002): 87–105.

52. Bruce Jennings, *Foundations of International Agricultural Research: Science*

and Politics in Mexican Agriculture (Boulder, CO, and London: Westview Press, 1988).

53. P. Rosset, "Cuba's Nationwide Conversion to Organic Agriculture," *Capitalism, Nature, Socialism* 5/3 (1994): 20.
54. Samir Amin, "Food Sovereignty: A Struggle for Convergence in Diversity," in *Food Movements Unite! Strategies to Transform Our Food Systems* (Oakland, CA: Food First Books, 2011), xi–xviii.
55. Beverly McIntire et al., "Agriculture at a Crossroads: International Assessment of Agricultural Knowledge, Science and Technology for Development," *Synthesis* (Washington, D.C.: Island Press, 2009), http://www.agassessment.org/.

Conclusion: Changing Everything

1. Epigraph: Karl Marx, "Theses on Feuerbach," in *Ludwig Feuerbach and the End of Classical German Philosophy* (Peking: Foreign Languages Press, 1976), https://msuweb.montclair.edu/~furrg/gned/marxtonf45.pdf, 65.
2. Nancy Fraser, "The End of Progressive Neoliberalism," *Dissent*, January 2, 2017, https://www.dissentmagazine.org/online_articles/progressive-neoliberalism -reactionary-populism-nancy-fraser.
3. Ibid.
4. E. Holt-Gimenez and A. Shattuck, "Food Crises, Food Regimes and Food Movements: Rumblings of Reform or Tides of Transformation?," *Journal of Peasant Studies* 38, no. 1 (January 2011): 109–44.
5. Howard Zinn, "Eugene V. Debs," in *A Power Governments Cannot Oppress* (San Francisco: City Lights, 2007).
6. David Macaray, "Labor Unions and Taft-Hartley," *Counterpunch*, January 1, 2008, https://www.counterpunch.org/2008/01/02/labor-unions-and-taft -hartley/.
7. Regin Schmidt, *Red: FBI and the Origins of Anticommunism in the United States, 1919–1943* (Copenhagen, DK: Museum of Tusculanum Press, 2000).
8. Eric Bentley, *Thirty Years of Treason: Excerpts from Hearings before the House Committee on Un-American Activities 1938–1968*, 1st ed. (New York: Penguin Books, Ltd., 1973).
9. Poppendiek, *Breadlines Knee-Deep in Wheat: Food Assistance in the Great Depression.*
10. Ben Stein, "In Class Warfare, Guess Which Class Is Winning," *New York Times*, November 26, 2006, http://www.nytimes.com/2006/11/26/business/yourmoney/26every.html.
11. Gerry Mullvany, "World's 8 Richest Have as Much Wealth as Bottom Half, Oxfam Says," *New York Times*, January 16, 2017, https://www.nytimes.com/2017/01/16/world/eight-richest-wealth-oxfam.html.
12. Jens Martens and Karolin Seitz, "Philanthropic Power and Development; Who Shapes the Agenda?" (Aachen/Berlin/Bonn/New York: Miserior, Global Policy Forum, November 2015), https://www.globalpolicy.org/images/pdfs/GPFEurope/Philanthropic_Power_online.pdf.

13. E. Holt-Giménez, "Racism and Capitalism: Dual Challenges for the Food Movement," *Journal of Agriculture, Food Systems, and Community Development* (2015), http://dx.doi.org/10.530 4/jafscd.2015.052.014.
14. Jurgen Habermas, *The Structural Transformation of the Public Sphere: An Inquiry into a Category of Bourgeois Society* (Cambridge, MA: MIT Press, 1989).
15. Nancy Fraser, "Transnationalizing the Public Sphere: On the Legitimacy and Efficacy of Public Opinion in a Post-Westphalian World," in *Transnationalizing the Public Sphere* (Cambridge: Polity Press, 2014), 1, http://journals.sagepub.com/doi/pdf/10.1177/0263276407080090.
16. Ibid.
17. Karl Marx, *The Eighteenth Brumaire of Louis Bonaparte* (New York: Marx-Engels Internet Archive, 1995), https://www.marxists.org/archive/marx/works/1852/18th-brumaire/.
18. Jason Hickel, "The True Extent of Global Poverty and Hunger: Questioning the Good News Narrative of the Millennium Development Goals," *Third World Quarterly* 37/5 (May 3, 2016): 749–67, doi:10.1080/01436597.2015.1109439.
19. Antonio Gramsci, *Selections from the Prison Notebooks*, ed. Q. Hoare (New York: International Publishers, 1971).
20. David Harvey, *The New Imperialism* (New York: Oxford University Press, 2003).

Index